Here's what fishing pundits are saying about
Fishing Vacations for All Budgets

"Alaska salmon, Florida redfish, Colorado trout, Georgia tarpon, Tennessee smallmouths, New York steelhead, California catfish, and everything else imaginable. Cleverly designed for ease of use and with quick-check sidebars, this book allows readers to select the best fishing vacation possible." *Bob Newman, regional editor for Fly Fish America and author of North American Fly-Fishing and Flyfishing Structure*

"In Fishing Vacations for All Budgets, H. Lee Simpson has compiled an amazing resource of fishing resorts, loaded with the skinny, and delivering pertinent information about resorts around the country...including many secret gems. I particularly found the guest comments useful. This book provides anglers with a valuable guidebook to the nation's fishing resorts. I plan to keep a copy on my desk." *Mark D. Williams, Author, Trout Fishing Sourcebook*

"No one can guarantee the fishing but H. Lee Simpson's new book will make sure there are no surprises with your vacation destination's accommodations and facilities." *Nick Karas, Outdoor Columnist (NY) Newsday*

"Finally a guide to fishing camps and resorts throughout the U.S. The information on the camps I've personally visited is accurate and current. A good place to start your vacation planning." *R.P. Van Gyetnbeek, Editor, Fly Fishing in Salt Water Magazine.*

Fishing Vacations contains a wealth of information for the traveling angler; a valuable reference for those on the go." *Steve Quinn, Editor, In-Fisherman Magazine*

FISHING VACATIONS FOR ALL BUDGETS

DIRECTORY OF U.S. FISHING RESORTS AUTHENTIC GUEST-RATED RESORT GUIDE

H. LEE SIMPSON

pilot books . . . *guides to the good life, all your life*

Library of Congress Catalog Card Number: 98-15713

Cover and text design by Karen K. Quigley

Library of Congress Cataloging in Publication Data

Simpson, H. Lee, 1969—
    Fishing vacations for all budgets: complete directory of U.S. fishing
    resorts: authentic guest-rated resort guide / H. Lee Simpson.
        p. cm.
    Includes index.
    ISBN 0-87576-220-4 (alk. paper)
    1. Fishing Lodges—United States—Directories. I. Title.
    SH463.S56   1998
    799.1'025'73—dc21
                                                                98-15713
                                                                CIP

Printed in the United States of America

ABOUT THE AUTHOR

H. Lee Simpson, who has published articles on a variety of subjects, comes from a long line of fishing enthusiasts. Her fishing career got off to an early start when, at 4, she was found scooping minnows out of the black and yellow bait bucket that was a permanent fixture at her grandfather's lakeside dock. Her Uncle Marty was startled to hear Heather, elbow deep in the minnow bucket, address the minnows in a less than lady-like fashion, "Get back here you little *%#*'s !" she bellowed. With some help, the minnow was captured, impaled on a hook and gracefully presented to an unsuspecting bluegill who lived under the dock.

The author graduated from Indiana University and currently lives in Indianapolis with her husband Mike and their son Noah.

ACKNOWLEDGMENTS

My heartfelt gratitude to the fishing resort owners and managers for their tremendous support, cooperation, advice and patience during this process. Without their help we would never have been able to put together such a comprehensive resource for fishing enthusiasts and their families. I am especially indebted to Dale Wheaton and Dick Wall for the thoughtful comments and suggestions they provided toward the beginning of this project. I am equally grateful to the hundreds of fishing resort guests who took the time to fill out our surveys and offer the insightful comments that bring each resort to life. And to Mike and Noah, to my grandparents, and especially to my parents for the loving example they live.

TABLE OF CONTENTS

INTRODUCTION

Americans are visiting fishing resorts in record numbers—and it's easy to see why. People of all ages, abilities and budgets are discovering the joy of hooking a hard-fighting largemouth, landing a rainbow on the fly or challenging a willful marlin. America's fishing resorts, from Florida to Alaska, are as varied and unique as the thousands of people who visit them each year. The destination *you* choose will mean the difference between a relaxing, fun-filled getaway—with just the kind of atmosphere and fishing you love—or a vacation that's only so-so...or worse. With so many options, how do you find the fishing vacation that's just right for you? By using this book.

Fishing Vacations for All Budgets, for the very first time, gives you a complete resource for information about U. S. fishing vacations that fit all budgets—from economy to luxury. In these pages you will find fishing getaways that appeal both to the die hard fishing enthusiast and to his or her traveling companion (who can't understand why anyone would enjoy standing by a body of water holding a stick with something slimy hanging off it).

We've packed our Fishing Directory/Guide with listings, information, photographs, indexes, *honest, unbiased* customer comments and insider tips on just about every facet of fishing resorts, USA. From informal little family retreats to once-in-a-lifetime luxury lodges; from remote fishing camps to companionable fly fishing schools; the multitude of fishing destinations listed in this book gives you ample choices and easy-to-use ways to weed out those vacation possibilities which don't appeal and focus on those which do.

This book is the result of over a year's exhaustive research and the first to combine a comprehensive listing of America's fishing resorts with direct feedback and ratings from their paying guests. Because *none of the resorts paid to be included in the Guide,* you can be confident that the same set of guidelines and requirements were applied to all, regardless of whether they are big or small, luxury or budget-priced.

And, while most guests liked the resort they rated, their response was spontaneous, given voluntarily and without compensation. You can believe their impartial comments and ratings because—unlike an author (who may have never laid eyes on the places he or she writes about) or the resort's own promotional materials (which are probably accurate but somewhat prejudiced in their own favor), these guests had absolutely nothing to gain from praising a resort's rooms, fishing equipment, staff or the pretty scenery they enjoyed during their stay.

HOW TO USE YOUR FISHING VACATIONS FOR ALL BUDGETS DIRECTORY/GUIDE

For easy reference, the book is divided into two parts: The Directory of U.S. Fishing Resorts; and the Authentic Guest-Rated Resort Guide.

THE DIRECTORY

This is the first complete listing that focuses only on fishing resorts, lodges, inns or camps in the United States. It is arranged alphabetically by state then resort and gives you basic information including: resort name, address, telephone number and—when available—price category, fishing waters and type of fishing. The price categories—in both the Directory and Guide—are represented by an appropriate amount of dollar signs, as follows:

$	*Economy*	Less that $50 a day per person
$$	*Average*	Between $50 and $125 a day per person
$$$	*High Average*	Between $125 and $250 a day per person
$$$$	*Luxury*	Over $250 a day per person

THE GUEST-RATED GUIDE...

is also arranged alphabetically by state then resort name, but it devotes an entire page to each resort including a recent photograph, icons that instantly show you how guests rated the resort (see below), special resort features and detailed descriptions including: **Price Category; Season; Transportation; Fishing; Accommodations; Amenities and Activities; Payment; and Guest Comments.** All information is arranged so you can quickly scan the page and find what's important to you.

GUEST RATINGS:

The guest ratings are the heart of the Fishing Guide. They are what give you a unique, insider's view and opinion of each resort, good and not so good. Here's how we gathered this information:

The resorts listed in the Guide are those which responded to our mailing (to, essentially, every fishing vacation resort, camp, lodge and inn in the United States) and had enough confidence in their facility and service to agree to be impartially rated by their recent guests. We supplied them with guest survey questionnaires which were mailed or given to a representative sampling of customers. The response was outstanding. We received hundreds of surveys *directly from the guests,* then objectively compiled and presented the results so you can read—in their own words—how people like you feel about the resort you're considering as a fishing vacation destination.

The survey asked guests to rate the resort—from poor through excellent —in 7 categories:

- **Room** (Was it clean, comfortable, attractive?)
- **Staff** (Were they friendly, helpful, efficient?)
- **Meals** (Were they appetizing, served well?)
- **Outside Areas** (Were they clean, attractive, well-maintained?)
- **Fishing Guides** (Were they knowledgeable, friendly, helpful?)
- **Fishing Equipment** (Was it well-maintained, in adequate supply?)
- **Children's Activities** (Were they well-supervised, varied, entertaining?)

In addition, guests were asked to comment about each category and the resort in general. These results are included in the **Guest Comments** section.

So you can see at a glance what "grade" the resort was given by its guests in the various categories, they are rated with an appropriate number of "fish."

GUEST RATING ICONS:

🐟	*Poor*	75% or more guests gave the facility a "poor" rating.
🐟🐟	*Average*	75% or more guests rated the facility as "average".
🐟🐟🐟	*Good*	75% or more guests gave the facility a "good" rating.
🐟🐟🐟🐟	*Excellent*	75% or more guests gave the facility an "excellent" rating.

The icons which identify the special features of a resort are:

RESORT FEATURES ICONS:

🍳	Fully equipped kitchens or kitchenettes.
👨‍👩‍👧	Resort offers a structured children's program, classes or baby-sitting services.
🍳	1,2 or 3 meals are included in the overnight room rates of these facilities.
🐾	Guests may bring pets. Note: Many resorts charge a "pet fee." Ask the resort management for details.
⛳	Golf course on the property for guest use.
🍸	Bar or other facility serving or selling alcohol available on premises.
🏕	Full (sewer, water, electric) or basic RV camping sites.

More specific information about a resort's special features are included in the resort description. For example, the **Amenities and Activities** section will tell you about nearby golf courses, saunas, nature walks, etc.

INDEXES

To help you pinpoint fishing vacation destinations that are right for *you*, we've indexed the resorts by 5 categories:

- The **Price Category Index** groups resorts by each of our 4 budget categories: Economy; Average; High Average; and Luxury.
- The **Resorts by State Index** arranges resorts alphabetically by state.
- The **Fish Species Index** identifies vacation sites by the kind of fish you'll (hopefully) be catching if you visit there.
- The **Bodies of Water/Geographic Index** lists resorts by the nearest fishing waters and geographic features such as national parks or wilderness areas.
- The **Resort Features Index** allows you to look up resorts by a specific feature that you want or need in a fishing facility, e.g: RV hookups; remote access; childcare; pets allowed; fly fishing schools.

BEFORE YOU START YOUR RESEARCH...

keep the following questions in mind, it'll make the pleasant task of pinpointing appropriate fishing vacations even easier:

When do you want to go?

You may not have a choice about when you vacation, since many of us follow work or school schedules, but, if your schedule is flexible, consider visiting a resort during its "off-season" when the pace is often more relaxed and the service more personal. Many resorts also offer discounts on lodging and rentals during the off-season. You'll find information on peak seasons for specific fish in the **Insider Tips** portion of the fishing section in the Guide and the **Season** section tells you which months the resort is open and which months off-season discounts are offered.

Where do you want to go?

If your vacation time is limited, you may want to choose a destination that will serve more than one purpose. For instance, if you've always dreamed of visiting the Grand Canyon, choose a destination that allows you to stop on your way to or from, your fishing retreat. Or, if you have family members or business associates that you would like to visit, plan a vacation at a nearby resort.

Are you eager to escape from the bustle and noise of the city? Check out remote fishing areas in the **Resort Features Index**. If, on the contrary, you prefer to stay close to the amenities and nightlife cities offer, find resorts where you fly in and out of a major city and spend a few days there, before or after your fishing trip. All resorts are arranged alphabetically by state.

Flip through some fishing or travel magazines and take a look at some bodies of water you haven't fished before. Again, to make your search easier, all resorts are arranged alphabetically by state and indexed by body of water.

What kind of fishing do you want to do?

Are you a dyed-in-the-wool fly fisherman or do you dream of landing a record-setting marlin? Many resorts listed in this book offer a very wide range of fishing opportunities, others are more specialized. The **Fishing** section includes information on the bodies of water, type of fishing and species of fish found at each location. In addition, the **Fishing** and **Insider Tips** sections include information on availability and cost of guides, equipment available for rent or purchase, peak fishing seasons and special tips from resort owners and previous guests. In the **Resort Features Index** you will find lists of locations that offer ice fishing, fly fishing schools and salt water fishing.

What sort of accommodations are you looking for?

This book lists a complete range of accommodations from luxury suites, where you're pampered to your heart's content, to rustic cabins (some with out-houses), even tents with wood stoves. It's important to think about the comfort level that you expect while on vacation and choose accordingly. If you're a couple who craves room service and sparkling evenings, you may find yourselves dissatisfied with a cozy cabin and well appointed kitchenette. Both locations are great, they're just different. Depends on you.

Who will be traveling with you?

If you plan to travel with one or several people who don't fish, pay special attention to the **Resort Features Index** as well as the **Amenities and Activities** section of each resort description. Given the variety of offerings, you should be able to easily find a resort where the on-site or area attractions will help settle your friends' or family's travel debate. These sections also contain information about the resort, lodge, camp or inn's options (if any) for children. Some locations offer structured kids' programs, others are able to arrange baby-sitting as needed.

How much do you want to spend?

As noted earlier, each resort has been given a price category based on average cost per person per day. If you're on a tight budget, look for resorts in the first two categories. Many of these locations are American Plan and include 1,2, or even 3 meals with each night's lodging. Another way to stretch your vacation dollar is to pick a location that offers kitchenettes where you can cook your own meals—and save the expense of eating out three times a day.

HAVE A GREAT TRIP!

The easy-to-read icons, detailed descriptions, insightful guest comments and handy indexes will help you research your next fishing vacation quickly, easily and thoroughly. After you have narrowed your choices to 5 or 6 different resorts, call the finalists and ask for a brochure. While you have your potential host on the phone, ask some questions about local fishing and sightseeing. If he or she is enthusiastic and willing to take some time to answer your questions, it is very likely they will also be a gracious host. If the person you're speaking with is "too busy to talk", presses for an immediate commitment from you, or is generally uncooperative, you can probably expect the same treatment in person.

Before you make your final decision, be sure that you have weighed all the options: rates; accommodations; location, fishing opportunities; and over-all impression. Then make your reservation with confidence. Before long, you'll be hanging out that "Gone Fishing" sign and on the way to *your* dream fishing getaway.

FISHING VACATIONS FOR ALL BUDGETS

DIRECTORY OF U.S. FISHING RESORTS

AUTHENTIC GUEST-RATED RESORT GUIDE

Note: Some resorts did not provide price, waters or fishing information in time for publication.

ALABAMA

Dead Lake Fishing Lodge
2350 Dead Lake Rd.
Creola, AL 36525
334-675-0320
Price Category: $
Waters: Dead Lake.

Lakepoint Resort State Park
151 West Chewalla
Euffaula, AL 36027
334-687-4425

Ossa-Win-Tha Resort
PO Box 203
Guntersville, AL 35976
205-582-4595
Price Category: $
Waters: Lake Guntersville.

White Oak Plantation
5215 CR 10
Tuskegee, AL 36083
334-727-9258
Price Category: $$
Waters: Private ponds.
Fish: Largemouth bass.

ALASKA

Afognak Wilderness Lodge*
General Delivery
Seal Bay, AK 99697
907-486-6442
800-478-6442
Price Category: $$$$
Waters: Kodiak Island waters in
Gulf of Alaska; North Afognak

Island streams and lakes.
Fish: Halibut; lingcod; sea bass;
eel; sockeye salmon; pink
salmon; silver salmon; rainbow
trout; dolly varden; steelhead.

Alagnak Lodge
505 Ward Ave., Ste. 207
Honolulu, HI 95814-4111
800-319-4617
Price Category: $$$$
Waters: Alagnak River; Moraine
Creek; Nanuktuk Creek; Naknek
River; American River;
Kulik River.
Fish: Rainbow trout; silver
salmon; sockeye salmon; pink
salmon; grayling; king salmon;
chum salmon; northern pike.

Alaska Reel Adventures
PO Box 211333
Auke Bay, AK 99821
800-877-2661
Price Category: $$$$
Waters: N/A
Fish: Arctic char; arctic grayling;
chum salmon; cutthroat trout;
dolly varden; halibut; king
salmon; lake trout; ling cod;
northern pike.

Alaskan Fishing Adventures
PO Box 2457
Soldotna, AK 99669
800-548-3474
Price Category: $$$$
Waters: Kasilof River; Kenai
River; Cook Inlet.
Fish: Halibut; king salmon; rain-

bow trout; dolly varden; silver salmon; steelhead.

Alaskan Fishing Smorgasbord
PO Box 1516
Cordova, AK 99574
907-424-5552
Price Category: $$$
Waters: N/A
Fish: King salmon; sockeye salmon; pink salmon; chum salmon; silver salmon; rainbow trout; dolly varden; grayling; halibut; lake trout.

Alaska's Lake Clark Inn*
1 Lang Lane, General Delivery
Port Alsworth, AK 99653-9999
907-781-2224
Price Category: $$$$
Waters: Bristol Bay; Cook Inlet.
Fish: King salmon; red salmon; chum salmon; pink salmon; silver salmon; rainbow trout; arctic char; dolly varden; lake trout; northern pike; shee fish.

Alaska's Wilderness Lodge*
PO Box 190748
Anchorage, AK 99519-0748
907-272-9912
800-835-8032
Price Category: $$$$
Waters: Bristol Bay; Lake Clark National Park waters; Katmai National Park waters.
Fish: Chinook salmon; sockeye salmon; chum salmon; silver salmon; northern pike; lake trout; rainbow trout; char; grayling.

Anchor Point Lodge
PO Box 211333

Auke Bay, AK 99821
800-877-2661

Angler's Lodge and Fish Camp*
PO Box 508
Sterling, AK 99672
907-262-1747
Price Category: $$
Waters: Kenai River; Kasilof River; Cook Inlet.
Fish: King salmon; silver salmon; red salmon; halibut; rainbow trout; dolly varden.

Arctic Tern Charters and Fish Camp*
PO Box 1122
Sterling, AK 99672
907-262-7631
Price Category: $$$$
Waters: Kenai River; Cook Inlet; Kechimak Bay; Resurrection Bay.
Fish: Halibut; king salmon; silver salmon; red salmon.

Baranof Wilderness Lodge*
PO Box 42
Norden, CA 95724
Business Office: 530-582-8132;
Summer: 907-738-3597
Price Category: $$$$
Waters: Chatham Straight area.
Fish: Silver salmon; red salmon; pink salmon; king salmon; chum salmon; trout; dolly varden; halibut; various bottom and rock fish.

Captain Bligh's Beaver Creek Lodge
PO Box 4300
Soldotna, AK 99669
Winter: 907-262-7919

*This resort is included in Guest-Rated Resort Guide

Summer: 907-283-7550
Price Category: $$$$
Waters: Kenai River; Cook Inlet.
Fish: Salmon; trout; halibut.

Chelatna Lake Lodge*
3941 Float Plane Dr.
Anchorage, AK 99502
907-243-7767
800-999-0785
Price Category: $$$$
Waters: Chelatna Lake and area
rivers and streams.
Fish: King salmon; silver
salmon; rainbow trout; red
salmon; chum salmon; pink
salmon; lake trout; grayling;
northern pike.

Chinita Bay Lodge
PO Box 233032
Anchorage, AK 99523
907-522-2715
Price Category: $$$$
Waters: Cook Inlet; Chinita Bay.
Fish: King salmon; red salmon;
chum salmon; silver salmon;
halibut.

Copper River Lodge
PO Box PVY
Iliamna, AK 99606
Summer: 907-571-1464
Winter: 406-222-0624
Price Category: $$$$
Waters: Copper River.
Fish: Rainbow trout; sockeye
salmon.

Creekside Inn
PO Box 39236
Ninilchik, AK 99639
907-567-7333
Price Category: $$$

Waters: Cook Inlet; Kenai River;
Kasilof River; Deep Creek.
Fish: Sockeye salmon; silver
salmon; king salmon; pink
salmon; chum salmon; dolly
varden; halibut.

Daniel's Lake Lodge
PO Box 1444
Kenai, AK 99611
800-774-5578

Deer Creek Cottages*
PO Box 19475
Thorne Bay, AK 99919
907-828-3393
Price Category: $$$$
Waters: Pacific Ocean's Clarence
Strait; Thorne River; Staney
Creek; Ratz Creek ; Hatchery
Creek.
Fish: Halibut; cod; yellow-eyed
rockfish; steelhead; coho
salmon; pink salmon; sockeye
salmon; cutthroat trout; dolly
varden.

Denali West Lodge*
Box 40AC
Lake Minuchumina, AK 99757
907-674-3112
Price Category: $$$$
Waters: Lake Minuchumina;
Nowitna River; Yukon River;
Kuskokwim River; Salmon
River; Tonzoa River.
Fish: Northern pike; shee fish.

**Evergreen Lodge at Lake
Louise***
HC 01; Box 1709
Glennallen, AK 99588
907-822-3250
Price Category: $$ - $$$$

This resort is included in Guest-Rated Resort Guide

Waters: Lake Louise; Clarence Lake; remote wilderness lakes. Fish: Lake trout; arctic grayling; rainbow trout; salmon.

Fishing Unlimited Lodge

PO Box 190301
Anchorage, AK 99519
907-243-5899
Price Category: $$$$
Waters: Lake Iliamna; Lake Clark.
Fish: Rainbow trout; lake trout; king salmon; silver salmon; pink salmon; northern pike.

Funny Moose Vacation Rentals*

HC #1, Box 1299
Soldotna, AK 99669
907-262-3701
800-770-3701
Price Category: $$ - $$$$
Waters: Kenai River; Kasilof River; Funny River; Moose River; Deep Creek; Ninilchik River; Kachemak Bay; Prince William Sound.
Fish: King salmon; red salmon; pink salmon; silver salmon; halibut; cod; steelhead; rainbow trout; grayling.

Glacier Bay Country Inn and Whalesong Lodge*

PO Box 5
Gustavus, AK 99826
907-697-2288
Price Category: $$
Waters: Streams and rivers of Chicagof Island; Glacier Bay.
Fish: Five salmon species; dolly varden; char; steelhead; cutthroat trout; halibut.

Goodnews River Lodge*

PO Box 770530
Eagle River, AK 99577
800-274-8371
Price Category: $$$$
Waters: Goodnews River.
Fish: Rainbow trout; dolly varden; king salmon; sockeye salmon; chum salmon; pink salmon; silver salmon.

Gustavus Inn*

PO Box 60
Gustavus, AK 99826
907-697-2254
800-649-5220
Price Category: $$
Waters: Icy Strait; Icy Passage; Glacier Bay.
Fish: Halibut; king salmon; coho salmon; pink salmon; chum salmon; ling cod.

Island Point Lodge*

(Petersburg, AK)
PO Box 929
Westborough, MA 01581
508-366-4522
Price Category: $$$$
Waters: Wrangell Narrows; Sumner Strait; Frederick Sound; Falls Creek; Blind Slough.
Fish: Salmon; halibut; cutthroat trout; dolly varden; steelhead.

Katmai Wilderness Lodge

Box 4332
Kodiak, AK 99615
800-488-8767

*This resort is included in Guest-Rated Resort Guide

Kenai Legend Lodge
PO Box 460
Kenai, AK 99611
907-776-5363
Price Category: $$
Waters: Island Lake.

Kenai Magic Lodge*
2440 East Tudor #205
Anchorage, AK 99507
907-248-9889
Price Category: $$$$
Waters: Kenai River; Kasilof
River; Moose River; Deep Creek;
Ninilchik River; Kachemak Bay;
Prince William Sound.
Fish: King salmon; red salmon;
silver salmon; pink salmon; rain-
bow trout; dolly varden;
grayling; pike; lake trout; char;
halibut.

King Ko Inn
PO Box 346
King Salmon, AK 99613
907-246-3377
Price Category: $$
Waters: Naknek River.

Kulik Lodge / Brooks Lodge
4550 Aircraft Dr.
Anchorage, AK 99502
800-544-0551
Price Category: $$$$

Mission Lodge
111201 SE 8th, Suite 100
Bellevue, WA 98004
800-819-0750
Price Category: $$$$
Waters: Bristol Bay area.
Fish: Pacific salmon; rainbow

trout; arctic trout; dolly varden;
arctic grayling; lake trout;
northern pike.

Misty Fjords Lodge
125 South Main
Ketchikan, AK 99901
888-295-5464
Price Category: $$$$
Waters: Mink Bay area waters.
Fish: Salmon; steelhead; trout.

Northland Ranch Resort
PO Box 2376
Kodiak, AK 99615
907-486-5578
Price Category: $$$
Waters: Gulf of Alaska; Kodiak
Island waters.
Fish: Salmon.

No See Um Lodge
6266 Riverside Dr.
Redding, CA 96001
916-241-6204
Price Category: $$$$
Waters: Kvichak River; Iliamna
Lake
Fish: Rainbow trout; dolly var-
den; arctic char; arctic grayling;
king salmon; silver
salmon; red salmon; pink
salmon; dog salmon.

Orca Lodge*
PO Box 4653
Soldotna, AK 99669
907-262-5649
Price Category: $$$$
Waters: Kenai River; Kachemac
Bay; Kasilof River; Alaska
Peninsula streams and lakes.

Fish: King salmon; red salmon; silver salmon; pink salmon; rainbow trout; halibut.

Port Lions Lodge
PO Box 875545
Wasilla, AK 99687
907-454-2264
Price Category: $$$$
Waters: Karluk River.
Fish: King salmon; steelhead; coho salmon; halibut.

Quinnatt Landing Resort
5520 Lake Otis Pkwy. #101
Anchorage, AK 99507
800-770-3474

Reel M Inn*
PO Box 221
King Salmon, AK 99613
907-246-8322
Price Category: $$$$
Waters: Naknek River; Illiamna drainage; Becharof drainage.
Fish: King salmon; pink salmon; red salmon; silver salmon; rainbow trout; arctic char; grayling.

Saltery Lake Lodge
1516 Larch St.
Kodiak , AK 99615
907-486-7083
Price Category: $$$$
Waters: Saltery River; Saltery Lake; Ugak Bay.
Fish: Sockeye salmon; pink salmon; chum salmon; silver salmon; dolly varden; rainbow trout; steelhead.

Saltwater Sportsman Lodge
PO Box 95
Seward, AK 99664
907-224-5271

Silver Salmon Creek Lodge*
PO Box 3234
Soldotna, AK 99669
907-262-4839
888-8-SALMON
Price Category: $$ - $$$$
Waters: Silver Salmon Creek; Shelter Creek; Johnson River; Cook Inlet.
Fish: Silver salmon; king salmon; pink salmon; chum salmon; dolly varden; halibut.

Silver Salmon Lodge
Box 378
Kodiak, AK 99615
907-680-2230

Soaring Eagle Lodge
HC 1, Box 1203
Soldotna, AK 99669
907-262-8474

Stephan Lake Lodge
PO Box 770695
Eagle River, AK 99577
907-733-2538
Price Category: $$$$
Fish: King salmon; silver salmon; rainbow salmon; grayling.

Talaview Resorts
PO Box 190088
Anchorage, AK 99519
907-733-3447

*This resort is included in Guest-Rated Resort Guide

Price Category: $$$$
Waters: Talachulitna River.
Fish: Salmon; rainbow trout;
arctic grayling.

Tanaku Lodge
PO Box 72
Elfin Cove, AK 99825
800-482 6258
Price Category: $$$$
Waters: Cross Sound.
Fish: Red salmon; pink salmon;
silver salmon; chum salmon;
halibut; ling cod.

The Point Lodge at Lake Louise
HC 01, Box 1706
Glenallen, AK 99588
907-822-5566

Tikchik Narrows Lodge
PO Box 220248
Anchorage, AK 99522
907-243-8450
Price Category: $$$$
Waters: Tikchik River; Togiak
River; Nushagak River; Tikchik
Lake system; Kokwok River;
Nuyakuk River; Naknek River.
Fish: King salmon; sockeye
salmon; chum salmon; pink
salmon; silver salmon; grayling;
char; rainbow trout; lake trout;
northern pike; arctic char; dolly
varden.

Tutka Bay Wilderness Lodge
Box 960 VP
Homer, AK 99603
907-235-3905

Price Category: $$$$
Waters: Kachemac Bay; Cook
Inlet.
Fish: Halibut; king salmon; kelp
bass; greenling; dolly varden.

Ugashik Lake Lodge
PO Box 90444-YP
Anchorage, AK 99509
800-437-2472
Price Category: $
Waters: Ugashik Lake; Bristol
Bay.
Fish: Chinook salmon; sockeye
salmon; arctic char; northern
pike; grayling.

Ultima Thule Outfitters
1007 H. St.
Anchorage, AK 99501
907-258-0636
Price Category: $$$$
Waters: Wrangler/St. Elias
National Park rivers; lakes and
Streams; Gulf of Alaska.
Fish: Salmon; steelhead; trout;
grayling.

Waterfall Resort
PO Box 6440
Ketchikan, AK 99901
800-544-5125
Price Category: $$$$
Waters: Prince of Wales Island
Area.
Fish: King salmon; pink salmon;
halibut; red snapper; ling cod;
various bottom fish.

Whaler's Cove Lodge
PO Box 101

*This resort is included in Guest-Rated Resort Guide

Angoon, AK 99820
800-423-4123

Wilderness Place Lodge
PO Box 19711
Anchorage, AK 99519
907-248-4335

Wooden Wheel Cove Lodge*
PO Box 118
Point Baker, AK 99927
907-489-2288
888-489-9288
Price Category: $$$$
Waters: Sumner Strait; West
Coast of Prince of Wales Island;
Flicker Creek; Alder Creek;
Staney Creek.
Fish: Halibut; various bottom
species; steelhead; cutthroat
trout; dolly varden; coho
salmon; pink salmon; king
salmon; sockeye salmon.

Yes Bay Lodge
PO Box 6440
Ketchikan, AK 99901
800-999-0784
Price Category: $$$$
Waters: McDonald Lake; Yes Bay.
Fish: Salmon; halibut; rockfish;
trout; steelhead.

ARIZONA

Hawley Lake Resort*
White Mountain Apache
Reservation
PO Box 448
McNary, AZ 85930
520-335-7511
Price Category: $ - $$

Waters: Hawley Lake; Diamond
Creek; White River; Early Park
Lake.
Fish: Apache trout; brook trout;
lake trout.

Lee's Ferry Lodge
Vemilion Cliffs, HC 67, Box 1
Marble Canyon, AZ 86036
520-355-2231

ARKANSAS

Anderson House Inn
201 East Main St.
Heber Springs, AR 72543-3116
501-362-5266
Price Category: $ - $$
Waters: Little Red River.
Fish: Trout; smallmouth bass

Brady Mountain Resort
4120 Brady Mountain Rd.
Royal, AR 71968
501-767-3422
Price Category: $
Waters: Ouachita River; Lake
Hamilton; Lake Catherine; Lake
DeGray.
Fish: Crappie; striped bass;
walleye.

Buffalo Outdoor Center
Hwy. 65, Rt. 1, Box 56
St. Joe, AR 72675
800-582-2244

Chit Chat Chaw Resort
Rt. 1, Box 157
Mountain Home, AR 72653-
5803
501-431-5584

This resort is included in Guest-Rated Resort Guide

Price Category: $
Waters: Bull Shoals Lake; White River.
Fish: Rainbow trout; brown trout; cutthroat trout; crappie; bass; walleye; catfish; bluegill.

Crystal Springs Resort*
1647 Crystal Springs Rd.
Royal, AR 71968
501-991-3361
Price Category: $
Waters: Lake Ouachita; Lake Hamilton; Lake Catherine; Arkansas River; Ouachita River.
Fish: Smallmouth bass; largemouth bass; black bass; white bass; striped bass; walleye; catfish; bream; crappie.

Degray Lake Resort State Park*
Rt. 3, Box 490
Bismarck, AR 71929-8194
501-865-2801
800-737-8355
Price Category: $
Waters: DeGray Lake.
Fish: Black bass; hybrid bass; crappie; catfish; bream.

Gaston's
1777 River Rd. A
Lakeview, AR 72642
501-431-5202
Price Category: $
Waters: White River; Bull Shoals Lake.
Fish: Rainbow trout; brown trout; cutthroat trout; bass; walleye; catfish; bluegill; crappie.

Gunga La Lodge
Rt. 1, Box 147

Lakeview, AR 72642
800-844-5606
Price Category: $
Waters: Bull Shoals Lake; White River; Crooked Creek.
Fish: Rainbow trout; cutthroat trout; brown trout; smallmouth bass; rock bass.

Holiday Shores Resort
Rt. 1, Box 283
Midway, AR 72651
870-431-5370
Price Category: $
Waters: Bull Shoals Lake.
Fish: Rainbow trout; cutthroat trout; brown trout; bass; crappie; walleye; bluegill; catfish; white bass.

Howard Creek
887 Howard Creek Rd.
Midway, AR 71625
888-437-3474
Price Category: $
Waters: Bull Shoals Lake; White River; Norfork Lake; Buffalo River; North Fork River.
Fish: Largemouth bass; smallmouth bass; rainbow trout; brown trout; cutthroat trout; walleye; crappie; white bass; striper; catfish; bluegill.

Lindsey's Rainbow Resort*
350 Rainbow Loop
Heber Springs, AR 72543
501-362-3139
800-305-8790
Price Category: $
Waters: Greers Ferry Lake; Little Red River.
Fish: Rainbow trout; brook trout; brown trout; cutthroat trout.

Mar Mar Resort and Tackle Shop
PO Box 168
Bull Shoals , AR 72634
800-332-BULL
Price Category: $
Waters: Bull Shoals Lake; White River.
Fish: Rainbow trout; cutthroat trout; brown trout; bass; crappie; bluegill; walleye; catfish; white bass.

Mountain Harbour Resort
PO Box 807 T
Mount Ida, AR 71957
501-867-1200
Price Category: $$$
Waters: Lake Ouachita.

North Shore Resort*
1462 C.R. 19
Mountain Home, AR 72653
870-431-5564
Price Category: $
Waters: Bull Shoals Lake; White River; Crooked Creek.
Fish: Bass (largemouth; smallmouth; spotted; white; striped); trout (rainbow; lake; brown); walleye; crappie; catfish.

Oak Ridge Resort*
275 C.R. 106
Mountain Home, AR 72653
870-431-5575
Price Category: $
Waters: White River; Bull Shoals Lake.
Fish: Largemouth bass; smallmouth bass; Kentucky bass; walleye; crappie; lake trout; catfish.

Ozark Angler
822 North Monroe
Little Rock, AR 77205
501-663-8403

PJ's Lodge
PO Box 61
Norfolk, AR 72658
870-499-7500
Price Category: $ - $$
Waters: White River.
Fish: Brook trout; brown trout; cutthroat trout.

Promise Lane Resort
323 CR 107
Mountain Home, AR 72653-6243
870-431-5576
Price Category: $
Waters: Lake Taneycomo; Bull Shoals Lake; Table Rock Lake.
Fish: Smallmouth bass; largemouth bass; Kentucky bass; bluegill; catfish; brown trout; crappie.

Rainbow Drive Resort*
669 Rainbow Landing Dr.
Cotte, AR 72626
870-430-5217
Price Category: $
Waters: Bull Shoals Lake; White River; Lake Norfork; North Fork River; Buffalo National River.
Fish: Rainbow trout; brown trout; cutthroat trout.

Scott Valley Resort and Guest Ranch*
PO Box 1447
Mountain Home, AR 72653
888-855-7747
Price Category: $$

This resort is included in Guest-Rated Resort Guide

Waters: White River; North Fork River.
Fish: Rainbow trout; brown trout; cutthroat trout; bass.

Shady Oaks Resort*
HC 62, Box 128
Flippin, AR 72634
870-453-8420
Price Category: $
Waters: Bull Shoals Lake; Norfork Lake; Buffalo River; White River; North Fork River.
Fish: Bass; crappie; walleye; trout; catfish.

Shangri La
Star Rt. 1, Box 257
Mt. Ida, AR 71957
501-867-2011
Price Category: $
Waters: Lake Ouachita.
Fish: Largemouth bass; striped bass; bluegill; crappie; catfish.

Sister Creek Resort*
9833 Promise Land Rd.
Mountain Home, AR 72653
870-431-5587
Price Category: $
Waters: Bull Shoals Lake.
Fish: Largemouth bass; smallmouth bass; trout; walleye; crappie; catfish; bluegill.

Sportsman's
HCR 62, Box 96
Flippin, AR 72634
501-453-2424
Price Category: $
Waters: Bull Shoals Lake.
Fish: Crappie; smallmouth bass; white bass; Kentucky bass; trout; walleye; catfish; bluegill.

Stetson's
HCR 62, Box 102
Flippin, AR 72634
501-453-8066
Price Category: $$$
Waters: White River.
Fish: German brown trout; rainbow trout; brook trout.

Tall Timbers Resort
Rt. 1, Box 48 - S
Oakland, AR 72661
501-431-5622
Price Category: $
Waters: Bull Shoals Lake.
Fish: Crappie; smallmouth bass; white bass; Kentucky bass; trout; walleye; catfish; bluegill.

White Buffalo Resort
418 White Buffalo Trail
Mountain Home, AR 72653-7719
870-424-6892

Wilson's Resort
Rt. 71, Box 660
Camdenton, MO 65020
573-873-5178
Price Category: $
Waters: Lake of the Ozarks.
Fish: Black bass; white bass; crappie; catfish; walleye.

Wimpy's Resort
Rt. 1, Box 141
Mountain Home , AR 72653
501-431-5325
Price Category: $
Waters: Bull Shoals Lake.
Fish: Crappie; smallmouth bass; white bass; Kentucky bass; trout; walleye; catfish; bluegill.

This resort is included in Guest-Rated Resort Guide

CALIFORNIA

Arcularius Ranch
Rt. 1, Box 230K
Mammoth Lakes, CA 93546
703-648-7807
Price Category: $$
Waters: Owens River.
Fish: Brown trout; rainbow trout.

Back Country
19560 8th St.
Sonoma, CA 95476
707-939-9408

Big Rock Resort*
PO Box 126
120 Big Rock Rd.
June Lake, CA 93529
706-648-1067
Price Category: $
Waters: June Lake; Gull Lake;
Silver Lake; Grant Lake; Rush
Creek.
Fish: Rainbow trout; brown
trout; cutthroat trout.

Camanche Northshore Resort
2000 Camanche Rd.
Ione, CA 95640
209-763-5166
Price Category: $
Waters: Lake Camanche; Lake
Alamador; Lake Pardee; Hogan
Reservoir.
Fish: Bass; trout; catfish;
bluegill; sunfish.

Clearwater House on Hat Creek
PO Box 90
Cassel, CA 96016
916-335-5500

Price Category: $$$
Waters: Hat Creek.
Fish: Rainbow trout; brook
trout; brown trout.

Coffee Creek Ranch
HC 2, Box 4940
Trinity Center, CA 96091
530-266-3343
Price Category: $
Waters: Coffee Creek; Trinity
River; Trinity Lake.
Fish: Brook trout; brown trout;
rainbow trout; bass; catfish.

Deer Lodge
753 Patrick Place Dr.
Trinidad, CA 95570
707-677-3554
Price Category: $$
Waters: Pacific Ocean; Klamath
River; Trinity River; Eel River;
Redwood Creek.
Fish: Salmon; bottom fish; steel-
head.

Doc and Al's
Local Box
Bridgeport, CA 93517
760-932-7051
Price Category: $
Waters: Robinson Creek; Twin
Lakes.
Fish: Trout.

Hat Creek House
18101 Doty Rd.
Cassel, CA 96016
916-335-5270
Price Category: $$$
Waters: Hat Creek.
Fish: Brown trout; rainbow
trout.

This resort is included in Guest-Rated Resort Guide

Henderson Springs
PO Box 220
Big Bend, CA 96011
916-337-6917
Price Category: $$$
Fish: Rainbow trout; brown
trout.

**High Sierra Family Vacation
Camp**
1485 Redwood Dr.
Los Altos, CA 94022
800-227-9900

Jim's Soda Bay Resort*
6380 Soda Bay Rd.
Kelseyville, CA 95451
707-279-4837
Price Category: $
Waters: Clear Lake.
Fish: Bass; bluegill; catfish; crap-
pie.

Ko-Ket Resort
14174 Islaton Rd.
Islaton, CA 95641
916-776-1488

Kona Kai Resort
1551 Shelter Island Dr.
San Diego, CA 96106
619-222-1191
Price Category: $$$
Waters: Pacific Ocean.

Lake Henshaw Resort
26439 Hwy. 76
Santa Isabell, CA 92070
618-782-3501

Lassen View Resort
7457 Hwy. 147
Lake Almashore, CA 96137
916-596-3437

Lava Creek Lodge
PO Box 1050
Fall River Mills, CA 96028
916-336-6288
Price Category: $
Waters: Eastman Lake;
Ahjumawi Springs; Baum Lake;
Fall River; Hat Creek; Pit River;
McCloud River.
Fish: Rainbow trout; brown
trout.

Little Rock Lake Resort
32700 Chesbrough
Palmdale, CA 93552
805-533-1923

Montecito - Sequoia
8000 General's Hwy.
Box 858
King's Canyon National Park,
CA 93633
415-967-0540
Price Category: $$
Waters: Stoney Creek; Dorst
Creek; Bid Meadow Creek;
Boulder Creek; Ten Mile Creek;
King's River.
Fish: Rainbow trout.

Oakridge Inn
PO Box 1560
780 N. Ventura Ave.
Oak View, CA 93022
805-649-4018
Price Category: $$
Waters: Lake Casitos.
Fish: Largemouth bass; rainbow
trout; crappie; sunfish; catfish.

Oasis Springs Lodge*
PO Box 20368
Oakland, CA 94620
510-653-7630

This resort is included in Guest-Rated Resort Guide

800-642-4150
Price Category: $$
Waters: South Fork of Battle
Creek
Fish: Rainbow trout; brown
trout.

Red's Kern Valley Marina
PO Box 3181
Lake Isabella, CA 93240
619-3749-1634
Price Category: $
Rick's Lodge
Glenburn Star Rt.
Fall River Mills, CA 96028
916-336-5300
Price Category: $$

Sea Ranch Lodge
PO Box 44
Sea Ranch, CA 95497
800-732-7262
Price Category: $$
Fish: Steelhead.

Sorensen's Resort
14255 Hwy. 88
Hope Valley, CA 96120
800-423-9949
Price Category: $-$$
Waters: Carson River.
Fish: Trout.

Tenaya Lodge at Yosemite*
1122 Hwy. 41
Fish Camp, CA 93623
209-683-6555
Price Category: $$
Waters: Sierra National Forest
and Yosemite National Park
lakes and streams.
Fish: Golden trout; brook trout;
brown trout; rainbow trout.

The Pines Resort
PO Box 109
Bass Lake, CA 93604
800-350-7463
Price Category: $$$
Waters: Bass Lake.

The Sea Ranch Lodge
PO Box 44
The Sea Ranch, CA 95497
800-732-7262
Price Category: $$
Waters: Gualala River.
Fish: Steelhead.
Will O Point Resort
#1 1st St.
Lakeport, CA 95453
707-263-5407
Price Category: $
Waters: Clear Lake; Blue Lake.
Fish: Trout.

Willow Springs Motel
Local Box
Bridgeport, CA 93517
760-932-7725
Price Category: $$
Waters: Green Creek; Green
Lake.
Fish: Trout

COLORADO

Broadmoor Resort
PO Box 1439
Colorado Springs, CO 80901
719-634-7711
Price Category: $$

Circle K Ranch
26916 Hwy. 145
Dolores, CO 81323
970-562-3808

*This resort is included in Guest-Rated Resort Guide

Price Category: $
Waters: Dolores River.

Columbine Creek Bed and Breakfast
PO Box 1675
Grand Lake, CO 80447
970-627-2429
Price Category: $$$

Cross D Bar Trout Ranch*
2299 County Road 328
Westcliffe, CO 81252
719-783-2007
Price Category: $
Waters: 4 private, spring fed lakes.
Fish: Rainbow trout; cutthroat trout; brown trout; golden trout; Donaldson trout; brook trout.

Elk Creek Lodge
PO Box 130
1111 CR 54
Meeker, CO 81641
970-878-5454
Price Category: $$$$
Waters: Elk Creek; White River.
Fish: Trout.

Elktrout Lodge
PO Box 614
Kremmling, CO 80459
970-724-3343
Price Category: $$$$
Waters: Private sections of the Colorado River.
Fish: Trout.

Fryingpan River Ranch
32042 Fryingpan River Ranch
Meredith, CO 81642
970-927-3441

Price Category: $$$
Waters: Fryingpan River.
Fish: Trout.

Gold Lake Mountain Resort
3374 Gold Lake Rd.
Ward, CO 80481
800-450-3544
Price Category: $$$$
Waters: Gold Lake.
Fish: Trout.

Little Grizzly Creek Ranch
777 County Rd. 1
Walden, CO 80480
970-723-4209
Price Category: $$$
Waters: North Platte River; Little Grizzly Creek.
Fish: Brook trout; rainbow trout; cutthroat trout.

Seven Lakes Lodge
General Delivery
Meeker, CO 81641
970-878-3635
Price Category: $$$$
Waters: White River.
Fish: Brook trout; cutthroat trout; rainbow trout.

Sunset Ranch
PO Box 876
Steamboat Springs, CO 80477
970-879-0954

Sylvan Dale Guest Ranch*
2939 North County Rd. 31D
Loveland, CO 80538
970-667-3915
Price Category: $
Waters: Private stretch of the Big Thompson River; 12 private lakes.

This resort is included in Guest-Rated Resort Guide

23

Fish: Rainbow trout; brown trout; brook trout; cutthroat trout; steelhead.

Three Rivers Resort*
130 Cty. Rd. 742
Almont, CO 81210
970-641-1303
888-761-FISH
Price Category: $
Waters: East River; Taylor River; Gunnison River; Taylor Reservoir; Spring Creek Reservoir.
Fish: Makinaw trout; rainbow trout; cutthroat trout; brook trout; brown trout; pike.

Triple J Trout Ranch
Salida, CO
719-539-3094
Price Category: $$$

CONNECTICUT

Old Riverton Inn*
Rt. 20, PO Box 6
Riverton, CT 06065
Price Category: $
Waters: West Branch of the Farmington; Sandy Brook.
Species: Brown Trout.

The Boulders
East Shore Rd.
New Preston, CT 06777
860-868-0541
Price Category: $$$
Waters: Lake Waramug.
Species: Brown trout; smallmouth bass; largemouth bass.

FLORIDA

Amelia Island Plantation
Hwy. A1A South
Amelia, FL 32034
904-261-6161
Price Category: $$$
Waters: Pacific Ocean.

Angler's Marina*
910 Okeechobee Blvd.
Clewiston, FL 33440
941-983-4613
800-741-3141
Price Category: $
Waters: Lake Okeechobee.
Fish: Largemouth bass; crappie; bluegill; shellcrackers.

Bass Haven Lodge
PO Box 458
Welaka, FL 32193
904-467-8812
Price Category: $
Waters: Rodman Reservoir; Big and Little Lake George; Ocklawaha River.
Fish: Largemouth bass; pickerel; striped bass; black bass.

Bienville Plantation*
PO Box 241
White Springs, FL 32096
904-397-4215
Price Category: $$$$
Waters: Private phosphate pit lakes.
Fish: Largemouth bass; crappie; bluegill.

Bull Creek Fish Camp
#3861 CR 2006

This resort is included in Guest-Rated Resort Guide

Bunnell, FL 32110
904-437-3451
Price Category: $

Camp Henry Resort and Marina*
HC 1, Box 522
Georgetown, FL 32139
904-467-2282
Price Category: $
Waters: St. John's River; Lake George; Little Lake George.
Fish: Largemouth bass; striped bass; crappie; bluegill; sunfish; catfish.

Cheeca Lodge
PO Box 527
Islamorada, FL 33036
800-327-2888
Price Category: $$$$
Waters: Atlantic Ocean.
Fish: Wahoo; marlin; bonefish; tarpon; sailfish; snapper; tuna.

Faro Blanco Resort
1996 Overseas Hwy.
Marathon, FL 33050
800-759-3276
Price Category: $$
Waters: Atlantic Ocean; Gulf of Mexico.
Fish: Bonefish; tarpon; permit.

Fish Haven Lodge*
1 Fish Haven Rd.
Auburndale, FL 33823
941-984-1183
Price Category: $
Waters: Lake Juliana.
Fish: Bass; bluegill; speckled perch; bream; catfish.

Fisherman's Cove Resort
29115 Eickelberger Rd.
Auburndale, FL 33923
800-254-9993
Price Category: $
Waters: Lake Harris.
Fish: Bass; catfish.

Flamingo Lodge
1 Flamingo Dr.
Flamingo, FL 33034
941-695-3101
Price Category: $
Waters: Florida Bay; Everglades National Park area waters.
Fish: Snook; redfish; grouper; tarpon; sea trout; snapper; amberjack.

Gainey's Talquin Lodge
Rt. 2, Box 1607
Quinch, FL 32351
904-627-3822

Georgetown Marina and Lodge
1533 Rd. 309
PO Box 171
Georgetown, FL 32139
Price Category: $
Waters: Lake George.

Hawk's Cay Resort*
61 Hawk's Cay Blvd.
Duck Key, FL 33050
305-743-9000
Price Category: $$$
Waters: Atlantic Ocean; Florida Bay; Florida Everglades National Park.
Fish: Dolphin; tuna; wahoo; kingfish; snapper; grouper; shark; tarpon; bonefish; permit;

marlin; barracuda; trout; snook; redfish.

Hidden Harbour Resort
3136 Shoth Marina Pkwy.
Lake Wales, FL 33853-8450
800-823-7576
Price Category: $$$

Howard Johnson Riverside Inn Resort*
5297 South Cherokee Way
Homosassa, FL 34448
352-628-2474
800-442-5020
Price Category: $
Waters: Homosassa River; Gulf of Mexico; Crystal River.
Fish: Black bass; trout; bream; tarpon; sheepshead; grouper; redfish; speckled trout; snapper; shark; cobia.

Moonrise Resort*
8801-18 East Moonrise Lane
Floral City, FL 34436
352-726-2553
800-665-6701
Price Category: $
Waters: Tsala Apopka Lake; Withlacoochee River.
Fish: Black bass; pickerel; bluegill; crappie; shellcracker; catfish.

Okee Tantie Recreation Area
10430 Hwy. 78 West
Okeechobee, FL 34947
813-763-2622
Price Category: $

Palm Grove Fishing Lodge
PO Box 194

Steinhatchee, FL 32359
352-498-3721
Price Category: $$$

Parramore's Campground*
1675 South Moon Rd.
Astor, FL 32102
904-749-2721
800-516-2386
Price Category: $ - $$
Waters: St. John's River, Lake Dexter, Lake George, Lake Woodruff.
Fish: Speckled perch; bream; bluegill; bass; catfish.

Pelican Cove Resort*
PO Box 633
84457 Old Overseas Hwy.
Islamorada, FL 33036
305-664-4435
800-445-4690
Price Category: $$$
Waters: Atlantic Ocean; Gulf of Mexico.
Fish: Sailfish; marlin; permit; bonefish; tarpon; snook.

Pine Island Fish Camp
6808 Lake Griffin Rd.
Lady Lake, FL 32159
352-753-2972
Price Category: $
Waters: Lake Griffin; Oklawaha River.

Pirates Cove Resort and Marina*
4307 SE Bayview St.
Stuart, FL 34997
516-287-2500
800-332-1414
Price Category: $$

This resort is included in Guest-Rated Resort Guide

Waters: Gulf Stream; Indian River Lagoon; St. Lucia River.
Fish: Dolphin; wahoo; kingfish; sailfish; marlin; trout; snook; tarpon; redfish; grouper.

Port of the Islands Hotel Resort and Marina*
25000 Tamiami Trail
East Naples, FL 34114-9602
941-394-3101
Price Category: $$
Waters: Gulf of Mexico; 10,000 Islands area.
Fish: Snook; redfish; tarpon; tripletail; trout.

Rainbow Bend Fishing Resort*
57784 Overseas Hwy., MM 58
Marathon, FL 33050
800-929-1505
Price Category: $$
Waters: Atlantic Ocean; Gulf of Mexico.
Fish: Bonefish; snook; barracuda; tarpon; permit; lobster; shark; sailfish; yellowtail; dolphin; wahoo; red snapper; red mangrove; marlin.

Richardson's Fish Camp
1550 Scotty's Rd.
Kissimee, FL 34744
407-846-6540
Price Category: $

Roland Martin's Lakeside Resort
920 East Del Monte Ave.
Clewiston, FL
941-983-3151
Price Category: $$

Waters: Lake Okeechobee.
Fish: Bass.

Sandestin Resort
9300 West Hwy. 98
Destin, FL 32541
850-267-8000
Price Category: $$$
Waters: Gulf of Mexico.

South Seas Plantation*
PO Box 194
Captiva Island, FL 33924
941-472-5111
800-237-8482
Price Category: $$
Waters: Pine Island Sound; Gulf of Mexico.
Fish: Snook; redfish; sea trout; snapper; grouper; shark; tarpon.

Trophy Bass Lodge
1533 CR 309
Georgetown , FL 32139
904-467-2002
Price Category: $

'Tween Waters Inn
PO Box 249
Captiva, FL 33924
941-472-5161
Price Category: $$ - $$$
Waters: Gulf of Mexico.
Fish: Snook; tarpon; redfish; grouper; sea trout.

GEORGIA

Burnt Pine Plantation
2941 Little River Rd.
Madison, GA 30650
706-342-2170
Price Category: $$$

This resort is included in Guest-Rated Resort Guide

Callaway Gardens*
PO Box 2000
Pine Mountain, GA 31822-2000
706-663-2281
800-CALLAWAY
Price Category: $$ - $$$$
Waters: Mountain Creek Lake
and 12 smaller ponds.
Fish: Largemouth bass; bluegill;
shellcracker; rainbow trout; cat-
fish; redbreast.

Gillionville Plantation
PO Box 3250
Albany, GA 31706-3250
912-439-2837
Price Category: $$$$
Fish: Largemouth bass.

Highland Marina and Resort
1000 Seminole Rd.
LaGrange, GA 30250
706-882-3437
Price Category: $
Waters: West Point Lake.
Fish: Largemouth bass; crappie.

Lake Lanier Islands Hilton
7000 Holiday Rd.
Lake Lanier Island, GA 30518
770-945-8787
Price Category: $$$

Red Gate Fishing Lodge
4201 Ogeechee Rd.
Savannah, GA 31405
Price Category: $$

**The Lodge on Little St. Simon's
Island***
PO Box 21078
Little St. Simon's Island,
GA 31522
912-638-7472

Price Category: $$$$
Waters: Atlantic Ocean;
Altamaha River; Hampton River.
Fish: Sea trout; speckled trout;
amberjack; redfish; shark; tar-
pon; flounder.

HAWAII

Kona Village Resort*
PO Box 1299
Kailua-Kona, HI 96745
808-325-5555
Price Category: $$$$
Waters: Pacific Ocean.
Fish: Marlin; swordfish; tuna;
dolphin; wahoo.

Uncle Billy's Kona Bay Resort
87 Banyan Dr.
Hilo, HI 96720
Price Category: $$$$
Waters: Pacific Ocean.

IDAHO

Beamer's Landing
Box 1243
Lewiston, ID 83501
800-522-6966
Price Category: $$
Waters: Snake River; Salmon
River; Grande Ronde River;
Copper Creek.
Fish: Steelhead.

Castle Creek Guest Ranch
PO Box 2008
Salmon, ID 83467
208-756-2548
Price Category: $$$

This resort is included in Guest-Rated Resort Guide

Elk Creek Ranch

PO Box 2
Island Park, ID 83429
208-558-7404
Price Category: $
Waters: Henry's Fork.
Fish: Brook trout; cutthroat
trout; rainbow trout.

Fish Creek Lodging

PO Box 833
Ashton, ID 83420
208-652-7566
Price Category: $$
Waters: Henry's Fork; Warm
River; Fall River.
Fish: Trout.

Hell's Canyon Lodge

PO Box 576
Lewiston, ID 83501
800-727-6190
Price Category: $$$$
Waters: Snake River.
Fish: Steelhead; rainbow trout;
smallmouth bass.

Henry's Fork Anglers

HC 66, Box 491
Island Park, ID 83429
208-558-7525
Price Category: $$
Waters: Henry's Fork.
Fish: Rainbow trout; brown
trout.

Henry's Fork Lodge

HC 66, Box 600
Island Park, ID 83429
415-434-1657
Price Category: $$$$
Waters: Henry's Fork; Madison
River; Gallatin River;

Yellowstone River; Slough Creek.
Fish: Rainbow trout.

Huckleberry Heaven Lodge

Box 165
Elk River, ID 83827
208-826-3405
Price Category: $$
Waters: Elk Creek.
Fish: Trout.

Jared's Wild Rose Ranch Resort*

HC 66, Box 140
Island Park, ID 83429
208-558-7201
Price Category: $
Waters: Henry's Lake; Henry's
Fork River; Quake Lake; Hebgen
Lake; Madison River; Snake
River.
Fish: Cutthroat trout; hybrid
trout; brook trout.

Last Chance Lodge

HC 66, Box 482
Island Park, ID 83429
208-926-4149

Middle Fork Lodge

PO Box 16278
Boise, ID 83715
208-362-9261

Mystic Saddle Ranch

General Delivery
Stanley, ID 83278
208-774-3591
Price Category: $$$
Waters: Salmon River; Sawtooth
Wilderness Area.
Fish: Cutthroat trout; rainbow
trout.

This resort is included in Guest-Rated Resort Guide

South Fork Lodge and Float Trips*
PO Box 22
Swan Valley, ID 83449
208-483-2112
Price Category: $ - $$$
Waters: South Fork of the Snake River.
Fish: Brown trout; cutthroat trout; rainbow trout; cutbow hybrid trout.

St. Joe Hunting and Fishing Camp*
HC 01, Box 109A
St. Maries, ID 83861
208-245-4002
Price Category: $$$
Waters: St. Joe River.
Fish: Trout.

Sulphur Creek Ranch
7151 West Emerald
Boise, ID 83704
208-377-1188
Price Category: $$
Waters: High altitude lakes; Sulphur Creek; Middle Fork of the Salmon River.
Fish: Cutthroat trout.

The Lodge at Palisades Creek*
PO Box 70
Irwin, ID 83428
208-483-2222
Price Category: $$$ - $$$$
Waters: South Fork of the Snake River; Henry's Fork; Teton River.
Fish: Brown trout; rainbow trout; cutthroat trout.

Three Rivers Ranch
PO Box 856K, Warm River

Ashton, ID 83420
208-652-3750

Twin Peaks Ranch
PO Box 774
Salmon, ID 83467
800-659-4899
Price Category: $$$
Waters: Salmon River; William's Lake.
Fish: Trout.

Wapiti Meadow Ranch*
HC 72
Cascade, ID 83611
208-633-3217
Price Category: $$ - $$$$
Waters: Middle Fork and South Fork of Salmon River; Salmon River watershed.
Fish: Cutthroat trout; rainbow trout; brook trout; bull trout.

William's Lake Lodge
PO Box 1230
Salmon, ID 83467
208-756-2007

ILLINOIS

Anthony Acres Resort*
PO Box 1371
Effingham, IL 62401
217-868-2950
Price Category: $
Waters: Lake Sara.
Fish: Largemouth bass; walleye; crappie; bluegill; catfish.

Eagle Ridge Inn and Resort*
Box 777
Galena, IL 61036
815-777-2444
Price Category: $$ - $$$$

This resort is included in Guest-Rated Resort Guide

Waters: Galena Lake; Mississippi River.
Fish: Smallmouth bass; perch; bluegill; catfish; crappie; rainbow trout; tiger muskie.

Kinkaid Lake Marina
2063 Marina Rd.
Murphyboro, IL 62966
618-687-4914

Rend Lake Resort
11712 E. Windy Lane
Whittington, IL 62897-9718
618-629-2211
Price Category: $
Waters: Rend Lake.

Starved Rock Lodge
PO Box 570
Utica, IL 61373
815-667-4211
Price Category: $
Waters: Illinois River.
Fish: Catfish; bullhead; white bass; sauger; crappie.

INDIANA

Edelweiss House
RR 1, Box 628
Cloverdale, IN 46120
765-795-2220

IOWA

Highrock Lake Lodge
PO Box 117
Underwood, IA 51576
800-483-2799

Northland Inn
Box 2051, Hwy. 9
Spiritlake, IA 51360
712-336-1450
Price Category: $
Waters: West Okoboji; East Okoboji.

KANSAS

Mosler Resort
Box 12
90th and Bethlehem
Columbus, KS 66725
316-597-2799
Price Category: $

KENTUCKY

Big Bear Resort and Marina*
30 Big Bear Resort Rd.
Benton, KY 42025
502-354-6414
800-922-BEAR
Price Category: $-$$
Waters: Kentucky Lake; Lake Barkley; Ohio River.
Fish: Largemouth bass; smallmouth bass; white bass; crappie; bluegill; catfish; perch; sauger; rockfish.

Cozy Cove Waterfront Resort
1917 Reed Rd.
Benton, KY 42025
800-467-8168
Price Category: $
Waters: Kentucky Lake.
Fish: Sunfish; striper; bluegill; shellcracker; crappie; sauger; catfish; largemouth bass.

Emerald Isle Resort and Marina
PO Box 282
Campbellsville, KY 42719
502-465-3412
Price Category: $
Waters: Green River Lake.
Fish: Bass; crappie; walleye; muskie.

Finn n' Feather Lodge
16695 US Hwy. 68 East
Aurora, KY 42028
502-474-2351
Price Category: $
Waters: Kentucky Lake.
Fish: Largemouth bass; crappie; sauger; white bass; smallmouth bass.

Green River Marina
2892 Lone Valley Rd.
Campbellsville, KY 42718
800-488-2512
Price Category: $

Green Turtle Bay Resort*
PO Box 102
Grand Rivers, KY 42045
502-362-8364
800-498-0428
Price Category: $$
Waters: Kentucky Lake; Tennessee River; Lake Barkley; Cumberland River.
Fish: Catfish; bass; striped bass; crappie; bluegill; spoonbill; sunfish.

Gwinn Island Resort
1200 Gwinn Island Rd.
Danville , KY 40422
606-236-4286

Price Category: $$
Waters: Herrington Lake.
Fish: Smallmouth bass; largemouth bass; crappie; catfish; perch; bluegill; white bass.

Hester's Spot in the Sun*
3500 Hester's Rd.
Benton, KY 42025
502-354-8280
800-455-7481
Price Category: $
Waters: Kentucky Lake; Lake Barkley.
Fish: Largemouth bass; smallmouth bass; catfish; crappie; bluegill; white bass.

Hickory Hill Resort*
90 Hickory Hill Lane
Benton, KY 42025
502-354-8207
800-280-4455
Price Category: $-$$
Waters: Kentucky Lake; Lake Barkley.
Fish: Crappie; smallmouth bass; largemouth bass; catfish; white bass; bluegill; sauger.

Holiday Hills
5631 KY 93 S
Eddyville, KY 42038
502-388-7236
Price Category: $
Waters: Lake Barkley
Fish: Sunfish; striper; bluegill; crappie; sauger; catfish; smallmouth bass.

Lake Barkley Marina
PO Box 1009
Cadiz, KY 42211

This resort is included in Guest-Rated Resort Guide

502-924-9954
Price Category: $
Waters: Lake Barkley.
Fish: Sunfish; striper; bluegill; crappie; sauger; catfish; smallmouth bass.

Lake Barkley State Resort Park
Box 790
Cadiz, KY 42211
800-325-1708
Price Category: $$
Waters: Lake Barkley.
Fish: Crappie; bass; bluegill; white bass; catfish.

Malcolm Creek Resort
RT 4, Box 153
Benton, KY 42025
800-733-6713
Price Category: $

Moon Bay Harbor Resort
PO Box 520
Kuttawa, KY 42055
502-388-7389

Paradise Resort*
1024 Paradise Dr.
Murray, KY 42071
502-436-2767
800-340-2767
Price Category: $
Waters: Kentucky Lake; Lake Barkley.
Fish: Largemouth bass; smallmouth bass; crappie; sauger; channel catfish; red ear sunfish; bluegill; striped bass; white bass.

Ponderosa Boat Dock
865 Ponderosa Rd.
Clarkson, KY 42726
502-242-7215
Price Category: $
Waters: Nolin Lake.
Fish: Largemouth bass; smallmouth bass; crappie; catfish.

Shawnee Bay Resort
1297 Shawnee Bay Rd.
Benton, KY 42025
800-272-4413
Price Category: $
Waters: Kentucky Lake.
Fish: Crappie; sauger; striped bass; bluegill.

Sportsman's Anchor
12888 US Hwy. 68 E
Benton, KY 42025
502-354-8493
Price Category: $
Waters: Kentucky Lake.
Fish: Crappie; sauger; striped bass; bluegill.

Sportsman's Quest
570 Moors Rd.
Gilbertsville, KY 42044
502-362-4740
Price Category: $

The Moors
570 Moors Rd.
Gilbertville, KY 42044
502-362-8361
Price Category: $
Waters: Kentucky Lake; Lake Barkley.
Fish: Crappie; bass; bluegill; white bass; catfish; red ear.

Town and Country Resort
1425 Gardner Rd.
Benton, KY 42025
502-354-8823
Price Category: $
Waters: Kentucky Lake.
Fish: Crappie; bass; bluegill;
white bass; catfish; striped bass.

Whispering Oaks
267 Miller's Rd.
Benton, KY 42025
Price Category: $
Waters: Kentucky Lake.
Fish: Crappie; bass; bluegill;
white bass; catfish; striped bass.

LOUSIANA

Abita Bed and Breakfast
27473 Quimet Dr.
Abita Springs, LA 70420
505-893-4604

Bridge Side Cabins
2012 LA 1
Grand Isle, LA 70358
504-787-2418

Chandler's Camp
5779 Hwy. 9
Creston, LA 71070
318-875-2222
Price Category: $
Waters: Red River.
Fish: Bass; bream; crappie; catfish; gou.

Cochiara Marina
Rt. 1, Box 526B
Lafitte, LA 70067
504-689-4272
Price Category: $

Waters: Gulf of Mexico.
Fish: Marlin; tuna; wahoo;
cobia; snapper.

D'Arbonne Lake Motel
101 Dori Driver
Farmerville, LA 71241
318-368-2236

Inn on the Bayou
1101 W Prien Lake Rd.
Lake Charles, LA 70601
318-493-5114

Joe's Landing
1170 Anthony Lane
Baratoria, LA 70036
504-689-4304

Point Cocodrie Inn
8250 Hwy. 56
Chauvin, LA 70344
504-594-4568
Price Category: $

Sportsman's Paradise
6830 Hwy. 56
Chauvin, LA 70344
504-594-2414
Price Category: $

Sunshine Marina
Sunshine West
Four Point Rd.
Dulac, LA 70353
504-563-4946
Price Category: $

Wildwood Resort
129 Wildwood Dr.
Zwolle, LA 71486
318-645-6114
Price Category: $

*This resort is included in Guest-Rated Resort Guide

MAINE

Aimhi Lodge
Box F
North Windham, ME 04062
207-892-6538

Alden Camps
RD 2, Box 1140SC
Oakland, ME 04963
207-465-7703
Price Category: $

Attean Lake Lodge
PO Box 457 - SC
Jackman, ME 04945
207-668-3792

Bear Mountain Lodge
RR 1, Box 1969
Smyrna Mills, ME 04780
Price Category: $
Waters: Rockabema Lake;
Skitacook Lake; Pleasant Lake;
Mud Lake.
Fish: Landlocked salmon; brook
trout.

Bosebuck Mountain Camps*
PO Box 1213
Rangeley, ME 04970
207-474-5903
Price Category: $$
Waters:Megalloway River;
Aziscohos Lake; Parmachenee
Lake.
Fish: Brook trout; landlocked
salmon.

Bowlin Camps
Box 251
Patten, ME 04765
207-528-2022

Price Category: $$
Waters: East Branch of the
Penobscot River; Bowlin Pond;
Madagamon Lake.
Fish: Landlocked salmon; small-
mouth bass; brook trout.

Bulldog Camps
PO Box 1229
Greenville, ME 04441
207-243-2853
Price Category: $
Waters: Enchanted Pond; Little
Enchanted Pond.
Fish: Brook trout.

Cap'n Fish's Motel
PO Box 660
Boothbay Harbor, ME 04538
Price Category: $$

Casey's Spencer Bay Camp
PO Box 1190
Greenville, ME 04413
207-695-2801
Price Category: $

Castle Island Camps
PO Box 251
Belgrade Lakes, ME 04918
207-495-3312
Price Category: $

Cobb's Pierce Pond Camps
PO Box 124
North New Portland, ME 04961
207-628-2819 or 207-628-3612
Price Category: $

Colonial Sportsman
Box 167
Grand Lake Stream, ME 04637
207-796-2655

Price Category: $
Waters: West Grand Lake; Big Lake; St. Croix River; Junior Lake; Grand Lake Stream; Sysladobsis Lake; Wabash Lake; Pocumcus Lake; First Machias Lake.
Fish: Lake trout; brook trout; pickerel; landlocked salmon; smallmouth bass; white perch.

Dad's Camps
PO Box 142
West Enfield, ME 04493
207-746-7278
Price Category: $
Waters: Penobscot River.
Fish: Smallmouth bass; brook trout.

Eagle Lodge
PO Box 686
Lincoln, ME 04457
207-794-2181

Fish River Lodge
Box 202
Eagle Lake, ME 04739
207-444-5207

Fisherman's Wharf Inn
40 Commercial St.
Boothbay Harbor, ME 04538
Price Category: $$

Frost Pond Camps*
Box 620, Star Route 76
Greenville, ME 04441
207-723-6622
Price Category: $
Waters: Frost Pond; Little Frost Pond; Chesuncook Lake; West Branch of the Penobscot; Harrington Lake.

Fish: Brook trout; landlocked salmon; lake trout.

Gentle Ben's Lodge
PO Box 212
Rockwood, ME 04478
Price Category: $
Waters: Kennebec River; Penobscot River; Moose River; Moosehead Lake.
Fish: Lake trout; brook trout; salmon; smallmouth bass; large-mouth bass.

Grant's Kennebago Camps
PO Box 786
Rangeley, ME 04970
207-864-3608
Price Category: $

Great Pond Lodge
HC 31
Aurora, ME 04408
207-584-3541
Price Category: $$

Great Pond Wilderness Lodge and Sporting Camp**
RR 2, Box 482
Eddington, ME 04428
207-745-6728
Price Category: $
Waters: Great Pond; Alligator Lake; Union River; Machias River; Penobscot River.
Fish: Smallmouth bass; brown trout; pickerel; brook trout; salmon.

Greenville Inn
PO Box 1194
Greenville, ME 04441
888-695-6000
Price Category: $$

This resort is included in Guest-Rated Resort Guide

Waters: Moosehead Lake.
Fish: Lake trout; brook trout;
smallmouth bass; landlocked
salmon.

Hardscrabble Lodge
PO Box 428
Moose River, ME 04945
207-243-3020

Harrison's Pierce Pond Sporting Camps*
PO Box 315
Bingham, ME 04920
207-672-3625
Price Category: $$
Waters: Pierce Pond and 6 satel-
lite ponds within walking dis-
tance.
Fish: Landlock salmon; brook
trout.

Idlease and Shorelands Guest Resort*
Route 9, Box 769
Kennebunkport, ME 04046
207-985-4460
Price Category: $
Waters: Mousam River; Atlantic
Ocean.
Fish: Mackerel; striper.

Kennebago River Kamps
1773 Burketville Rd.
Appleton, ME 04862
207-845-6035
Price Category: $

Lakewood Camps
Middledam
Andover, ME 04216
207-243-2959
Price Category: $
Waters: Richardson Lakes; Rapid

River.
Fish: Landlocked salmon; brook
trout.

Leen's Lodge
Box 40
Grand Lake Stream, ME 04637
800-99-LEENS
Price Category: $$

Libby Camps*
PO Box V
Ashland, ME 04732
207-435-8274
Price Category: $$
Waters: Aroostook River;
Allagash River; Penobscot River.
Fish: Brook trout; landlocked
salmon; lake trout; smallmouth
bass.

Little Lyford Pond Camps
PO Box 1269
Greenville, ME 04441
207-695-2821
Price Category: $

Long Lake Camps
Box 817
Princeton, ME 04668
207-796-2051
Price Category: $

Macannamac Camps*
PO Box B FR
Haymock Lake T8R11
Patten, ME 04765
207-528-2855
Price Category: $
Waters: Allagash Lakes Region
including Haymock Lake; Cliff
Lake; Spider Lake; Allagash
River; Bib Pleasant Lake; Big
Eagle Lake; Churchill Lake.

Fish: Brook Trout; whitefish; lake trout; landlocked salmon.

McNally's Ross Stream Camps*
HCR 71, Box 632
Greenville, ME 04441
207-944-5991
Price Category: $
Waters: Allagash River; St. John River; Ross Stream; Cunliffe Lake; Long Lake; Umsaskis Lake.
Fish: Lake trout; brook trout; whitefish.

Medawisla
HCR 76, Box 592
Greenville, ME 04441
207-695-2690

Moose Point Camps
PO Box 170
Portage, ME 04732
207-435-6156

Moose River Landing*
PO Box 295
Rockwood, ME 04478
207-534-7577
Price Category: $
Waters: Moose River; Kennebac River.
Fish: Salmon; togue; brook trout.

Mt. Chase Lodge
RR 1, Box 281
Patten, ME 04765
207-582-2183

Nahmakanta Lake Camps*
PO Box 544

Millinocket, ME 04462
207-746-7356
Price Category: $$
Waters: Nahmakanta Lake; surrounding streams and 10 remote ponds.
Fish: Brook trout; salmon; lake trout.

Nesowadnehunk Lake Wilderness Campground
Box 616, Langdon Rd.
Richmond, ME 04357
207-737-8309
Price Category: $

Nicatous Lodge
PO Box 100
Burlington, ME 04417
207-732-4771

Northern Outdoors
Route 201, PO Box 100
The Forks, ME 04985
800-765-2244
Price Category: $
Waters: Kennebec River; Androscoggin River.
Fish: Smallmouth bass.

Northern Pines Lodge
HC 76, Box 588 HF
Greenville, ME 04441
207-695-2890
Price Category: $
Waters: First Roast Pond; Moosehead Lake.
Fish: Brook trout; landlocked salmon; togue.

Nugent's Camps*
HCR 76, Box 632
Greenville, ME 04441

This resort is included in Guest-Rated Resort Guide

207-944-5991
Price Category: $-$$
Waters: Allagash River; West Branch of the Penobscot River; Chamberlain Lake; Eagle Lake.
Fish: Lake trout; brook trout; whitefish.

Packard's Camps

RFD #2, Box 176
Guilford, ME 04443
207-997-3300
Price Category: $
Waters: Sebec Lake.
Fish: Lake trout; salmon; smallmouth bass.

Red River Camps

PO Box 320
Portage, ME 04768
207-528-2259
Price Category: $
Fish: Brook trout; landlocked salmon.

Rideout's Lodge*

East Grand Lake
Danforth, ME 04424
800-594-5391
Price Category: $-$$
Waters: East Grand Lake.
Fish: Smallmouth bass; landlocked salmon; lake trout.

Sally Mountain Cabins

Box 50
Jackman, ME 04945
800-644-5621
Price Category: $
Waters: Big Wood Lake.
Fish: Salmon; brook trout; lake trout; splake; cusk.

Salmon Pool Camps

HCR 69, Box 558
Medway, ME 04460
207-746-5860

Sebago Lake Lodge and Cottages

PO Box 110
North Windham, ME 04062
207-892-2698

Sebago Lake Camps

Box 905
North Sebago, ME 04029
207-787-3211
Price Category: $
Waters: Sebago Lake
Fish: Landlocked salmon; lake trout; smallmouth bass; largemouth bass; white perch; whitefish; cusk; brook trout; brown trout; pickerel; calico bass; bullhead.

Seboomook Wilderness Campground

HC 85, Box 560 HF
Rockwood, ME 04478
207-534-8824
Price Category: $
Waters: Moosehead Lake.
Fish: Lake trout; brook trout; salmon.

Shoreland Guest Resort

PO Box 769
Kennebunkport, ME 04046
800-992-3224

South Branch Lake Camps

HCR 66, Box 195
Seboeis, ME 04448
207-732-3446

*This resort is included in Guest-Rated Resort Guide

Price Category: $
Fish: Smallmouth bass.

Spruce Lodge Camps
RR 1, Box 716
Springfield, ME 04487
207-738-3701

**The Lakeside - Country Inn
and Sporting Camps***
PO Box 36
2 Park St.
Princeton, ME 04668
207-796-2324
Price Category: $
Waters: Big Lake; Long Lake;
Lewey Lake; Grand Falls
Flowage; St. Croix River; West
Grand Lake; Grand Lake Stream;
Pocomoonshine Lake.
Fish: Smallmouth bass; large-
mouth bass; landlocked salmon;
brooktrout; lake trout; Atlantic
salmon.

The Last Resort
Box 777 MSCA
Jackman, ME 04945
207-668-5091
Price Category: $
Waters: Long Pond; Moose
River.
Fish: Landlocked salmon; trout;
perch.

The Pines Sporting Camps*
PO Box 158
Grand Lake Stream, ME 04637
207-796-5006
Price Category: $ - $$
Waters: Sysladobsis Lake;
Pocumcuss Lake; West Grand
Lake; Grand Lake Stream.

Fish: Smallmouth bass; landlocked salmon.

Tim Pond Camps
Box 22
Eustis, ME 04936
207-243-2947
Price Category: $$
Waters: Tim Pond.
Fish: Trout.

Tomhegan Wilderness Resort
Box 310
Brockwood, ME 04478
207-534-7712
Price Category: $$
Waters: Moosehead Lake.
Fish: Brook trout; salmon; lake
trout.

Two Falls Camps
RFD Box 178
Guilford, ME 04443
207-997-3625

Weatherby's
PO Box FH69
Grand Lake Stream, ME 04637
207-746-5558
Price Category: $$
Fish: Smallmouth bass; land-
locked salmon; brook trout.

West Branch Pond Camps
Box 1153
Greenville, ME 04441
207-695-2561

Wheaton's Lodge*
HC 81, Box 120
Brookton, ME 04413
Summer Phone: 207-448-7723
Winter Phone: 207-843-5732

*This resort is included in Guest-Rated Resort Guide

Price Category: $$
Waters: East Grand Lake;
Spednik Lake; Baskahegan Lake;
Upper St. Croix watershed
and streams.
Fish: Landlocked salmon; small-
mouth bass.

Whisperwood Lodge and Cottages
Taylor Woods Rd.
Belgrade, ME 04917
800-355-7170
Price Category: $$
Waters: Salmon Lake.
Fish: Smallmouth bass; largemouth bass; brown trout; white
perch; yellow perch;
pickerel.

White House Landing Wilderness Camps
Box 749
Millinocket, ME 04462
207-324-9077
Price Category: $

Willard Jalbert Camps
6 Winchester St.
Presque Isle, ME 04769
207-764-0494
Price Category: $

MARYLAND

Carmel Cove Inn*
PO Box 644
Oakland, MD 21550
301-387-0067
Price Category: $-$$
Waters: Deep Creek Lake;
Youghiogheny River and
Reservoir.

Fish: Trout; bass; walleye; crappie; pickerel; catfish.

Chesapeake House Hotel
2151 Chesepeake House Dr.
PO Box 310
Tilghman, MD 21671
410-886-2121

Pine Oaks Lodge
855 Deepcreek Dr.
McHenry, MD 21541
301-387-5115

Savage River Lodge
18237 Lyles Dr.
Hagerstown, MD 21740
301-790-1037
Price Category: $$-$$$
Waters: Deep Creek Lake;
Savage River; Potomac River;
Casselman River;
Youghiogheny River; New
Germany Lake; Savage
Reservoir; Bear Creek; Jennings-
Randolf Reservoir.
Fish: Muskielunge; northern
pike; brown trout; brook trout;
rainbow trout; largemouth bass;
smallmouth bass.

The Lodge at Sawmill Hollow*
400 Sawmill Hollow Rd.
Swanton, MD 21561
301-387-8455
Price Category: $
Waters: Deep Creek Lake;
Youghiogheny River; Casselman
River; Savage River; Jennings-
Randolf Lake.
Fish: Bass; bluegill; carp; catfish;
crappie; perch; pickerel; pike;
walleye; trout.

Wisp Resort*
290 Marsh Hill Rd.
McHenry, MD 21541
800-462-9477
Price Category: $$$
Waters: Deep Creek Lake; North Branch of the Potomac; Youghiogheny River; Savage River.
Fish: Perch; smallmouth bass; largemouth bass; bluegill; walleye; trout; chain pickerel; northern pike.

MASSACHUSETTS

Copper Lantern Motor Lodge
PO Box 1138
West Brookfield, MA 01585
508-867-6441
Price Category: $
Waters: Quabbin Reservoir; Quaboag River; Lake Wickaboag; Quaboag Lake; Seven Mile River; Swift River; Browning Post; South Pond; Long Pond; Comet Pond.
Fish: Largemouth bass; smallmouth bass; perch; pickerel; lake trout; landlocked salmon; rainbow trout; brook trout; northern pike; catfish; shad.

Fleming's Camps
12 C St.
Hopkinton, MA 01748
508-435-3717

King's Landing Marina
80 King's Landing
Norwell, MA 13302
781-659-7273

The Williamsville Inn*
Route 41
West Stockbridge, MA 01266
413-274-6118
Price Category: $-$$
Waters: Williams River; Housatonic River; Green River; Laurel Lake; Stockbridge Bowl.
Fish: Brook trout; brown trout; rainbow trout; bass; pickerel; perch.

MICHIGAN

Arnold's Landing Resort
Box 73, HC 52
Drummond Island, MI 49726
906-493-5654
Price Category: $
Waters: Lake Huron.
Fish: Walleye; northern pike; smallmouth bass; catfish; sunfish; perch.

Camp Mana Pine
998 Emmons Rd.
Wellston, MI 49689
616-848-4141
Price Category: $
Waters: Manistee River; Pine River.
Fish: Trout; steelhead; bass.

Gates Au Sable Lodge
471 Stephan Bridge Rd.
Grayling, MI 49738
517-348-8462
Price Category: $$
Waters: Au Sable River.
Fish: Brown trout; rainbow trout.

This resort is included in Guest-Rated Resort Guide

Johnson's Pere Marquette Lodge
Rt. 1, Box 1290
Baldwin, MI 49304
616-745-3972
Price Category: $
Waters: Pere Marquette.
Fish: Brown trout; rainbow trout; steelhead; salmon.

Lake Fanny Hooe Resort and Campground
PO Box 31
Copper Harbor, MI 49918
800-426-4451

Riverside Motel and Marina*
520 Water St.
Manistee, MI 49660
616-723-3554
Price Category: $
Waters: Lake Michigan; Big Manistee River.
Fish: Brown trout; salmon; steelhead; lake trout.

Trout Creek Condominium Resort
4749 Pleasant
Harbor Springs, MI 49740
800-748-0245
Price Category: $$

White Birch Haven Resort
248 Rysberg Dr.
Crystal Falls, MI 49920
906-875-6855
Price Category: $
Waters: Buck Lake.
Fish: Northern pike; bass; crappie; perch; bluegill.

MINNESOTA

A Place in the Woods
11380 Turtle River Lake Rd., NE
Bemdiji, MN 56601
218-586-2345

Anderson's Northland Lodge
HCR 84, Box 376
Walker, MN 56484
800-247-1719

Angle Outpost Resort*
RR 1, Box 36
Angle Inlet, MN 56711
218-223-8101
Price Category: $ - $$$
Waters: Lake of the Woods.
Fish: Walleye; smallmouth bass; northern pike; sauger; jumbo perch.

Arcadia Resort
Rt. 1, Box 620
Bigfork, MN 56628
218-888-3852

Arrowood
Box 639
Alexandria, MN 56308
320-762-1124
Price Category: $$$
Waters: Lake Darling; Lake L'Homme Dieu; Lake Geneva.

Ashby Resort and Campground
PO Box 57
Ashby, MN 56623
218-747-2959

Ballard's Resort
RR1, Box 176

Baudette, MN 56623
800-776-2675
Price Category: $
Waters: Rainy River; Lake of the
Woods.
Fish: Walleye; northern pike;
sauger; perch; smallmouth bass;
sturgeon.

Bally Creek Camp / Bear Track Outfitting
937 EM
Grand Marais, MN 55604
218-387-1162
Price Category: $
Waters: Boundary Waters Canoe
Area.
Fish: Walleye; smallmouth bass;
northern pike; lake trout.

Barneveld's Resort
RR 1, Box 346
Aitkin, MN 46431
218-678-2433
Price Category: $
Waters: Mille's Lac Lake.
Fish: Walleye; northern pike;
perch.

Barrett's Fish Inn
PO Box 93
Federal Dam, MN 56641
218-654-3755

Bay Store and Resort
PO Box 21
Oak Island, MN 56741
218-223-8621
Price Category: $
Waters: Lake of the Woods.
Fish: Walleye.

Bayview Lodge
Rt. 1, Box 75 B

Baudette, MN 56623
218-634-2194

Beaver Creek Resort
Rt. 1, Box 48
Hines, MN 56647
218-835-6681

Big Lake Wilderness Lodge*
PO Box 359
Ely, MN 55731
800-446-9080
Price Category: $
Waters: Big Lake; Lapond Lake;
Big Rice Lake; other Boundary
Waters Canoe Area lakes.
Fish: Walleye; smallmouth bass;
northern pike; yellow perch.

Big Wolf Lake Resort and Campground
12150 Walleye Lane, SE
Bemidji , MN 56601
218-751-5749

Birch Knoll Ranch
820 Old Crystal Bay Rd.
Wayzata, MN 55391
612-475-2054
Price Category: $ - $$
Fish: Brook trout; brown trout.

Bonnie Brae Resort
Box 56 X
Oak Island, MN 56741
218-864-5534

Borderland Lodge
7480 Crane Lake Rd.
Crane Lake, MN 55725
218-993-2233

Bowsers on Crane Lake
7529 Bowser Ct.

This resort is included in Guest-Rated Resort Guide

Crane Lake, MN 55725
218-993-2226

Break on the Lake Resort
Rt. 2, Box 254
Cass Lake, MN 56633
800-443-5101

Buck Point Lodge and Resort
Rt. 3, Box 153 MRA
Osakis, MN 56360
320-859-2530

Camp Van Vac
2714 Van Vac Lane
Ely, MN 55731
218-365-3782
Price Category: $
Waters: Burntside Lake.
Fish: Smallmouth bass; northern
pike; walleye; crappie; lake trout.

**Carlson's Lake of the Woods
Resort**
Box 65
Angle Inlet, MN 56711
218-223-8961

Chippewa Paws
HC 3, Box 3, 56 EM
Pennington, MN 56663
218-335-6897
Price Category: $$
Waters: Cass Lake; Kitchie Lake.
Fish: Northern pike; perch; bass;
sunfish; crappie; muskie.

Deer Horn Resort
10024 Gappa Rd.
Ray, MN 56669
218-875-3861
Price Category: $
Waters: Lake Kabetogama.

Fish: Walleye; perch; northern
pike; smallmouth bass.

Deer Ridge Resort
PO Box 238
Ely, MN 55731
800-382-2041
Price Category: $
Waters: Garden Lake; White
Iron Lake; Farm Lake.
Fish: Northern pike; walleye;
largemouth bass; smallmouth
bass.

**Eagle Ridge at Lusten
Mountains**
Box 106
Lusten, MN 55612
800-360-7666
Price Category: $
Waters: Poplar River.
Fish: Brook trout; brown trout;
steelhead; chinook salmon.

**El Reno Resort and
Campground**
Rt. 1, Box 80
Glenwood, MN 56334
800-291-5616
Price Category: $
Waters: Lake Reno.
Fish: Walleye; northern pike;
bass; crappie.

**Elk Horn Resort and
Campground**
Rt. 2, Box 323
Waubun, MN 59589
218-935-5437
Price Category: $
Waters: South Twin Lake.
Fish: Walleye; northern pike;
crappie; bass.

Fair Hills and Five Lakes
PO Box 6 MR
Detroit Lakes, MN 56501
218-847-7638
Price Category: $$
Waters: Pelican Lake.
Fish: Walleye; crappie; northern pike; bass.

Four Winds Resort
9990 Gappa Rd.
Ray, MN 56669
218-875-2821

Golden Eagle Lodge
325 Gunflint Trail
Grand Marais, MN 55604
218-388-2203
Price Category: $ - $$
Waters: Flour Lake.
Fish: Lake trout; northern pike; walleye.

Governor's Point Resort
RR 1, Box 31
Vergas, MN 56587
800-308-9624
Price Category: $-$$
Waters: Loon Lake.
Fish: Northern pike; walleye; largemouth bass; crappie; bluegill; bullhead.

Heath's Resort
RR 1, Box 285
Pine River, MN 56474
218-587-2286

Herseth's Tomahawk Resort
10078 Gappa Rd.
Ray, MN 56669
218-875-2352

Hillcrest Resort
Rt. 3, Box 754
McGregor, MN 55760
218-426-3323

Jackpine Lodge
PO Box 570
Ely, MN 55731
218-365-5700

Jakes Northwest Angles
1 Walleye Bay
Angle Inlet, MN 56711
800-729-0864
Price Category: $
Waters: Northwest Angle Creek; Lake of the Woods.
Fish: Walleye; smallmouth bass; muskie.

Judd's Resort
HCR 1, Box 35
Bena, MN 56626
218-665-2216
Price Category: $$
Waters: Lake Winibigoshish.
Fish: Walleye; northern pike; perch.

Karpen's Sunset Bay
45401 Mille Lacs Pkwy.
Isle, MN 56342
320-676-8834

Kavanaugh's
2300 Kavanaugh Dr. SW
Brainerd, MN 56401
218-829-5226
Price Category: $$
Waters: Sylvan Lake.
Fish: Smallmouth bass; northern; walleye.

Kitchie Landing Resort
Pennington Rt., HC 3, Box 166
Blackduck, MN 56630
218-835-6595

Kohls Resort
15707 Big Turtle Dr., NE
Bemidji, MN 56601
218-243-2131

Lakecrest Resort
Rt. 1, Box EA
Detroit Lakes, MN 56501-9703
800-435-5459
Price Category: $
Waters: Long Lake.
Fish: Walleye; northern; large-
mouth bass; smallmouth bass;
crappie; sunfish.

**Latourell's Resort and
Outfitters**
Box 239
Ely, MN 55731
218-365-4531
Price Category: $$
Waters: Moose Lake.
Fish: Smallmouth bass; north-
ern; walleye.

Madden's Gull Lake
8001 Pine Beach Peninsula
Brainerd, MN 56401
218-829-2811
Price Category: $$$
Waters: Gull Lake.

Madsen Grove Resort
PO Box 1598
Detroit Lakes, MN 56502
218-847-5830

Morningside Resort
R-3 Box 2405
Aitkin, MN 56431
218-927-2708

North Country Lodge
5865 Moose Lake Rd.
Ely, MN 55731
800-777-4431
Price Category: $$
Waters: Moose Lake; Basswood
Lake chain.
Fish: Northern pike; smallmouth
bass; lake trout.

Northern Lights Lodge
PO Box 186
Ely, MN 55731
800-777-4406

Northernair Lodge
2123 Haapala Rd.
Ely, MN 55731
218-365-4882

Northland Lodge*
HCR 84, Box 376
Walker, MN 45684
218-836-2332
800-247-1719
Price Category: $
Waters: Leech Lake.
Fish: Walleye; muskie; bass;
northern pike.

Northwind Lodge
PO Box 690
Ely, MN 55731
218-365-5489
Price Category: $
Waters: Jasper Lake.
Fish: Walleye.

Norway Point Resort
11033 Slade Rd.
Orr, MN 55771
218-757-3434
Price Category: $
Waters: Pelican Lake.
Fish: Bluegill; sunfish; crappie; smallmouth bass; largemouth bass; pike; walleye.

Oak Haven Resort
14333 Roosevelt Rd. SE
Bemidji, MN 56601
218-335-2092
Price Category: $
Waters: Mississippi River; Cass Lake; Andrusia Lake; Pine Bay Lake; Kitchie Lake.
Fish: Walleye; bass; pike; muskie.

Old Town Resort
Rt. 2, Box 42 (M5)
Clitherall, MN 56524
800-545-4062
Price Category: $
Waters: Lake Clitherall.
Fish: Walleye; northern; yellow perch; smallmouth bass; large-mouth bass; bluegill; sunfish.

Paradise Resort
HC 3, Box 204
Pennington, MN 56630
218-835-6514

Park Point Resort
10498 Waltz Rd.
Ray, MN 56669
800-272-4533

Peter's Sunset Beach
2500 South Lakeshore Dr.

Glenwood, MN 56334
800-356-8654
Price Category: $$
Waters: Lake Minnewaska.
Fish: Walleye.

Pimushe Resort
Rt. 4, Box 312M
Bemidje, MN 56601
218-586-2094

Rockwood Lodge
625 Gunflint Trail
Grand Marais, MN 55604
800-942-2922
Price Category: $ - $$
Waters: Eastern portion of Boundary Waters Canoe Area.
Fish: Brook trout; brown trout; rainbow trout; walleye; northern pike; smallmouth bass.

Rocky Point Resort
12953 Ness Rd.
Ray, MN 56669
800-762-5977
Price Category: $
Waters: Lake Kabetogama.
Fish: Walleye, northern pike.

Rocky Reef Resort
Rt. 1, Box 220
Onamia, MN 56359
320-532-3431

Rutger's Bay Lake Lodge
PO Box 400
Deerwood, MN 56444
800-950-7244
Price Category: $$
Waters: Bay Lake.
Fish: Bass; walleye; northern pike; sunfish; crappie.

This resort is included in Guest-Rated Resort Guide

Sherrick's Wilderness Resort
8131 Forest Road #203
Crane Lake, MN 55725
 218-374-3531

Silver Rapids Lodge and Campground
HC1, Box 2992
Ely, MN 55731
218-365-4877

Sportsman's Lodge
RR 1, Box 167
Baudette, MN 56623-9622
218-634-1342
Price Category: $
Waters: Lake of the Woods; Rainy River.
Fish: Walleye; pike; smallmouth bass; sauger; perch; sturgeon.

Steamboat Bay Resort
HCR 7, Box 585
Walker , MN 56484
1-800-705-9925

The Quarterdeck on Gull*
1588 Quarterdeck Rd. West
Nisswa, MN 56468
800-950-5596
Price Category: $
Waters: Gull Lake; Gull Lake Chain.
Fish: Bass; walleye; northern pike; crappie; bluegill; rock bass; perch; bullhead.

Thunderbird Lodge
2170 Cty. Rd. 139
International Falls, MN 56649
800-351-5133
Price Category: $$
Waters: Rainy Lake.

Fish: Walleye; crappie; smallmouth bass; northern pike.

Timber Trail Lodge
HC 1, Box 3111
Ely, MN 55731
800-777-7348
Price Category: $$
Waters: South Farm Lake; White Iron Lake; Farm Lake; Garden Lake.
Fish: Walleye; northern pike; smallmouth bass; largemouth bass.

Timber Wolf Lodge
PO Box 147
Ely, MN 55731
800-827-3512

Tomahawk Resort
10078 Gappa Rd.
Ray, MN 56669
218-875-2352
Price Category: $
Waters: Lake Kabetogama.
Fish: Northern pike; walleye; largemouth bass; smallmouth bass.

Tom's Bait and Resort
Box 192
Emily, MN 56447
218-763-2355
Price Category: $
Waters: Lake Emily; Dahler Lake.

Trout Lake Resort
230 Gunflint Trail
Grand Marais, MN 55604
1-800-258-7688

Williams Narrows Resort
HCR 3, Box 652 RG
Deer River, MN 56636
800-325-2475
Price Category: $
Waters: Lake Winnibigoshish;
Cut-foot Sioux Lake.
Fish: Walleye; perch; northern
pike; tullibee (cisco).

Zippel Bay Resort
HC 2, Box 51
Williams, MN 56686
218-783-6235
Price Category: $ - $$
Waters: Lake of the Woods.
Fish: Walleye; northern pike;
sauger; perch; smallmouth bass.

MISSOURI

Alpine Lodge Resort
HCR 1, Box 795, Indian Point
Branson, MO 65616
417-338-2514
Price Category: $
Waters: Table Rock Lake.
Fish: Bass; walleye; catfish.

Angler's Resort
Rt. 2, Box 2832
Wheatland, MO 65779
417-282-5507

Aqua Finn Resort
1190 Bittersweet Rd.
Lake Ozark, MO 65049
573-365-2605

Artilla Cove Resort
HC 1, Box 839
Branson, MO 65616

417-338-2346
Price Category: $
Waters: Table Rock Lake.
Fish: Largemouth bass; small-
mouth bass; Kentucky bass;
crappie; bluegill; catfish.

Bass Point Resort
RR 1, Box 127
Sunrise Beach, MO 65079
573-374-5205

Bavarian Village Resort
HCR 1, Box 797
Branson, MO 65616
800-322-8274

Bell Harbour Resort
HC 76, Box 2550
Pittsburg, MO 65724
417-852-4880

Big Cedar Lodge
612 Devil's Pool Rd.
Ridgedale, MO 65739
417-335-2777
Price Category: $ - $$
Waters: Table Rock Lake.
Fish: Largemouth bass; rainbow
trout; brown trout.

Blue Haven Resort
PO Box 38
Branson, MO 65615
417-334-3917

Bonaire Resort
Rt. 2, Box 316
Camdenton, MO 65020
573-346-5248

Brass Lantern Resort
5133 Brass Lantern Rd.

This resort is included in Guest-Rated Resort Guide

Cedarcreek, MO 65627
417-794-3961

Breezy Point Resort
Rt. 71, Box 663
Camdenton, MO 65020
800-345-5173

Brills Rainbow Resort
414 North Sycamore
Branson, MO 65616
417-334-3955

Bucksaw Point Resort and Marina
670 SE 803
Clinton, MO 64735
816-477-3323

Buttermilk Springs Resort
Rt. 3, Box 4420
Galena , MO 65052
573-346-2123

Cedar Green Resort
Rt.1, Box 50
Camdenton, MO 65020
573-346-2849
Price Category: $$
Waters: Lake of the Ozarks;
Lake Green.
Fish: Bass; catfish; crappie.

Cedar Resort*
HCR 9, Box 1418
Lake 265-12
Branson, MO 65616
417-338-2653
Price Category: $
Waters: Table Rock Lake.
Fish: Walleye; crappie; small-
mouth bass; largemouth bass;
catfish.

Chimney Rock Resort
Rt.76, Box 627
Camdenton, MO 65020
573-873-5130

Clearwater Resort
PO Box 118
Camdenton, MO 65020
573-346-2112
Price Category: $
Waters: Lake of the Ozarks.
Fish: Crappie; bluegill; black
bass; white bass; catfish.

Cooper's Cove Resort
RR 1, Box 472
Flemington, MO 65650
417-282-5210

Crow's Nest Resort
HCR 1, Box 792
Branson, MO 65616
417-338-5254

Del Mar Resort*
1993 Lakeshore Dr.
Branson, MO 65616
417-334-6241
800-892-9542
Price Category: $
Waters: Lake Taneycomo.
Fish: Rainbow trout; German
brown trout.

Digger O'Dells
Lake Road 578
Camdenton, MO 65020
573-873-5380

Drift-In Resort
Rt. 1, Box 54
Camdenton, MO 65020
615-346-2269

Drop Anchor Resort
Rt. 3, Box 6
Gravois Mills, MO 65037
573-372-6620
Price Category: $

Eagle's Nest at Lake Pomme de Terre*
HC 76, Box 2690
Pittsburg, MO 65724
800-259-6936
Price Category: $
Waters: Lake Pomme de Terre.
Fish: Bass; crappie; muskie.

Edgewater Beach Resort and Marina*
Box 159
Lake Ozark, MO 56049
800-822-6044
Price Category: $
Waters: Lake of the Ozarks.
Fish: Drum; muskie; catfish; paddlefish; black crappie; white crappie; bass; bluegill; walleye.

Empire Resort
HCR 80, Box 481
Camdenton, MO 65020
573-346-2177
Price Category: $
Waters: Lake of the Ozarks.
Fish: Bass; catfish; crappie.

Fin and Feather Resort
HCR 3, Box 710
Kimberling City, MO 65686
417-739-4477
Price Category: $
Waters: Table Rock Lake.
Fish: Bass; walleye; catfish.

Fish Hook Resort*
HCR 7, Box 1710
Lake Road DD Hwy.
Reeds Spring, MO 65737
417-338-2354
Price Category: $
Waters: Table Rock Lake; Bull Shoals Lake; Roaring Fork River; Beaver Lake; James River; Taneycomo Lake.
Fish: White bass; paddlefish; spotted bass; walleye; large- mouth bass; smallmouth bass; crappie; catfish.

Fish N' Fun Resort
HCR 1, Box 4170
Shell Knob, MO 65747
800-545-6137
Price Category: $
Waters: Table Rock Lake.
Fish: Bass; walleye; catfish.

Fisherman's Haven Resort
Rt. 1, Box 1050
Golden, MO 65658
417-271-3599

Fisherman's Luck Resort
Rt. 5, Box 346
Reeds Springs, ME 65737
417-739-4485
Price Category: $
Waters: Table Rock Lake.
Fish: White bass; largemouth bass; catfish; sunfish; bluegill; crappie.

Fisherwaters Resort
Rt. 80, Box 754
Camdenton, MO 65020
573-346-2166

*This resort is included in Guest-Rated Resort Guide

Price Category: $
Waters: Lake of the Ozarks.
Fish: Bass; catfish; crappie.

Flame Resort
Rt. 71, Box 520
Camdenton, MO 65020
573-873-5065
Price Category: $
Waters: Lake of the Ozarks.
Fish: Bass; catfish; crappie.

Forever Resorts
PO Box 3229
Camdenton, MO 56020
800-255-5561

Golden Rule Resort
299 Golden Rule Rd.
Lake Ozark, MO 65049
573-365-2451

Golden Horseshoe Resort
79 Barba Le Lane
Lake Ozark, MO 65049
573-365-2642
Price Category: $-$$
Waters: Lake Ozark.
Fish: Smallmouth bass; largemouth bass; bluegill; catfish;
crappie; perch.

Goody's Resort
RR 1, Box 434
Flemington, MO 65650
417-282-6338

Grand River Resort
PO Box 962
Warway, MO 65355
816-438-2741
Price Category: $
Waters: Truman Lake and area

waters.
Fish: Bass; crappie; walleye.

Happy Hollow Resort
248 Hammock Way
Blue Eye, MO 65611
417-779-4360
Price Category: $
Waters: Table Rock Lake.
Fish: Bass; crappie; catfish;
bluegill.

Heavenly Days Resort
Rt. 71, Box 799
Camdenton, MO 65020
573-873-5325

Heritage on the Lake
PO Box 325
Osage Beach, MO 65065
573-348-3600

Hiawatha Resort
HCR 1, Box 849
Branson, MO 65616
417-338-2605

Hickory Grove Resort
HC 76, Box 2650
Pittsburg, MO 65724
417-852-4440

**Highway 83 Marina and
Resort**
Rt. 2, Box 408
Flemington, MO 65650
417-282-6341

Holiday Hills Resort
620 East Rockford Dr.
Branson, MO 65616
417-334-4013

Hyd-A-Way Cove
Rt. 2, Box 648
Camdenton, MO 65020
573-346-2673

Indian Hill Resort
HC 77, Box 990
Pittsburg, MO 65724
417-852-4444

Indian Trails Resort
HCR 1, Box 999
Branson, MO 65616
417-338-2827

Jonathan's Landing
500 Walnut Rd.
Lake Ozark, MO 65049
573-365-6772

Kalfran Lodge
PO Box 221
Osage Beach, MO 67065
573-348-2266
Price Category: $
Waters: Lake of the Ozarks.
Fish: Bass; catfish; crappie.

Knotty Pines Resort
Rt. 71, Box 860
Camdenton, MO 65020
573-873-5181
Price Category: $
Waters: Lake of the Ozarks.
Fish: Bass; catfish; crappie.

Kon Tiki
Rt. 71, Box 793
Camdenton, MO 65020
573-873-5320

Lakefront Resort and Campground
HCR 2, Box 127

Blue Eye, MO 65611
800-488-4514
Price Category: $
Waters: Table Rock Lake.
Fish: Walleye; bass; catfish;
bluegill.

Lamplighter Resort
HCR 71, Box 15
Camdenton, MO 65020
573-873-5150

Lazy Lee's Resort*
HC 7, Box 1840
Reeds Springs, MO 65737
417-338-2253
Price Category: $
Waters: Table Rock Lake; Lake
Taneycomo; Bull Shoals Lake;
James River; White River.
Fish: Smallmouth bass; crappie;
catfish; walleye; sun-perch.

Lodge of the Four Seasons
PO Box 215
Lake Ozark, MO 65049
800-843-5253
Price Category: $$$
Waters: Lake of the Ozarks.
Fish: Bass; catfish; crappie.

Lodge of the Ozarks
PO Box 306
Lake Ozark, MO 65049
573-365-6729

Lost Creek Lodge
HC 3, Box 22
Greenville, MO 63944
573-297-3351

Millstone Lodge
PO Box 1157
Laurie, MO 65038

This resort is included in Guest-Rated Resort Guide

573-372-5111
Price Category: $$
Waters: Lake of the Ozarks.
Fish: Bass; catfish; crappie.

Mimosa Beach Resort
Rt. 1, Box 106D
Climax Springs, MO 65324
573-345-3400

Plaza Beach Resort*
Rt. 76, Box 420
Camdenton, MO 65020
573-873-5308
Price Category: $
Waters: Lake of the Ozarks.
Fish: Largemouth bass; white
bass; crappie; catfish; bluegill;
walleye.

**Rainbow Trout and Game
Ranch**
PO Box 100
Rockbridge, MO 65741
417-679-3619
Price Category: $$$
Waters: Spring Creek.
Fish: Rainbow trout.

Rippling Waters Resort
Rt. 80, Box 123
Camdenton, MO 65020
573-346-2642
Price Category: $
Waters: Lake of the Ozarks.
Fish: Bass; catfish; crappie.

Rivertowne Resort
4012 River Rd.
Saint Joseph, MO 64505
816-364-6500

Robin's Resort*
4935 Robin's Circle

Osage Beach, MO 65065
573-348-1696
Price Category: $
Waters: Lake of the Ozarks.
Fish: Catfish; walleye; spoonbill;
bluegill; crappie; white bass;
striper; hybrid bass; black bass.

Rocky Ridge Ranch Resort
#1 Rocky Ridge Ranch
Sainte Genevieve, MO 63670
573-483-2019

Rod N Reel Resort
HCR 1, Box 4322
Shell Knob, MO 65747
417-858-6295
Price Category: $$
Waters: Table Rock Lake.
Fish: Bass; catfish; crappie.

Rod'n Reel Resort
Rt. 71, Box 687
Camdenton, MO 65020
800-906-LAKE

Russ T Resort
RR 1, Box 1616
Wheatland, MO 65779
417-282-6241

Sand Spring Resort
Rt. 16, Box 1040
Lebanon, MO 65536
417-532-5857
Price Category: $
Waters: Niangua River.

Shore Acres Resort*
Rt. 4, Box 2010
Reeds Spring, MO 65737
417-338-2351
Price Category: $
Waters: Table Rock Lake.

This resort is included in Guest-Rated Resort Guide

Fish: Bass; catfish; bluegill; crappie.

South Fork Resort
Rt. 1, Box 93
Stoutsville, MO 65283
573-565-3500
Price Category: $
Waters: Mark Twain Lake.

Sportsmen's Cove
Lake Rd. 54-29, Box 7400
Osage Beach, MO 65065
800-472-0833

Sterett Creek Resort
Rt. 4, Box 353
Warsaw, MO 65335
816-438-2821

Still Waters Vacation Resort*
HCR 1, Box 928
Branson, MO 65616
417-338-2323
800-777-2320
Price Category: $$
Waters: Table Rock Lake.
Fish: Largemouth bass; small-mouth bass; walleye; crappie; catfish.

Sun Dance Resort
PO Box 871
Lake Ozark, MO 65049
573-365-2946
Price Category: $$
Waters: Lake of the Ozarks.
Fish: Bass; catfish; crappie.

Sunflower Resort
Rt. 2, Box 2681
Wheatland, MO 65779
417-282-6235

Taneycomo Resort
PO Box 158
Branson, MO 65616
417-334-7375
Price Category: $
Waters: Lake Taneycomo; Table Rock Lake; Bull Shoals Lake.
Fish: Trout; bass; crappie; cat-fish; bluegill.

Tebo Creek Lodge
27 S-E Hwy. PP
Clinton, MO 64735
816-477-3516
Price Category: $
Waters: Truman Lake.
Fish: Catfish; bass; crappie.

The Harbour
PO Box 126
Gravois Mills, MO 63057
573-372-3000

Theodosia Marina and Resort
Box 390
Theodosia, MO 65761
417-273-4444
Price Category: $
Waters: Bull Shoals Lake.
Fish: Catfish; bass; crappie; bluegill.

Thunder Bay Resort
HCR 1, Box 1300
Isabella, MO 65676
417-273-4222

Up The Creek
Rt. 1, Box 34M
Edwards, MO 65326
573-345-3370

Whip-Poor-Will Resort
HC 3 3636
Shell Knob, MO 65747
417-858-6590
Price Category: $
Waters: Table Rock Lake.
Fish: Walleye; catfish; bluegill.

Whispering Pines
Hwy. 160 W.
Isabella, MO 65676
417-273-4222

White Branch Marina
PO Box 1806
Warsaw, MO 65355
816-438-6344

Willow Winds Resort
Lake Rd. 254 - 15
Wheatland, MO 65779
417-282-5591
Price Category: $
Waters: Lake Pomme de Terre.
Fish: Muskie; bass; crappie;
walleye; catfish; bluegill; drum.

Wind Rush Farm
Rt. 2, Box 34
Cook Station, MO 65449
573-743-6555
Price Category: $ - $$
Waters: Benton Creek.
Fish: Rainbow trout.

Wing and Fin Resort
HCR 1, Box 1290
Isabella, MO 65676
417-273-4242
Price Category: $
Waters: Bull Shoals Lake.
Fish: Black bass; white bass;
crappie.

MONTANA

Above the Rest Lodge
8 Above the Rest Lane
Gardiner, MT 59030
406-848-7747

Alta Meadow Ranch*
9975 West Fork Rd.
Darby, MT 59829
409-349-2464
Price Category: $$-$$$
Waters: Bitter Root River, lake,
ponds.
Fish:Cutthroat, rainbow, brown
trout

Averill's Flathead Lake Lodge*
150 Flathead Lake Lodge Road
Bigfork, MT 59911
406-837-4391
Price Category: $$$
Waters: Flathead Lake; Van
Lake; Swan Lake; Swan River.
Fish: Rainbow trout; lake trout;
bull trout; cutthroat trout.

Babcock Creek Outfitters
280 Twin Lakes Rd.
Whitefish, MT 59937
406-862-7813

Bar N Ranch
3111 Targee Pass Hwy.
West Yellowstone, MT 59758
800-BIGSKYS
Price Category: $$
Waters: South Fork of Madison;
Hebgen Lake.
Fish: Brown trout; cutthroat
trout; rainbow trout.

This resort is included in Guest-Rated Resort Guide

Battle Creek Lodge
Box 670
Chotequ, MT 59422
406-266-4426
Price Category: $$
Waters: Deep Creek; high mountain lakes; private pond.
Fish: Brown trout; brook trout; cutthroat trout; rainbow trout.

Beartooth Plateau Outfitters*
PO Box 127
Cooke City, MT 59020
800-253-8545
Price Category: $$
Waters: Slough Creek; Lamar River; Cache Creek; Miller Creek; Pebble Creek; several alpine lakes in the Absaroka - Beartooth wilderness.
Fish: Cutthroat trout; brook trout; rainbow trout; golden trout; arctic grayling.

Big Horn River Lodge
Box 7756
Fort Smith, MT 59035
406-666-2368

Bighorn River Fin and Feather Lodge
1925 Central
Billings, MT 59101
406-656-8280

Billingsley Ranch Outfitters
Box 768
Glasgow, MT 59230
406-367-5577

Bob Marshall Wilderness Ranch
General Delivery
St. Ignatius, MT 59865
406-745-4466

C-B Ranch
PO Box 146
Cameron, MT 59720
888-723-3474
Price Category: $$$
Waters: Indian Creek; Madison River; Henry's Fork.
Fish: Brown trout; rainbow trout.

Canyon Creek Ranch
PO Box 126
Melrose, MT 59743
888-225-3172
Price Category: $$
Waters: Bighole River; Beaverhead River; Ruby River; Blacktail River; Jefferson River; Canyon Creek; Lamarche Creek; Pattengail Creek; Trapper Creek; Abundance Lake;Crescent Lake; Lion Lake; Grayling Lake.
Fish: Brown trout; rainbow trout; brook trout; cutthroat trout; cutbow trout; grayling.

Chef's Guest Ranch
4274 Eagle Pass Trail
Charlo, MT 59824
406-644-2557

Chico Hot Springs Lodge
PO Drawer D
Pray, MT 59065
406-333-4933
Price Category: $-$$
Waters: Firehole River; Madison River.
Fish: Brook trout; brown trout; cutthroat trout; rainbow trout.

Cinnamon Lodge
Box 33
Gallatin Gateway, MT 59730
406-995-4253

Price Category: $
Waters: Gallatin River.
Fish: Rainbow trout; cutthroat trout; brown trout; mountain whitefish.

Crane Meadow Lodge
Box 303
Twin Lodges, MT 59754
406-684-5773

Diamond J Ranch
Box 577
Ennis, MT 59729
406-682-4867
Price Category: $$$
Waters: Jack Creek; Madison River.
Fish: Trout.

Double Arrow Resort
PO Box 747
Seeley Lake, MT 59868
406-677-2777
Price Category: $-$$
Waters: Blackfoot River
Fish: Brown trout; rainbow trout.

Eagle Nest Lodge
PO Box 509
Hardin, MT 59034
406-665-3711
Price Category: $$$
Waters: Bighorn River.
Fish: Brown trout; rainbow trout.

Fairmont Hot Springs Resort
1500 Fairmont Rd.
Anaconda, MT 59071
800-332-3272
Price Category: $$
Waters: Big Hole River;

Georgetown Lake.
Fish: Trout.

Firehole Ranch
Box 686
West Yellowstone, MT 59758
406-646-7294
Price Category: $$$$
Waters: Madison River; Yellowstone River; Gibbon River; Firehole River.
Fish: Brown trout; rainbow trout.

Fly Fisher's Inn
2629 Old Hwy. 91
Cascade, MT 59421
406-468-2529
Price Category: $$
Waters: Missouri River between Holter and Cascade.
Fish: Rainbow trout; brown trout.

Ford Creek Ranch
Box 329
Augusta, MT 59410
406-562-3672

Great Northern Chalets at Glacier National Park
Box 278M
West Glacier, MT 59936
800-735-7897
Price Category: $$
Waters: Flathead River.
Fish: Cutthroat trout; rainbow trout.

Hawley Mountain Guest Ranch*
PO Box 4
McLeod, MT 59052
406-932-5791

Price Category: $$$
Waters: Upper Boulder River;
Blue Lake; Meatrack Creek;
Yellowstone River. High moun-
tain streams and lakes.
Fish: Brook trout; cutthroat
trout; rainbow trout; cutbow
trout.

Healing Waters Fly Fishing Lodge
270 Tyke St.
Twin Bridges, MT 59754
406-684-5960
Price Category: $$$$

Holiday Resort
17001 East Shore Rd.
Bigfork, MT 59911
406-982-3710
Price Category: $$
Waters: Flathead Lake.
Fish: Rainbow trout; lake trout;
makinaw.

Hubbard's Yellowstone Lodge
RR 1, Box 662
Emigrant, MT 59027
406-848-7755
Price Category: $$$$
Waters: Merrell Lake;
Yellowstone River; Ram's Horn
Lake; Tom Miner Creek.
Fish: Rainbow trout; brown
trout; cutthroat trout.

Jumping Rainbow Ranch
110 Jumping Rainbow Rd.
Livingston, MT 59047
Price Category: $-$$
Waters: Yellowstone River.
Fish: Brown trout; cutthroat
trout; rainbow trout.

Kingfisher Inn
Box 7524
Fort Smith, MT 57035
406-666-2326
Price Category: $$
Waters: Bighorn River.
Fish: Brown trout; rainbow
trout.

Lone Mountain Ranch
Box 160069
Big Sky, MT 59716
800-514-4644
Price Category: $$$$
Waters: Madison River; Gallatin
River.
Fish: Trout.

Missouri River Lodge
3103 Old US 91
Cascade, MT 59421
406-468-9385
Price Category: $ - $$
Waters: Missouri River.
Fish: Brown trout; rainbow
trout.

Mountain Sky Guest Ranch
Box 1128
Bozeman, MT 59715
800-548-3392
Price Category: $$$$
Waters: Yellowstone River.
Fish: Rainbow trout; brown
trout; cutthroat trout.

Mountain Timbers Wilderness Lodge
PO Box 94
West Glacier, MT 59936
406-387-5830
Price Category: $$
Waters: Flathead River; Glacier

This resort is included in Guest-Rated Resort Guide

National Park area.
Fish: Trout.

Old Kirby Place
West Fork Bridge
Cameron, MT 59720
406-682-4194
Price Category: $$$
Waters: Madison River.
Fish: Brown trout; rainbow
trout.

Parade Rest Guest Ranch
7979 Grayling Creek Rd.
Drawer K
West Yellowstone, MT 59758
800-753-5934
Price Category: $$
Waters: Grayling Creek;
Madison River.
Fish: Trout.

Pepperbox Ranch
9959 West Fork Rd.
Darby, MT 59829
406-349-2920

Point Of Rocks Lodge
2017 US 89 South
Emigrant, MT 59027
406-333-4361
Price Category: $$ - $$$
Waters: Yellowstone River.
Fish: Brown trout; cutthroat
trout; rainbow trout.

Red Lodging*
PO Box 1477
115 West 9th
Red Lodge, MT 59068
406-446-1272
800-6-REDLODGE
Price Category: $

Waters: Yellowstone River;
Stillwater River drainage; Rock
Creek; Stillwater River; Wild
Bill Lake; several high altitude
lakes.
Fish: Cutthroat trout; rainbow
trout; brook trout; golden trout.

Rock Creek Fishing Company
PO Box 9138
Missoula, MT 59807
406-825-3019

Ruby Springs Lodge*
Box 119
Alder, MT 59710
800-278-7829
Price Category: $$$$
Waters: Bighole River;
Beaverhead River; Ruby River;
Madison River; Jefferson River.
Fish: Brown trout; rainbow
trout; grayling.

Sheep Mountain Lodge
PO Box 787
Superior, MT 59872
406-822-3382
Price Category: $$$
Waters: Clark Fork River.
Fish: Rainbow trout; cutthroat
trout; brown trout.

Skalkaho Lodge
Skalkaho Rd.
Hamilton, MT 59840
406-363-3522
Price Category: $$$
Waters: Bitteroot River.
Fish: Rainbow trout; brown
trout; cutthroat trout.

This resort is included in Guest-Rated Resort Guide

Sleepy Hollow Lodge
PO Box 1080
124 Electric Street
West Yellowstone, MT 59758
406-646-7707
Price Category: $$
Waters: Madison River; Firehole River; Gibbon River; Yellowstone River; Slough Creek; Lamar River; Gallatin River; Henry's Fork; Henry's Lake; Hebgen Lake.
Fish: Rainbow trout; brown trout; cutthroat trout; golden trout.

Soda Butte Lodge
PO Box 1119
209 Hwy. 212
Cooke City, MT 59020
406-838-2251
Price Category: $$

Spotted Bear Ranch
2863 Foothill Rd.
Kalispell, MT 59901
406-755-7337
Price Category: $$$
Waters: South Fork of the Flathead River.
Fish: Westslope cutthroat trout; dolly varden; Montana grayling; whitefish.

Sun Canyon Lodge
Box 327
Augusta, MT 59410
406-562-3654

Tamarack Lodge
32855 South Fork Dr.
Troy, MT 59935
406-295-4880

Price Category: $$$
Waters: Yaak River.
Fish: Bull trout; brook trout; cutthroat trout.

The Creekside Retreat
PO Box 1477
Red Lodge, MT 59068
406-446-1272

Triple Creek Ranch
5551 West Fork Stage Rd.
Darby, MT 59829
406-821-4600
Price Category: $$$$
Waters: West Fork of the Bitterroot River.
Fish: Brown trout; cutthroat trout; rainbow trout.

Trout Springs Bed and Breakfast
721 Desta St.
Hamilton, MT 59840
406-375-0911
Price Category: $$
Waters: Bitterroot River.
Fish: Trout.

Under Wild Skies Lodge and Outfitters*
PO Box 849
Phillipsburg, MT 59858
406-859-3000
Price Category: $$
Waters: Rock Creek; Middle Fork River; Big Hole River.
Fish: Mountain whitefish; rainbow trout; dolly varden; brook trout; cutthroat trout.

Yellowstone Valley Ranch
3840 Hwy. 89 S.

Livingston, MT 59047
800-626-3526
Price Category: $$$
Waters: Yellowstone River.
Fish: Brown trout; cutthroat trout; rainbow trout.

NEBRASKA

Alkali Fish Camp
HC 37, Box 32
Valentine, NE 69201
402-376-3479

Kingsley Lodge
N. Hwy. #61
Ogallala, NE 69153
308-284-2775
Price Category: $
Waters: North Platte River; Lake McConaughy.
Fish: Walleye; smallmouth bass; northern pike; tiger muskie; white bass; perch; trout; striper; catfish.

Merritt Resort
HC 32, Box 23
Valentine, NE 69201
402-376-3437
Price Category: $
Waters: Merritt Reservoir.
Fish: Catfish; walleye; perch; crappie; northern; largemouth bass; smallmouth bass.

Trade Winds Lodge
HC 37, Box 2
Valentine, NE 69201
402-376-1600

NEVADA

Overton Beach Resort
Overton Beach Marina
Overton, NV 89040
702-394-4040
Price Category: $
Waters: Lake Mead.

NEW HAMPSHIRE

Isaac Merril House
PO Box 8
Kearsarge, NH 03847
603-356-9041

Lopstick Lodge
1st Connecticut Lake
Pittsburg, NH 03592
800-538-6659

Nereledge Inn
PO Box 547
N. Conway, NH 03860
603-356-2831
Price Category: $
Waters: Saco River.

South Bay Resort*
822 Laconia Rd.
Tilton, NH 03276
603-528-2449
Price Category: $$
Waters: Lake Winnisquam.
Fish: Largemouth bass; smallmouth bass; mackerel.

Tall Timber Lodge
231 Beach Rd.
Pittsburg, NH 03593
800-83-LODGE

Price Category: $$
Waters: Connecticut Lakes
Region.
Fish: Rainbow trout; lake trout;
brook trout; brown trout; land-
locked salmon.

The Balsams Grand Resort Hotel*
Lake Gloriette - Route 26
Dixville Notch, NH 03576
603-225-3400
Price Category: $$$
Waters: Lake Gloriette; Lake
Umbagog; Connecticut Lakes;
Mohawk River; Connecticut
River.
Fish: Rainbow trout; brook
trout; brown trout; salmon;
pickeral; northern pike.

The Glen
First Connecticut Lake
Pittsburg, NH 03592
800-445-4536
Price Category: $$
Waters: First Connecticut Lake.
Fish: Salmon; lake trout; rain-
bow trout; squaretail; brown
trout; landlocked salmon.

The Manor on Golden Pond
Rt. 3, Box T
Holderness, NH 03245
800-545-2141
Price Category: $$
Waters: Squam Lake.

Woodbound Inn*
62 Woodbound Rd.
Rindge, NH 03461
603-532-8341

800-688-7770
Price Category: $$
Waters: Lake Contoocook.
Fish: Bass; trout; various pan-
fish.

NEW MEXICO

Blackfire Flyfishing Guest Ranch*
Box 981
Angel Fire, NM 87710
505-377-6870
Price Category: $$$
Waters: Private lake on property;
Cimarron River; Red River;
Coyote Creek.
Fish: Rainbow trout; brown
trout; cutthroat trout.

Gila Wilderness Lodge
HC 30, Box 471
Winston, NM 87943
505-772-5772
Price Category: $$
Waters: Gila River; Wall Lake.
Fish: Trout; smallmouth bass;
bluegill; crappie.

La Cueva Lodge
38690 Hwy. 126
Jemez Springs, NM 87025
505-829-3814

Los Pinos Ranch*
Rt. Box 8
Terrero, NM 87573
505-757-6213
Price Category: $$
Waters: Pecos River and tribu-
taries; high mountain lakes.

This resort is included in Guest-Rated Resort Guide

Fish: Rainbow trout; pecos brown trout; cutthroat trout.

Rizuto's San Juan River Lodge
PO Box 6309
Navajo Dam, NM 87419
505-632-3893
Price Category: $$
Waters: San Juan River.
Fish: Rainbow trout.

Spruce Lodge
PO Box 365
Chama, NM 87520
505-756-2593

Step Back Inn
103 West Aztec Blvd.
Aztec, NM 87410
505-334-1200
Price Category: $$
Waters: San Juan River.
Fish: Trout.

The Lodge at Chama
Box 127K
Chama, NM 87520
505-756-2133
Price Category: $$$$
Fish: Rainbow trout; brown trout; cutthroat trout.

Unser's Oso Ranch
PO Box 808
Chama, NM 87520
505-756-2954

Vermejo Park Ranch
PO Drawer E
Raton, NM 87740
505-445-5028

NEW YORK

1880 House Fisherman's Lodge
1 S. Jefferson St.
Pulaski, NY 13142
315-298-3511

Adirondack Fancy
21 Deer St.
Tupper Lake, NY 12986
518-359-7557

Beaverkill Valley Inn
136 Beaverkill Rd.
Lew Beach, NY 12753
914-439-4844
Price Category: $$
Waters: Beaverkill.
Fish: Brook trout; brown trout.

Double Eagle Lodge
3178 Star Rt. 13
Pulaski, NY 13142
315-298-3326
Price Category: $$
Waters: Salmon River.

Eldred Preserve
1040 Route 55
Eldred, NY 12732
914-557-8316
Price Category: $$
Waters: Private lakes and ponds.
Fish: Largemouth bass; trout; catfish.

Fish Inn Post
2035 Co. Rt. 22
Altmar, NY 13302
315-298-6406

Fort Geronimo Sports Lodge
RR 1, Box 47
McCaw Rd.
Redfield, NY 13437

Frost Haven
Box 241
14380 West Bay Rd.
Fair Haven, NY 13064

Huff House
100 Lake Anawanda Rd.
Roscoe, NY 12776
800-358-5012
Price Category: $$
Waters: Private ponds.
Fish: Trout.

Hungry Trout
Route 86
Whiteface, NY 12997
518-946-2217
Price Category: $$
Fish: Brown trout; rainbow trout; brook trout.

Indian Springs Camp*
RR 1, Box 200AA
Hancock, NY 13783
215-679-5022
Price Category: $$-$$$
Waters: Upper Delaware River.
Fish: Rainbow trout; brown trout; shad.

K & G Sportfishing Lodge*
94 Creamery Rd.
Oswego, NY 13126
800-346-6533
Price Category: $ - $$$
Waters: Lake Ontario; Oswego River; Salmon River.
Fish: Smallmouth bass; salmon;

steelhead; brown trout.

Lake Placid Lodge*
PO Box 550
Lake Placid, NY 12946
518-523-2700
Price Category: $$$$
Waters: Lake Placid; West Branch of AuSable River.
Fish: Lake trout; rainbow trout; brook trout; brown trout; pike; largemouth bass; smallmouth bass.

Laurdon Heights
PO Box 22
Pulaski, NY 13142
315-298-6091
Price Category: $$
Waters: Salmon River; Oswego River; Lake Ontario.
Fish: Rainbow trout; brown trout; steelhead; king salmon; Atlantic salmon.

LoPinta Farms Lodge
355 Sheldon
Freeville, NY 13068
607-347-6556
Price Category: $$

Sojourn Cottages
PO Box 175
Chippewa Bay, NY 13623
315-324-5229

The Portly Angler Lodge
PO Box 27
Pulaski, NY 13142
315-298-4773
Price Category: $
Waters: Salmon River; Lake Ontario.

This resort is included in Guest-Rated Resort Guide

Fish: Coho salmon; bass; king salmon; brown trout; steelhead.

The Thomas Inn
309 Seneca
Oswego, NY 13126
315-343-4900

The Wild River Inn
7743 SR 3
Pulaski, NY 13142
315-248-4195
Price Category: $
Waters: Salmon River; Lake Ontario.
Fish: Steelhead; king salmon; brown trout; smallmouth bass; walleye.

Thousand Islands Inn*
PO Box 69
335 Riverside Drive
Clayton, NY 13624
315-686-3030
800-544-4241
Price Category: $ - $$$
Waters: Lake Ontario; New York and Ontario regions of the St. Lawrence River.
Fish: Largemouth bass; smallmouth bass; northern pike; walleye; muskie.

West Branch Angler
150 Faulkner Rd.
Deposit, NY 13754
607-467-5525
Price Category: $$
Waters: West Branch of the Delaware River; Beaverkill River; Willowemoc River; Delaware River.
Fish: Trout

NORTH CAROLINA

Fontana Village Resort
Hwy. 28, Box 68
Fontana Dam, NC 28733
800-849-2258
Price Category: $$
Waters: Fontana Lake.
Fish: Trout.

Harker's Island Fishing Center
PO Box 400
Harker's Island, NC 28531
919-728-3907
Price Category: $
Waters: Atlantic Ocean.
Fish: Albacore; trout; drum; cobia; bluefish; Spanish mackeral; king mackeral; dolphin; wahoo; tuna; billfish.

High Hampton Inn
PO Box 338
Cashiers, NC 28717
800-334-2551
Price Category: $$
Waters: Hampton Lake.
Fish: Rainbow trout; bass; bream.

Santee State Park
251 State Park Rd.
Santee, SC 29142
803-854-2408
Price Category: $
Waters: Lake Moultrie; Lake Marion.
Fish: Landlocked bass; largemouth bass; catfish; crappie.

Sapphire Valley Resort
4000 Hwy. 64 West
Sapphire, NC 28774

800-533-8268
Price Category: $$
Waters: Fairfield Lake.

NORTH DAKOTA

Ashtabula Crossing Resort
301 N Central Ave.
Crossing
Valley City, ND 58072
701-845-0056

Bayshore Resort Marina
791 22nd St. SE
Valley City, ND 58072
701-845-1066

Dakota Waters Resort
PO Box 576
Beulah, ND 58523
701-873-5800
Price Category: $
Waters: Lake Sakakawea.
Fish: Walleye; salmon; sauger;
northern pike.

Golden Lake Resort
RR 2, Box 300
Hatton, ND 58240
701-543-4136

Indian Hills Resort
Box 700
Garrison, ND 58540
701-743-4122
Price Category: $
Waters: Lake Sakakawea.
Fish: Walleye; sauger.

Kautzman's Heart River Ranch
HC 4, Box 204
Mandan, ND 58554

Lund's Landing Marina
HC 1, Box 22
Ray, ND 58849
701-568-3474

Pouch Point Marina Resort
Box 794
New Town, ND 58763
701-627-3553

Woodland Resort
RR 1, Box 245
Devil's Lake, ND 58301
701-662-5996
Price Category: $
Waters: Devil's Lake; Woodland
Resort.
Fish: Perch.

OHIO

Gayles Bed and Breakfast
PO Box 85
Put-In-Bay, OH 43456
419-285-7181
Price Category: $ - $$
Waters: Lake Erie.
Fish: Walleye; smallmouth bass.

Sawmill Creek Resort
400 Sawmill
Huron, OH 44839
419-433-3800
Price Category: $$
Waters: Lake Erie.

OKLAHOMA

Belly View Resort
Rt. 1, Box 821
Eucha, OK 74342-9767
918-435-4318

This resort is included in Guest-Rated Resort Guide

Callis Striper Inn
HC 71, Box 744
Kingston, OK 73439
405-564-4883

Honey Creek Resort and Motel
2511 South Main
Grove, OK 74344
918-786-5119
Price Category: $
Waters: Grand Lake.
Fish: Catfish; crappie; black
bass; largemouth bass; smallmouth bass; white bass; hybrid
bass; walleye; buffalo; spoonbill.

Lake Texoma State Park
PO Box 248
Kingston, OK 73439
405-564-2311
Price Category: $$
Waters: Lake Texoma.
Fish: Catfish; striper.

Tera Miranda
Rt. Box 2200
Afton, OK 74331
918-257-4271

OREGON

CJ Lodge*
PO Box 130
Maupin, OR 97037
541-395-2404
Price Category: $$
Waters: Deschutes River.
Fish: Redside trout; steelhead;
salmon.

Eagle Rock Lodge
49198 McKenzie Hwy.

Vida, OR 97488
503-822-3962

Elkqua Lodge
Box 546
Elkton, OR 97436
503-584-2161
Price Category: $$$$
Waters: Umpqua River.
Fish: Steelhead; sturgeon;
striped bass; Chinook salmon;
silver salmon; shad.

Grande Ronde Lodge
PO Box 2935
LaGrande, OR 97850
541-963-7878
Price Category: $$$$
Waters: Grande Ronde River.
Fish: Steelhead; trout; small-
mouth bass.

Hannah Camps
PO Box 1
Elkton, OR 97436
503-459-2525

Horseshoe Ranch*
PO Box 495
Fort Klamath, OR 97626
541-381-2297
Price Category: $$$
Waters: Wood River; Williamson
River; Sprague River; Klamath
Lake; Agency Lake.
Fish: Rainbow trout; German
brown trout; brook trout.

Hunter's Hot Springs
PO Box 1189
Lakeview, OR 97630
541-947-4800

This resort is included in Guest-Rated Resort Guide

Lodge at Half Moon Bar
PO Box 10
Agness, OR 97406
503-247-6968

Lucas Pioneer Ranch and Lodge
PO Box 37
Agness, OR 97406
503-247-7443

Nightingale's Fish Camp
83130 Siltcoos Station Rd.
Westlake, OR 97493
503-997-2892

Odell Lake Lodge
PO Box 72
Crescent Lake, OR 97425
541-433-2540
Price Category: $
Waters: Odell Lake; Crescent Lake; Diamond Lake.
Fish: Rainbow trout; kokanee salmon; mackinaw trout; white fish.

Paradise Lodge*
PO Box 456
Gold Beach, OR 97444
541-247-6022
800-525-2161
Price Category: $$
Waters: Rogue River; Paradise Creek; Jackson Creek.
Fish: Coho salmon; steelhead; brook trout.

Riverside Inn
971 E 6th St.
Grant's Pass, OR 97526
800-331-4567
Price Category: $$
Waters: Rogue River.

Fish: Salmon; Steelhead.

Rocky Point Resort
28121 Rocky Point Rd.
Klammath Falls, OR 97603
541-345-2287

Summer Lake Bed and Breakfast Inn*
31501 Hwy. 31
Summer Lake, OR 97640
541-943-3983
800-261-2778
Price Category: $-$$
Waters: Ana River; Ana Reservoir; Chewacan River; Sycan River; Sprague River; Thompson Reservoir.
Fish: Rainbow trout; brook trout; brown trout.

The Big K
20029 Hwy. 138 W
Elkton, OR 97436
1-800-390-2445
Price Category: $$$
Waters: Umpqua River.
Fish: Steelhead; sturgeon; Chinook salmon; striped bass; shad; smallmouth bass.

The Lodge at Summer Lake*
36980 Hwy. 31
Summer Lake, OR 97640
541-943-3993
Price Category: $
Waters: Ana Resevoir; Ana River; Chewaucan River; private pond.
Fish: Bass; rainbow trout; brook trout; brown trout.

Willamette Pass Inn
PO Box 35
Crescent Lake, OR 97425

This resort is included in Guest-Rated Resort Guide

541-433-2211

Yamsi Ranch*
Box 371
Chiloquin, OR 97624
541-783-2403
Price Category: $$$
Waters: Williamson River headwaters; Spring Creek.
Fish: Rainbow trout; brook trout.

PENNSYLVANIA

Allenberry Resort Inn and Playhouse
PO Box 7
Boiling Springs, PA 17007
717-258-1464
Price Category: $$
Waters: Yellow Breeches Creek.
Fish: Brown trout; rainbow trout.

Big Moore's Run Lodge
Rt. 3, Box 204 A
Coudersport, PA 16915
814-647-5300

Cliff Park Inn
RR 4, Box 7200
Milford, PA 18337
717-296-3982
Price Category: $$
Waters: Delaware River.
Fish: Smallmouth bass; trout; walleye.

Falling Spring Inn
1838 Falling Spring Rd.
Chambersburg, PA 17201
717-267-3654
Price Category: $ - $$
Waters: Letort.

Fish: Brown trout; rainbow trout.

Fernwood
Rt. 209
Bushkill, PA 18324
800-233-8103
Price Category: $$

Golden Pheasant Inn
763 River Rd.
Erwinna, PA 18920
610-294-9595
Price Category: $$
Waters: Delaware River.
Fish: Smallmouth bass; striped bass; muskie.

Kane Manor Inn*
230 Clay St.
Kane, PA 16735
814-837-6522
Price Category: $$
Waters: Kinzua Reservoir; Tionesta Creek - East and South Branches; Chappel Fork; Mead Run.
Fish: Trout; salmon; muskielunge; walleye.

Roebling Inn on the Delaware
Scenic Dr.
Lackawaxen, PA 18435
717-685-7900
Price Category: $$
Waters: Delaware River.
Fish: Smallmouth bass; walleye; trout.

Skytop Lodge
One Skytop
Skytop, PA 18357
717-595-7401
Price Category: $$$$

This resort is included in Guest-Rated Resort Guide

Waters: Skytop Lake.
Fish: Rainbow trout.

Starlight Lodge
PO Box 86
Starlight, PA 18461
717-798-2350
Price Category: $$
Waters: Delaware River.
Fish: Rainbow trout; brook
trout.

The Feathered Hook
PO Box 84
Coburn, PA 16832
814-349-8757

Yellow Breeches House*
PO Box 221
213 Front St.
Boiling Springs, PA 17007
800-258-1639
Price Category: $ - $$
Waters: Yellow Breeches; LeTort;
Big Spring; Green Spring; Clarks
Creek.
Fish: Brown trout; rainbow
trout; brook trout; palomino
trout.

SOUTH CAROLINA

Brays Island Plantation
PO Box 30
Sheldon, SC 29941
803-846-3100

Broxton Bridge Planation
PO Box 310
Ehrhardt, SC 29081
803-366-5072

Deerfield Plantation
PO Box 152
Ridgeville, SC 29472
803-571-6620

Saluda River Resort
1283 Saluda River Rd.
Silver Street, SC 29145
803-276-7917

Santee State Park*
251 State Park Rd.
Santee, SC 29142
803-854-2408
Price Category: $
Waters: Lake Marion; Lake
Moultrie; Santee River.
Fish: Largemouth bass; striped
bass; black crappie; bream;
catfish.

SOUTH DAKOTA

Big Bend Ranch
1301 N. 4th St.
Aberdeen, SD 57401
605-229-3035

Lewis and Clark Resort
PO Box 754
Yankton, SD 57078
1-605-665-2680

Oahe Lodge
19602 Lake Place
Pierre, SD 57501-6200
605-224-9340
Price Category: $$
Waters: Lake Oahe.
Fish: Walleye.

Pheasant Cove Lodge
PO Box 158

This resort is included in Guest-Rated Resort Guide

Glenham, SD 57631
605-762-3325

Pike Haven Resort
27645 Pike Haven Place
Pierre, SD 57501
615-264-5465

Radisson Cedar Shore Resort
PO Box 308
Chamberlain, SD 57325
605-734-6376
Price Category: $-$$
Waters: Lake Francis.
Fish: Walleye.

Roy Lake Resort
RR 2, Box 96
Lake City, SD 57247
605-448-5498

South Whitlock Resort on Lake Oahe
HCR 3, Box 72
Gettysburg, SD 5742
605-765-9762

Spring Creek Resort
610 North Jackson
Pierre, SD 57501
605-224-8336

Stateline Resort
HC 80, Box 33
Pollock, SD 57648
701-336-7765
Price Category: $
Waters: Lake Oahe.
Fish: Walleye.

Thunderstik Lodge
Rt. 1, Box 10P

Chamberlain, SD 57325
800-734-5168

TENNESSEE

Arrowhead Resort
261 Bennett Dr.
Spring City, TN 37381
423-365-6484

Bayside Marina
134 Bayside Dr.
Ten Mile, TN 37880
423-376-7031
Price Category: $
Waters: Watts Bar Lake.
Fish: Largemouth bass; smallmouth bass; crappie; catfish; rockfish; striped bass; sauger; bluegill.

Birdsong Resort
255 Marina Rd.
Camden , TN 38320
800-225-7469

Buchannon Resort
785 Buchannon Resort Rd.
Springville, TN 38256
901-642-2828

Charit Creek Lodge
250 Apple Valley Rd.
Seveirville, TN 37862
423-429-5704
Price Category: $
Waters: Charit Creek; Station Camp Creek.

Cedar Hill Resort*
2371 Cedar Hill Rd.
Celina, TN 38551

615-243-2301
800-872-8393
Price Category: $ - $$
Waters: Dale Hollow Lake.
Fish: Smallmouth bass; walleye;
bluegill; crappie; catfish; trout.

Clydeton Dock Resort
10669 Clydeton Rd.
Waverly, TN 37185
615-296-2211

Crooked Creek Marina
Rt. 1, Box 247
Lobelville, TN 37097
615-593-2112

Cypress Bay Resort
110 Cypress Resort Loop
Buchanon, TN 38222
901-232-8221

Dancing Fish Lodge
627 Wisteria Lane
Waverly, TN 37185
615-296-3533

Defeated Creek Marina
156 Marina Lane
Carthage, TN 37030
615-774-3131

Eagle Cove Resort
5652 East Port Rd.
Alping, TN 38543
800-736-7951

Hales Bar Marina
1205 Hales Bar Rd.
Chattanooga, TN 37340
423-942-4040

Hamilton's Resort
Rt. 1, 4992 Hamilton Rd.

Hornbeck , TN 38232
901-538-2325
Price Category: $
Waters: Reelfoot Lake.
Fish: Largemouth bass; crappie;
catfish.

Holiday Landing and Resort
PO Box 1556
Tullahoma, TN 37388
615-455-3151
Price Category: $
Waters: Tim's Ford Lake.
Fish: Smallmouth bass; striper;
catfish; bluegill.

Horse Creek Resort
1150 Horse Creek Rd.
Celina, TN 38551
800-545-2595
Price Category: $
Waters: Dale Hollow Lake.
Fish: Brown trout; striped bass;
muskie; walleye; crappie;
bluegill; lake trout.

**Leatherwood Resort and
Marina***
751 Leatherwood Bay Rd.
Dover, TN 37058
931-232-5137
Price Category: $
Waters: Kentucky Lake; Lake
Barkley.
Fish: Largemouth bass; small-
mouth bass; catfish; crappie;
bluegill; white bass.

Mansard Island Resort
60 Mansard Island Dr.
Springville, TN 38256
901-642-5590
Price Category: $
Waters: Kentucky Lake.

*This resort is included in Guest-Rated Resort Guide

Fish: Largemouth bass; bluegill; crappie; catfish.

Mountain Lake Marina and Campground*
136 Campground Rd.
Lake City, TN 37769
Phone: 423-426-6510
Price Category: $
Waters: Clinch River; Norris Lake.
Fish: Walleye; crappie; smallmouth bass; largemouth bass; striper.

Oak Haven Resort
248 Oak Haven Rd.
Buchannan, TN 38222
901-642-1550
Price Category: $
Waters: Kentucky Lake.
Fish: Crappie; bass; sauger; bream; striped bass.

Rhea Harbor Resort
385 Lakeshire Dr.
Spring City, TN 37381
423-365-6851

Shamrock Resort
220 Shamrock Rd.
Buchanan, TN 38222
901-232-8211

Spring City Resort
2109 New Lake Rd.
Spring City, TN 37381
423-365-5150
Price Category: $
Waters: Watts Bar Lake.

Star Point Resort
4490 Star Point Rd.

Byrdstown, TN 38549
615-864-3115

Sugar Hollow Dock*
Rt. 2, Box 344 H
Lafolette, TN 37766
423-562-3466
Price Category: $
Waters: Norris Lake.
Fish: Smallmouth bass; largemouth bass; rock bass; crappie.

Sunset Marina and Resort*
2040 Sunset Dock Rd.
Byrdstown, TN 38549
931-864-3146
Price Category: $
Waters: Dale Hollow Lake; Pendergrass Creek; Hurricane Creek; Franklin Creek.
Fish: Smallmouth bass; largemouth bass; Kentucky bass; muskie; walleye; bluegill; crappie; catfish; trout.

Toestring Cottages
296 Toestring Valley Rd.
Spring City, TN 37381

Tri Lakes Marina
38 Marina Lane
Winchester, TN 37398
615-967-7127

Watauga Lakeshores Marina
2285 Hwy. 321
Hampton, TN 37658
423-725-2223
Price Category: $
Waters: Watuaga Lake.
Fish: Rainbow trout; smallmouth bass; largemouth bass; walleye; crappie; bluegill.

*This resort is included in Guest-Rated Resort Guide

Watts Bar Resort
6767 Watts Bar Hwy.
Watts Bar Dam, TN 37395
800-365-9598
Price Category: $
Waters: Watts Bar Lake.

TEXAS

777 Ranch*
777 - P.R. 5327
Hondo, TX 78861
210-426-3476
Price Category: $$$
Waters: 30 Private lakes and ponds.
Fish: Largemouth bass.

Booger Hollow Bed and Breakfast
PO Box 259
Atlanta, TX 75551
903-796-3409
Price Category: $
Waters: Caddo Lake.
Fish: Bass.

Chain O Lakes
PO Box 218
Romayor, TX 77368
713-592-2150

Del Lago Resort
600 Del Lago Blvd.
Montgomery, TX 77356
409-582-6100
Price Category: $$
Waters: Lake Conroe.
Fish: Bass.

Joshua Creek Ranch
PO Box 1946

Boerne, TX 78006
210-537-5090
Price Category: $$$
Waters: Joshua Creek; Joshua Lake.
Fish: Rainbow trout.

Lake Fork Lodge Bass and Breakfast*
PO Box 160
Alba, TX 75410
903-473-7236
Price Category: $$
Waters: Lake Fork.
Fish: Largemouth bass; crappie; bluegill; catfish.

Lake Fork Sportsman Lodge
Rt. 1, Box 198-2A
Emory, TX 75440
800-842-2778

Lakeway Inn Resort
101 Lakeway Dr.
Austin, TX 78734
512-261-600

Llano Grande Plantation
Rt. 4, Box 9400
Nacogdoches, TX 75961
409-569-1249

Los Patios Lodge
18907 Tranquility Dr.
Humble , TX 77346
409-286-5787

Lowe's Creek Park
Rt. 4, Box 383
Hemphill, TX 75948
409-787-2600
Price Category: $
Waters: Toledo Bend Creek.

Mossy Brake Lodge
Rt. 2, Box 63AB
Uncertain, TX 75661
903-789-3440
Price Category: $
Waters: Caddo Lake.
Fish: Bream; white bass; black
bass.

Pine Needle Lodge
Rt. 3, Box 447
Jefferson, TX 75657
903-665-2911
Price Category: $
Waters: Caddo Lake.

Possum Walk Ranch
Rt. 1, Box 174
Huntsville, TX 77340
409-291-1891

South Shore Harbour Resort
2500 South Shore Blvd.
League City, TX 77573
713-334-1000

**The Back Forty Ranch at
Fredericksburg***
457 Bob Moritz Dr.
Fredericksburg, TX 78624
830-997-6373
Price Category: $$
Waters: Private lake; Baron's
Creek.
Fish: Hybrid bass; bluegill; cat-
fish.

The Inn at Preston Bend
Rt. 2, Box 432
Pottsboro, TX 75076
903-786-2448

Trophy Lodge
Rt. 3, Box 3856
Quitman, TX 75783
903-878-2277

Waterfront Marina
Box 510
Karnack, TX 75661
903-679-3957
Price Category: $
Waters: Caddo Lake.
Fish: Bream; white bass; black
bass.

Wild Horse Lodge
PO Box 432
Bishop, TX 78343
512-584-3098
Price Category: $$

UTAH

Altamont Flyfishers
Falcon's Ledge
Box 67
Altamont, UT 84001
801-454-3737

Angler's Inn
2292 South Highland Dr.
Salt Lake City, UT 84106
801-466-3927

Beaver Dam Lodge
PO Box 859
Tamguitch Lake, UT 84759
801-676-8339

Boulder Mountain Lodge*
PO Box 1397
Boulder, UT 84716

This resort is included in Guest-Rated Resort Guide

801-335-7460
Price Category: $$
Waters: High elevation lakes and streams; low elevation canyon streams.
Fish: Rainbow trout; brook trout; brown trout; cutthroat trout.

Deer Trail Lodge*
PO Box 647
Clear Creek Canyon Rd.
Panguitch Lake, UT 84759
435-676-2211
Price Category: $
Waters: Panguitch Creek; Sevier River; Clear Creek; Panguitch Lake; Mammoth Creek.
Fish: Rainbow trout; German trout; cutthroat trout; brown trout.

Falcon's Ledge
PO Box 67
Altamont, UT 84001
801-454-3737
Price Category: $$$
Waters: Green Lake; private waters.
Fish: Cutthroat trout; brook trout; rainbow trout; brown trout.

Flaming Gorge Lodge*
155 Greendale; US 191
Dutch John, UT 84023
435-889-3773
Price Category: $$
Waters: Green River; Flaming Gorge Reservoir; private ponds located on the Bar S.
Fish: Kokanee salmon; rainbow trout; brown trout; lake trout;

brook trout; cutthroat trout; smallmouth bass.

LC Ranch*
PO Box 63
Altamont, UT 84002
435-454-3750
Price Category: $$$$
Waters: 28 private lakes and ponds.
Fish: Brook trout; rainbow trout; brown trout.

Pine Valley Lodge
960 E. Main
Pine Valley, UT 84028
916-246-8457

Rock Creek Ranch
PO Box 1736
Price, UT 84501
801-637-1236

VERMONT

Golden Maple Inn*
Rt. 15, Main St.
Wolcott Village, VT 05680-0035
800-639-5234
Price Category: $ - $$
Waters: Lamoille River; Winooski River; Dog River; Black River; Clyde River; area ponds and lakes.
Fish: Rainbow trout; brook trout; brown trout.

Lake St. Catherine Inn
Box 129
Poultney, VT 05764
802-287-9347
Price Category: $$

This resort is included in Guest-Rated Resort Guide

Waters: Lake St. Catherine.
Fish: Bass; trout.

The Inn at Manchester
Historic Rt. 7A
Manchester, VT 05254
800-273-1793
Price Category: $ - $$
Waters: Battenkill.
Fish: Brown trout; brook trout.

Vermont Sportsman Lodge*
HCR 70, Box 42
Morgan, VT
802-895-4209
Price Category: $ - $$
Waters: Lake Seymour; Lake
Memphremagog; Echo Lake;
Connecticut River.
Fish: Landlocked salmon; lake
trout; brown trout; brook trout;
rainbow trout; smallmouth
bass.

VIRGINIA

**Burton House Bed and
Breakfast**
PO Box 182
11 Brooklyn Ave.
Wachapreague, VA 23480
757-787-4560

Cherrystone
PO Box 545
Cheritone, VA 233316
757-331-3063
Price Category: $-$$
Waters: Chesapeake Bay.
Fish: Drum; flounder; trout;
spot; blue; sea mullet.

Fort Lewis Lodge
HCR 03, Box 21A
Millboro, VA 24460

Lavender Hill Farm
Rt. 631, RR 1, Box 515
Lexington, VA 24450
540-464-5877
Price Category: $

Red Oak Ranch
Hightown, VA 24444
540-434-3669

Shenandoah Lodge
100 Grand View Dr.
Luray, VA 22835
540-743-1920
Price Category: $$$
Waters: Shenandoah River.
Fish: Smallmouth bass; brook
trout.

**Sea Gull Cottages and
Marina***
PO Box 182
Wachapreague, VA 23480
757-787-4848
Price Category: $
Waters: Atlantic Ocean; Brad
Ford Bay; Burton Bay.
Fish: Flounder; trout; spot;
croaker; shark; tuna; dolphin;
marlin.

The Homestead
PO Box 2000
Hot Springs, VA 24445
800-838-1766
Price Category: $$$ - $$$$

The Inn at Narrow Passage*
PO Box 608, US Rt. 11

*This resort is included in Guest-Rated Resort Guide

Woodstock, VA 22664
540-459-8000
800-459-8000
Price Category: $$
Waters: Shenandoah River.
Fish: Smallmouth bass; perch;
bluegill.

The Tide's Inn
PO Box 480
Irvington, VA 22480
804-438-5000
Price Category: $$$
Waters: Rappahannock River;
Chesapeake Bay; Carter's Creek.
Fish: Fresh and salt water
species.

WASHINGTON

Brightwater House
PO Box 1222
440 Brightwater Dr.
Forks, WA 98331
360-374-5453
Price Category: $$
Fish: Steelhead; Chinook; sock-
eye salmon; silver salmon; cut-
throat.

Bristol Bay Lodge
2422 Hunter Rd.
Ellensburg, WA 98926
509-964-2094

Coulee Lodge Resort
33017 Park Lake Rd. NE
Coulee City, WA 99115-9608
509-632-5565

Cross Sound Lodge
15917 NE Union Rd., Suite 115
Ridgefield, WA 98642

Enchanted Lake Lodge
3222 West Lake Sammish, SE
Bellevue, WA 98008
206-643-2172
Price Category: $$$$
Waters: Bristol Bay area.
Fish: Trout; salmon; grayling;
arctic char; northern pike.

Lake Dale Resort
2627 Roche Harbor Rd.
Friday Harbor, WA 98250
360-378-2350
Price Category: $
Fish: Rainbow trout; bass.

Lost River Resort
672 Lost River Rd.
Mazama, WA 98833
800-996-2567

North Cascade Base Camp
255 Lost River Rd.
Mazama, WA 98833
509-996-2334
Price Category: $$

Ocean Shores Resort
2428 SR 109
Ocean City, WA 98569
360-289-3335

Port Ludlow Resort
200 Olympic Place
Port Ludlow, WA 98365
800-732-1239
Price Category: $$
Waters: Port Ludlow Bay.

Rain Forest Resort Village *
516 South Shore Rd.
PO Box 40
Quinault, WA 98575
360-288-2535

*This resort is included in Guest-Rated Resort Guide

800-255-6936
Price Category: $ - $$
Waters: Lake Quinault; Queets
River; Hoh River; Bogachiel
River.
Fish: Rainbow trout; cutthroat
trout; dolly varden; salmon;
steelhead.

**Roche Harbor Resort and
Marina***
PO Box 4397
Roche Harbor, WA 98250
360-378-2155
Price Category: $ - $$
Waters: Pacific Ocean near San
Juan Island.
Fish: Rock cod; ling cod; silver
salmon; king salmon; coho
salmon.

Roylance Ranch Lodge
2613-A 204th SW
Lynnwood, WA 98036
206-744-0846

Silver Lake Resort
3201 Spirit Lake Hwy.
Silver Lake, WA 98645
360-274-6141

Silver Salmon Resort
Bayview and Roosevelt
Neah Bay, WA 98357
360-645-2388

Soap Lake Resort
22818 Hwy. 17 N
Soap Lake, WA 98851
509-246-1103

The Blue Ribbon Jewel
4932 Hwy. 25 North
Northport, WA 99157

**Walker Lake and Diamond
Bell Lodge**
PO Box 104
Wauconda, WA 98859
509-486-1270

Westview Resort
2312 West Woodin Ave.
Rt. 1, Box 14
Chelan, WA 98816
509-682-4396
Price Category: $$
Waters: Lake Chelan.

WISCONSIN

Barker Lake Country Lodge
W 6841 Golf Course Rd.
Winter, WI 54896
715-266-4152

**Bay Park Resort and
Campground**
N 4347 Bay Park Rd.
Trego, WI 54888
715-635-2840

**Big Chetac Resort and
Campground**
Rt. 1, Box 185
Birchwood, WI 54817
800-424-3822

Birch Bay
Rt. 7, Box 7403
Hayward, WI 54843
715-462-3669

Birch Point Resort and Motel
Rt. 3, Box 3229
Hayward, WI 54843
715-634-4182
Price Category: $-$$

Waters: Nelson Lake.
Fish: Walleye; bluegill; crappie; bass; northern; perch.

Black Bear Lodge Resort and Campground
Rt. 5, Box 5393
Hayward, WI 54843
715-945-2676

Blueberry Hill Resort and Campgroud
11301 West Pine Knoll Rd.
Couderay, WI 54828
715-945-2686
Price Category: $
Waters: Blueberry Lake.
Fish: Bluegill; crappie; bass; walleye; perch; rainbow trout; northern pike.

Chief Lake Lodge
Rt. 5, Box 5374
Hayward, WI 54843
715-945-2221

Eagen's Riverview Cabins
Rt. 1, Box 123AA
Couderay, WI 54828
715-945-3178

East Fork Resort and Campground
W 7270 East Fork Rd., HL
Winter, WI 54896
715-266-5723

Ghost Lake Lodge*
Rt. 7, Box 7450
Hayward, WI 54843
715-462-3939
Price Category: $ - $$
Waters: Ghost Lake; Chippewa River; Chippewa Flowage; Teal

Lake; Lost Land Lake.
Fish: Muskie; bass; crappie; walleye; bluegill; perch.

Hansen's Haven
5928 Sunset Blvd.
Racine, WI 53406
715-462-9172

Hemlock Haven Resort
W 7101 Hemlock Haven Rd.
Winter, WI 54896
715-266-5701

Indian Trail Resort
Rt. 1, Box 93
Couderey, WI 54828
715-945-2665

Jamieson House Inn
407 N. Franklin St.
Poynette, WI 53955
608-635-4100
Price Category: $-$$
Waters: Rowan Creek
Fish: Rainbow trout; brook trout.

Lakeview on Grindstone
Rt. 2, Box 2264
Hayward, WI 54843
715-634-4555

Lakewoods Resort
HC 73, Box 715
Cable, WI 54821
715-794-2561

Northlake Lodge
3001 Wilnor Dr.
Oregon, WI 53575
800-878-5737

Palmquist's
N 3516 Diner Rd.

Brantwood, WI 54513
800-519-2558
Price Category: $$

Paust's Woods Lake Resort
Rt. 3
Crivitz, WI 54114
715-757-3722
Price Category: $
Waters: Woods Lake; Deer Lake;
Caldron Falls Flowage.
Fish: Muskie; northern pike;
bass; walleye; bluegill; crappie;
perch.

Ross' Teal Lake Lodge
Rt. 7 Ross Rd.
Hayward, WI 54843
715-462-3631

Sand Bay Beach Resort
3798 Sand Bay Point Rd.
Sturgeon Bay, WI 54235
414-743-5731

Serendipity Farm
RR 3, Box 162
Viroqua, WI 54665
608-637-7708
Price Category: $
Waters: West Fork of the
Kickapoo River.
Fish: Trout.

**Smoky Lake Wilderness
Reserve**
680 Reserve Kabe
Phelps, WI 54554
715-545-2333
Price Category: $$
Waters: Porcupine Lake; Smoky
Lake; Long Lake; Moose Lake;
Trout Lake.

Tiger Musky Resort
Rt. 1, Box 59
Couderay, WI 54828
715-945-2555

Whiplash Lake Resort
Rt. 7, Box 7640
Hayward, WI 54843
715-462-4302
Price Category: $$
Waters: Whiplash Lake
Fish: Bass; bluegill; walleye.

WEST VIRGINIA

Cranberry Wilderness Lodge
PO Box 265
Fenwick, WV 26202

WYOMING

Breteche Creek
PO Box 596
Cody, WY 82414
307-587-3844

Brush Creek Ranch
Star Route, Box 10
Saratoga, WY 82331
800-726-2499
Price Category: $$$
Waters: Brush Creek; North
Platte.
Fish: Brook trout; brown trout;
cutthroat trout; rainbow trout.

Canyon Springs Guest Ranch
354 Snooks Rd.
Sundance, WY 82729
307-283-1912

Crescent H Ranch
PO Box 347
Wilson, WY 83014
307-733-3674
Price Category: $$$$
Waters: Snake River; Green
River; South Fork.
Fish: Cutthroat trout; brown
trout; rainbow trout.

CK Hunting and Fishing Camp
PO Box 458
Big Piney, WY 83113
307-276-3723

Flying A Ranch
Rt. 1, Box 7
Pinedale, WY 82941
307-367-2385

Heart Six Ranch
Box 70
Moran, WY 83013
307-543-2477
Price Category: $$
Waters: Snake River.
Fish: Trout.

Lozier's Box R Ranch*
Box 100
Cora, WY 82925
307-367-4868
Price Category: $$
Waters: Willow Creek; Willow
Lake; Green River Lakes; Green
River; New Fork Lakes; New
Fork River; several alpine lakes.
Fish: Brook trout; German trout;
cutthroat trout; golden trout;
grayling; lake trout; rainbow
trout.

**Mountain Meadow Guest
Ranch**
Box 203
Centennial, WY 82055
307-742-6042

Q Ranch
PO Box 2850
Mills, WY 82644
307-235-0899
Price Category: $$$
Fish: Brook trout; brown trout;
cutthroat trout; rainbow trout.

Rimrock Ranch
2728 Northfork Rt.
Cody, WY 82414
307-587-3970

Spotted Horse Ranch
Star Rt. 43
Jackson Hole, WY 83002
800-528-2084
Price Category: $$$
Waters: Hoback River; Snake
River; Salt River.
Fish: Trout.

FISHING VACATIONS FOR ALL BUDGETS

DIRECTORY OF U.S. FISHING RESORTS

AUTHENTIC GUEST-RATED RESORT GUIDE

ALASKA

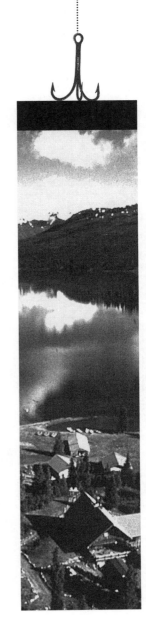

Guest Ratings

Room	🎣🎣🎣🎣
Staff	🎣🎣🎣🎣
Meals	🎣🎣🎣🎣
Outside areas	🎣🎣🎣🎣
Fishing Guides	🎣🎣🎣🎣
Fishing Equipment	🎣🎣🎣🎣
Children's Activities	🎣🎣🎣🎣

Resort Features

🐟	
👫	✓
🍴	
🎒	
🔦	
🍸	
🚐	

AFOGNAK WILDERNESS LODGE

General Delivery • Seal Bay, AK 99697
Phone: 907-486-6442 Reservations: 800-478-6442 • Fax: 907-486-2217
www.kodiak.org/kodiak • Email: afognak@usa.net

PRICE CATEGORY: $$$$

SEASON: May 15 through September 24.

TRANSPORTATION: From Kodiak, AK fly on scheduled mail plane ($70) or chartered floatplane (25 minute flight).

FISHING: Where: Kodiak Island waters in Gulf of Alaska. Streams and lakes on North Afognak Island. **Type:** Bait casting; spin casting; fly casting; deep sea. **How:** Walk and wade; boat; shore. **Species:** Halibut; lingcod; sea-bass; eel; sockeye salmon; pink salmon; silver salmon; rainbow trout; dolly varden; steelhead. **Guides:** Alaska licensed guides included in packages. **Equipment:** Deep sea; spinning; fly fishing gear provided. **Insider's Tip:** "Take lots of medium sized orange pixies during silver salmon season."

ACCOMMODATIONS: Main lodge and private log cabins with carpeting, indoor bath. $450 per person per day includes meals, guided fishing, wildlife viewing and hiking trips.

AMENITIES AND ACTIVITIES: Babysitting available with prior notice. Hot tub; wetsuits for water-skiing; knee boards; banana-boat; horseshoes; badminton; trampoline, birding; beach combing. **Insider's Tip:** "...Don't be afraid to request specific trips, the staff is very accommodating."

PAYMENT: MasterCard; Visa; personal check; cash.

GUEST COMMENTS: Cabins "look rustic but are actually very luxurious." Meals got unanimous approval: "everything's fresh;" "so much food and it's all good." "Wonderful viewing of seals; whales; dolphins and bears as well as hikes to the Salmon ladders." "Fishing guides were "knowledgeable;" "extremely helpful..." "even the kids caught fish..." "Scenery not to be missed;" "spacious; attractive accommodations;" and "tremendous fishing."

ALASKA'S LAKE CLARK INN

1 Lang Lane, General Delivery • Port Alsworth, AK 99653-9999
Phone: 907-781-2224 • Fax: 907-781-2252
www.LakeClark.com • E-mail: MarkLang@LakeClark.com

PRICE CATEGORY: $$ – $$$$

SEASON: Open all year.

TRANSPORTATION: Anchorage, AK (private flight to lodge).

FISHING: Where: Bristol Bay; Cook Inlet. **Type:** Fly; bait or spin casting. **How:** Walk and wade; boat; shore. **Species:** King salmon; red salmon; chum salmon; pink salmon; silver salmon; rainbow trout; arctic char; dolly varden; lake trout; northern pike; shee fish. **Guides:** US Coast Guard licensed, Alaska certified guides ($195 per person/day). Fly out river float trip ($295 per person). **Equipment:** Lodge provides spin casting gear; boat and canoe rentals.

ACCOMMODATIONS: Deluxe cabins ($3895 per person/week) includes 7 nights lodging; 6 days guided fly out fishing; fishing equipment; all meals; round-trip flight from Anchorage. Tent camp on Nushagak River ($2900 per person/week) includes 7 nights lodging; 6 days guided fishing; all meals. Deluxe cabin with fully equipped kitchen and bath ($125 per night single or double occupancy). Advance reservations required. Custom packages upon request.

AMENITIES AND ACTIVITIES: Hot tub; solarium dining room. Baby-sitting available with prior notice. Evening fly tying presentations; films; hiking; birding; panning for gold; hunting packages; flight seeing. **Places to Visit:** Tanalian Falls; Lake Clark National Park and Preserve.

PAYMENT: MasterCard; Visa; personal check; cash.

GUEST COMMENTS: The "cabins were especially well appointed, very new." An "exquisitely maintained facility," "exceptional hosts" and food that is "delicious and plentiful." Fishing and variety of activities earned high ratings. "Guides were extremely helpful and knowledgeable." "The owner; who acts as guide and pilot; is an absolute expert." Children feel "welcome and involved." "Everyone went out of their way to include our 11 year old daughter..."

Guest Ratings

Room	♦♦♦♦
Staff	♦♦♦♦
Meals	♦♦♦♦
Outside areas	♦♦♦♦
Fishing Guides	♦♦♦♦
Fishing Equipment	♦♦♦
Children's Activities	♦♦♦

Resort Features

🐟	✓
👥	✓
🍳	✓

Guest Ratings

Room	ᗧᗧᗧᗧ
Staff	ᗧᗧᗧᗧ
Meals	ᗧᗧᗧᗧ
Outside areas	ᗧᗧᗧᗧ
Fishing Guides	ᗧᗧᗧ
Fishing Equipment	ᗧᗧᗧ
Children's Activities	NA

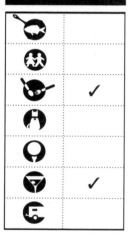

Resort Features

🐟	
👪	
🍳	✓
🎣	
🍷	
✈	✓
🚲	

ALASKA'S WILDERNESS LODGE

PO Box 190748 • Anchorage, AK 99519-0748
Phone: 907-272-9912 • Reservations: 800-835-8032
www.fishawl.com • E mail: fishawl@worldnet.att.net

PRICE CATEGORY: $$$$

SEASON: 1st week in June through early October.

TRANSPORTATION: Anchorage, AK (1 hour charter flight).

FISHING: Where: Bristol Bay; Lake Clark National Park waters; Katmai National Park waters; others by request. **Type:** Spin; fly or bait casting. **How:** Shore; boat; fly out trips. **Species:** Chinook salmon; sockeye salmon; chum salmon; silver salmon; northern pike; lake trout; rainbow trout; char; grayling. **Guides:** Included in package rates. **Equipment:** Fishing license; use of lodge rods and reels included in packages. **Instruction:** Fly tying tips and fly fishing instruction included.

ACCOMMODATIONS: Private cabins with carpeted floors; heaters; full baths ($4800 per person for seven nights) includes transportation to and from Anchorage; fishing license; lodging; meals; wine/beer; guides; equipment; fly out trips; fish packaging.

AMENITIES AND ACTIVITIES: Sauna; main lodge; dining area; sitting room; tackle and gift shop; lounge. Hiking; flight seeing.

PAYMENT: MasterCard and Visa (for hold deposits and gift shop purchases only); all other charges personal checks; cash.

GUEST COMMENTS: Cabins were "attractive" with "very good housekeeping" services. "Delicious" meals; complimented by "outstanding" service and an "excellent wine selection." The staff was "efficient" and made them "feel very comfortable". The fishing guides were "exceptional" "enjoyable to be around," and "willing to share information." "Exceptionally high standards for staff; meals and facilities."

ANGLER'S LODGE AND FISH CAMP

PO Box 508 • Sterling, AK 99672
Phone: 907-262-1747 • Fax: 907-262-6747
www.alaska.net/~anglers • Email: *anglers@alaska.net*

Guest Ratings

Room	♦♦♦♦
Staff	♦♦♦♦
Meals	♦♦♦♦
Outside areas	♦♦♦
Fishing Guides	♦♦♦
Fishing Equipment	♦♦♦♦
Children's Activities	NA

PRICE CATEGORY: $$

SEASON: Open all year. Fishing season is April 14-October 15.

TRANSPORTATION: Anchorage, AK (2 hour drive).

FISHING: Where: Kenai River; Kasilof River; Cook Inlet. **Type:** Bait casting; spin casting; fly casting; trolling (king salmon). **How:** Shore; boat. **Species:** King salmon; silver salmon; red salmon; halibut; rainbow trout; dolly varden. **Guides:** US Coast Guard licensed guide ($125 per half day for 1 to 4 anglers) includes rods; reels; tackle.

ACCOMMODATIONS: Lodge rooms with private baths; continental breakfast included ($80 double occupancy). Fishing package with 3 nights lodging; 2 days guided fishing and all meals ($999 double occupancy).

AMENITIES AND ACTIVITIES: Hot tub; deck. Hiking. **Places to visit:** Morgan's Landing State Park (bank fishing). **Insider's Tip:** Bring a book or deck of cards. The lodge is "away from it all," night life is "quiet".

PAYMENT: MasterCard; Visa; American Express; personal checks; cash.

GUEST COMMENTS: "The room was large—plenty of storage—bathroom very clean with lots of hot water." An "excellent value"; "much cheaper (than other lodges)" and "very reasonable for Alaska." Guests gave the "hearty, home-style" menu excellent ratings, with one guest cautioning that "breakfast is generally quick; light fare." Fishing equipment was "well maintained" and "the best and latest ." "Introduced anglers to a variety of Alaskan fishing" with "many other areas and streams to pick from as well as the salt water fishery and world famous Kenai River." "Guides went the extra mile" and "worked extra hard to get us fish." The general consensus: "Great location; great fishing at a reasonable rate."

Resort Features

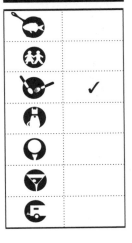

🐟	
👫	
🍳	✓
🎣	
⊙	
▽	
🚐	

Guest Ratings

Room	🐟🐟🐟🐟
Staff	🐟🐟🐟🐟
Meals	🐟🐟🐟🐟
Outside areas	🐟🐟🐟🐟
Fishing Guides	🐟🐟🐟🐟
Fishing Equipment	🐟🐟🐟🐟
Children's Activities	NA

Resort Features

	✓

ARCTIC TERN CHARTERS AND FISH CAMP

PO Box 1122 • Sterling, AK 99672
Phone: 907-262-7631 • Fax: 907-262-7631
www.alaskaone.com/arctern

PRICE CATEGORY: $$$$

SEASON: May 1st through August 31.

TRANSPORTATION: Anchorage, AK (3 hour drive or fly into Kenai where Arctic Tern Charters will meet your party).

FISHING: Where: Kenai River; Cook Inlet; Kachemak Bay; Resurrection Bay. **Type:** Spin; bait; fly. **How:** Boat; shore. **Species:** Halibut; king salmon; silver salmon; red salmon. **Guides:** US Coast Guard Licensed, Alaska certified guide included in lodging package. **Equipment:** Fresh and salt water equipment provided except for fly rods/reels. **Insider's Tip:** Bring warm layered clothing and book trips 12 to 18 months in advance.

ACCOMMODATIONS: Bunkhouse sleeps 1-4 guests ($295 per person/day) or ($250 per person/day for groups of 3 or 4) includes lodging; meals; fishing guide; fishing tackle; bait; fish processing; transportation to/from Kenai.

AMENITIES AND ACTIVITIES: Hiking; photography; sauna. wildlife viewing.

PAYMENT: Cash or personal checks.

GUEST COMMENTS: "This is a small scale, homelike fishing camp with no extra frills. You create you own fun and excitement with a very knowledgeable fishing guide." Rooms were "'clean and comfortable, "The Russian steam bath "Bonya" was awesome." The meals were "excellent; more than we could eat," "homemade baked goods" served by guide and host Perry Flotre's sister receiving special mention. Perry Flotre was "knowledgeable, "exceptional"; "sincere" and "expert." Guests said they could "fish as long or as much" as they wanted and were "never disappointed with the catch." 98% of the guests who responded rated the camp as "much better" than other lodges they had visited and 100% said they would consider a return trip. The consensus: "quality" —"a complete fishing experience."

BARANOF WILDERNESS LODGE

Room	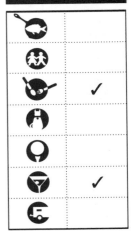
Staff	
Meals	
Outside areas	
Fishing Guides	
Fishing Equipment	
Children's Activities	NA

PO Box 42 • Norden, CA 95724
Phone: 530-582-8132 • Summer: 907-738-3597
www.flyfishalaska.com

Resort Features

PRICE CATEGORY: $$$$

SEASON: May 1 through October 1.

TRANSPORTATION: Sitka, AK (floatplane to lodge)

FISHING: Where: Chatham Straight area. **Type:** Salt and fresh water spin casting; fly casting; shrimping; crabbing; clamming. **How:** Boat; walk and wade. **Species:** Silver salmon; red salmon; pink salmon; king salmon; chum; trout; dolly varden; halibut; various bottom and rock fish. **Guides:** Licensed, insured guides included in lodging package. **Equipment:** All salt water tackle and bait provided. **Instruction:** Week long fly fishing school; covering casting; various fly fishing techniques. **Insider's Tip:** Peak fresh water season is July and August.

ACCOMMODATIONS: Guest cabins and lodge rooms with heat; electricity; hot showers; flush toilets. Lodge package ($2850 per person for 5 nights); Kelp bay base camp package ($2495 per person for 7 nights); Packages include meals; guides; lodging; float plane fly outs and charters; fish processing and packaging.

AMENITIES AND ACTIVITIES: Hot tubs; meeting facilities; gathering room; fly-tying bench; fishing dock; boardwalk hiking trail, float trips; hot springs; kayaking; tide pool exploring; beach-combing; whale watching fly-tying lessons; fly casting lessons; wildlife photography school. Host week long Elderhostel. **Places to Visit:** Togiak National Wildlife Refuge; Tlingit Indian Museums and Totem Pole Park; Hot Springs.

PAYMENT: American Express; cash.

GUEST COMMENTS: "A perfect trip." Staff members were "...helpful; always available but never in the way." "More than adequate accommodations; clean and comfortable." "A tremendous variety of fishing opportunities are offered, estuaries; rivers; lakes." "A different area to explore nearly everyday." "...whale watching; beach combing; and great fishing too." "My heartiest recommendation."

Guest Ratings

Room	🐟🐟🐟🐟
Staff	🐟🐟🐟🐟
Meals	🐟🐟🐟🐟
Outside areas	🐟🐟🐟🐟
Fishing Guides	🐟🐟🐟🐟
Fishing Equipment	🐟🐟🐟
Children's Activities	NA

Resort Features

🍳	
⚕	
🎣	✓
🎿	
⛷	
▼	✓
☕	

CHELATNA LAKE LODGE

3941 Float Plane Dr. • Anchorage, AK 99502
Phone: 907-243-7767 • Reservations: 800-999-0785 • Fax: 907-248-5791
www.alaska.net/~chelatna • Email: Chelatna@Alaska.net

PRICE CATEGORY: $$$$

SEASON: First Thursday of June through the Sunday before Labor Day.

TRANSPORTATION: Anchorage, AK (float plane flight to lodge).

FISHING: Where: Chelatna Lake; several area rivers and streams. **Type:** Spin casting; fly casting. **How:** Boat; shore; walk and wade; fly out. **Species:** King salmon; silver salmon; rainbow trout; red salmon; chum salmon; pink salmon; lake trout; grayling; northern pike. **Guides:** Included in package. **Equipment:** All tackle provided; 4 aircraft for fly out trips; rafts for float trips; small fishing boats. **Insider's Tip:** Early to mid June is peak season for King Salmon. Red; Silver and Pink Salmon fishing peaks in late July; early August.

ACCOMMODATIONS: Cedar chalets ($4290 double occupancy for 7 day and nights) includes all meals; guided fishing; fly out trips; all activities. Partial week packages ($2190 Sunday Thursday).

AMENITIES AND ACTIVITIES: Beer or wine available with dinner, hot tub; sauna; gathering room with game tables; fly tying table. White water raft trips; flight seeing; day hiking; bear viewing.

PAYMENT: MasterCard; Visa; Discover; personal check; cash.

GUEST COMMENTS: "The definition of luxury—and it is in the middle of nowhere!" Guests raved about the "warm, well decorated rooms;" described the meals as "5 star every time." Staff was "eager to please," "The staff was "great...the fishing was even better." Guests felt the guides were "helpful;" "excellent teachers for children and adults. Able to teach fly fishing; spinning; baiting and lure techniques equally well." "I'd recommend a visit even for a non-fisher." "Great bear viewing stand; loved watching the beaver." "The plane trip to view the mountain is great." All the survey respondents rated the lodge "much better" than others and would consider a return trip.

DEER CREEK COTTAGES

PO Box 19475 • Thorne Bay, AK 99919
Phone: 907-828-3393 • Fax: 907-828-3438

Guest Ratings

Room	🎣🎣🎣🎣
Staff	🎣🎣🎣🎣
Meals	NA
Outside areas	🎣🎣🎣🎣
Fishing Guides	NA
Fishing Equipment	NA
Children's Activities	NA

Resort Features

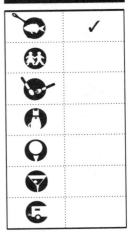

🐟	✓
👪	
🎣	
🍴	
♀	
▼	
Ⓕ	

PRICE CATEGORY: $$ - $$$$

SEASON: Open all year.

TRANSPORTATION: Ketchikan; AK (30 minute charter to lodge).

FISHING: Where: The Pacific Ocean's Clarence Strait; Thorne River; Staney Creek; Ratz Creek; Hatchery Creek. **Type:** Spin casting; fly casting; deep sea. **How:** Boat. **Species:** Halibut; cod; yellow-eyed rockfish; steelhead; coho salmon; pink salmon; sockeye salmon; cutthroat trout; dolly varden. Clamming and crabbing along nearby shorelines. **Guide Service:** Licensed; bonded and insured guides (freshwater; $300.00 per day for up to four people. Saltwater; $450.00 per day for up to four people) includes gear; bait; tackle and filleting. **Equipment:** Salt water fishing equipment can be rented at the office.

ACCOMMODATIONS: 2-3 bedroom cottages ($500/600 per day for 1-4 people) includes linens; washer; dryer; TV; VCR; phone; fully equipped kitchen; barbecue; Little Chief Smoker; map; 19' skiff with motor; fish box; salmon net; gaff hook; crab pots; cooler.

AMENITIES AND ACTIVITIES: Passenger van; game preparation room; hiking; sightseeing and photography excursions; **Places to Visit:** Anan Creek Bear Observatory; Klawock Totem Pole Park; El Capitan Caves; Salt-Chuck Mines.

PAYMENT: MasterCard; Visa; cash.

GUEST COMMENTS: "Cabins were great; really well equipped; well maintained and comfortable." The staff was "outstanding;" "happy to answer all our fishing and sightseeing questions." Fishing reviews varied from "weren't biting" to "hooked 15 steelheads and caught 8." "Recommend you go see the bears at Anan Island—great trip." "Liked having free run with the van and boat." "Good place for the do-it-yourself sort of traveler."

Guest Ratings

Room	🐟🐟🐟🐟
Staff	🐟🐟🐟🐟
Meals	🐟🐟🐟🐟
Outside areas	🐟🐟🐟🐟
Fishing Guides	🐟🐟🐟🐟
Fishing Equipment	🐟🐟🐟🐟
Children's Activities	NA

Resort Features

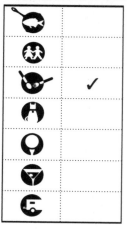

🐟	
👥	
🍳	✓

DENALI WEST LODGE

Box 40 • Lake Minchumina, AK 99757
Phone: 907-674-3112
www.alaskan.com/denaliwest • E-mail: Minchumina@aol.com

PRICE CATEGORY: $$$$

SEASON: Open all year.

TRANSPORTATION: Anchorage, AK (small aircraft flight to lodge).

FISHING: Where: Lake Minchumina; Nowitna River; Yukon River; Kuskokwim River; Salmon River; Tonzona River. **Type:** Spin casting; fly casting. **How:** Boat; shore. **Species:** Northern pike; shee fish. **Equipment:** Spinning rigs available for loan. **Insider's Tip:** Suggested lures include pixies in 5/8 to 7/8 oz. silver or gold with red or orange inserts; crocodiles, 1oz. any color; rapalas all types. Suggested flies include deer hair mouse; large bass poppers; streamers; minnow patterns; woolly boogers all on #6-#4 hooks..

ACCOMMODATIONS: Private log cabins with spruce pole beds and hand made quilts ($2000 for 5 nights) includes meals; guided fishing. All cabins have outhouses; shared sauna/bath house with men's and women's dressing rooms that have shower; sink; hot and cold running water.

AMENITIES AND ACTIVITIES: Main lodge with dining room. Dog mushing packages include instruction; trips. Canoeing; hiking; flightseeing; wildlife viewing; birding.

PAYMENT: MasterCard; Visa; American Express; Discover; personal checks; cash.

GUEST COMMENTS: "Wonderful; unique experience." "Cozy; comfortable rooms and clean shower houses." "The birding was great! I'll never forget the peregrine falcons or the wonderfully colored horned grebes." Food was "delicious; wonderful," " superb; the companionship even better." Staff made guests "feel at home; very accommodating; great hospitality."

EVERGREEN LODGE AT LAKE LOUISE

HC 01 Box 1709 • Glennallen, AK 99588
Phone: 907-822-3250
www.alaskaoutdoors.com/EL/

PRICE CATEGORY: $$ – $$$$

SEASON: March through November.

TRANSPORTATION: Anchorage, AK (3 1/2 hour drive).

FISHING: Where: Lake Louise; Clarence Lake and remote wilderness lakes. **Type:** Bait casting; spin casting; fly casting. The state record lake trout was landed at Clarence Lake. **How:** fly-out; boat; shore. **Species:** Lake trout; arctic grayling; rainbow trout; salmon. **Guides:** Guides included in fly-out fishing packages. **Equipment:** Rods, reel, line, lures available. **Insider's Tip:** Wear warm; layered clothing and bring a deck of cards with you to the remote cabin.

ACCOMMODATIONS: Remote fly-in cabin with three bedrooms; living room; fully equipped kitchen ($495 double occupancy); Lodge rooms with private baths (from $89 double occupancy) includes full breakfast; use of bicycles and canoe. Fishing package ($1890 per person) includes 5 nights lodging; meals; fly-out fishing; guide; all activities.

AMENITIES AND ACTIVITIES: Lounge area; guest bar; boat dock; canoe; small motorboat; bicycles; reading room with small library and card table; sauna. Canoeing; walking; boating; glacier flight seeing; wildlife viewing flights.

PAYMENT: MasterCard; Visa; personal checks; cash.

GUEST COMMENTS: Rooms were "clean" with "great views". Staff were praised for "wonderful hospitality." "The wild life flight was great—moose; bald eagles and bear." "Peaceful and beautiful; great food; enchanting." "An unforgettable experience."

Guest Ratings

Room	🎣🎣🎣🎣
Staff	🎣🎣🎣🎣
Meals	🎣🎣🎣
Outside areas	🎣🎣🎣
Fishing Guides	🎣🎣🎣
Fishing Equipment	NA
Children's Activities	NA

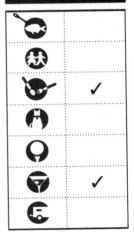

Resort Features

🐟	
👫	
🍳	✓
🍸	
🔦	
▼	✓
🅵	

Guest Ratings

Room	🐟🐟🐟🐟
Staff	🐟🐟🐟🐟
Meals	NA
Outside areas	🐟🐟🐟🐟
Fishing Guides	🐟🐟🐟🐟
Fishing Equipment	NA
Children's Activities	NA

Resort Features

🐟 (frying pan)	✓
(people)	
(pan)	
(axe)	
(circle)	
(martini)	
(dollar)	

FUNNY MOOSE VACATION RENTALS

HC #1, Box 1299 • Soldotna, AK 99669
Phone: 907-262-3701 Reservations: 800-770-3701 Fax: 907-262-3701
www.alaska1.com//funnymoose Email: funmoose@alaska.net

PRICE CATEGORY: $$ – $$$

SEASON: Mid-May through September 30. Discounts offered May 15-June 15 and September.

TRANSPORTATION: Anchorage, AK (2 1/2 hour drive).

FISHING: Where: Kenai River; Kasilof River; Funny River; Moose River; Deep Creek; Ninilchik River; Kachemak Bay; Prince William Sound. **Type:** Bait; spin; fly; salt charters. **How:** Boat; shore. **Species:** King salmon; red salmon; pink salmon; silver salmon; halibut; cod; steelhead; rainbow trout; grayling. **Guides:** Local guides; equipment included in fishing packages. **Equipment:** Rod/reel rentals available. **Insider's Tip:** Peak season for king salmon—June; red salmon—July; silver salmon—August and September. Recommends 7 or 71/2 ft. spin rod with 20# test line or 8 weight fly rod for bank fishing.

ACCOMMODATIONS: 2 bedroom cabins with kitchens; linens; full baths. (7 nights lodging, 3 days fishing is $725.) (Cabin only for 1-4 adults is $595 per week.)

AMENITIES AND ACTIVITIES: Fly out bear watching; remote fishing; whale watching; hiking; photography. **Places to Visit:** Mt. McKinley; Denali National Park; Anchorage; Homer; Seward; Kenai Fjords; Chugach Forest; National Moose Range.

PAYMENT: MasterCard; Visa; cash; personal check.

GUEST COMMENTS: "Clean; comfortable cabins at extremely reasonable rates;" "for the do-it-yourself guest" "Not luxurious—but clean and well maintained." Fishing was "typical for Alaska" and simply "great." "Friendly; knowledgeable guides", a host "willing to share information about area fishing." "Great fishing; great place."

GLACIER BAY COUNTRY INN AND WHALESONG LODGE

PO Box 5 • Gustavus, AK 99826
Phone: 907-697-2288 • Fax: 907-697-2289
www.glacierbayalaska.com • E Mail: gbci@thor.he.net

Guest Ratings

Room	♦♦♦
Staff	♦♦♦♦
Meals	♦♦♦♦
Outside areas	♦♦♦
Fishing Guides	NA
Fishing Equipment	NA
Children's Activities	NA

Resort Features

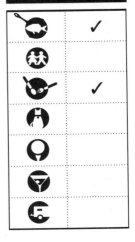

🐟	✓
👥	
🍳	✓

PRICE CATEGORY: $$

SEASON: May 15 through September 30.

TRANSPORTATION: Commercial flight into Juneau, Haines or Skagway. Alaska Air or ferry from Juneau.

FISHING: Where: Streams and rivers of Chicagof Island; Glacier Bay. **Type:** Fly casting, baitcasting, fresh and salt water. **How:** Boat, shore, wading. **Species:** Five salmon species; dolly varden; char; steelhead, cutthroat trout; halibut. **Guides:** Professional fly fishing guides available. **Equipment:** Provided except for fly fishing.

ACCOMMODATIONS: Whalesong Lodge: standard hotel style rooms (start at $109 per person) includes breakfast. Glacier Bay Country Inn: bed and breakfast style rooms. Includes three meals with each night's lodging, transfers to and from Gustavus airport, bicycles.

AMENITIES AND ACTIVITIES: Biking; hiking; wildlife viewing, whale watching; kayaking, flightseeing, glacier tours. **Places to Visit:** Glacier Bay National Park; Point Adolphus.

PAYMENT: MasterCard; Visa; American Express; personal checks; cash.

GUEST COMMENTS: Staff is "first class; friendly; helpful;" and "took good care of us." "So many beautiful touches." "wonderful exchanges during dinner with people from all over the world," "boat was excellent; allowed us to see Glacier Bay and whales at Point Adolphus." "Visit to Glacier Bay National Park was magnificent."

Guest Ratings

Room	🐟🐟🐟🐟
Staff	🐟🐟🐟🐟
Meals	🐟🐟🐟🐟
Outside areas	🐟🐟🐟🐟
Fishing Guides	🐟🐟🐟
Fishing Equipment	🐟🐟🐟
Children's Activities	NA

Resort Features

🐟	
👨‍👩‍👧	
🍳	✓
🎒	
⚓	
🍷	
🚐	

GOODNEWS RIVER LODGE

PO Box 770530 • Eagle River, Alaska 99577
Phone: 800-274-8371

PRICE CATEGORY: $$$$

SEASON: Mid-June through mid-September.

TRANSPORTATION: Anchorage, AK (Goodnews Lodge Charter flight; jet boat to lodge.)

FISHING: Where: Goodnews River; a three branch river system. **Type:** Catch and release fly fishing. **How:** Drift and jet boat. **Species:** Rainbow trout; dolly varden; king salmon; sockeye salmon; chum salmon; pink salmon; silver salmon. **Guides:** Included in trip package. **Equipment:** All terminal tackle provided.

ACCOMMODATIONS: Tent cabin lodging ($3650 per person/per week) all meals included.

AMENITIES AND ACTIVITIES: Dining hall; kitchen; restrooms and showers; drying room. Fly-tying; storytelling.

PAYMENT: Visa; MasterCard; personal checks.

GUEST COMMENTS: "Great companionship in an incredible location." "Hearty; well prepared meals." "Accommodating; friendly staff." "Guides are extremely knowledgeable; patient; excellent teachers;" and "good fishing partners." "Outstanding salmon fishing." "accommodate both the novice and more experienced fly fisher." "Very professional lodge for serious fishermen." "Once in a life-time fishing complimented by comfortable accommodations; great food and a wonderful staff."

GUSTAVUS INN

PO Box 60 • Gustavus, AK 99826
Phone: 907-697-2254 • Reservations: 800-649-5220 • Fax: 907-697-2254

Guest Ratings

Room	🎣🎣🎣🎣
Staff	🎣🎣🎣🎣
Meals	🎣🎣🎣🎣
Outside areas	🎣🎣🎣🎣
Fishing Guides	NA
Fishing Equipment	🎣🎣🎣🎣
Children's Activities	NA

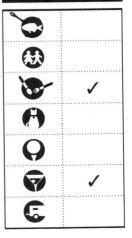

Resort Features

🍳	
🧗	
🍴	✓
🚪	
🔍	
🔻	✓
🔥	

PRICE CATEGORY: $$

SEASON: Mid May through mid September.

TRANSPORTATION: Juneau, AK. Call lodge for arrangements.

FISHING: Where: Icy Strait; Icy Passage; Glacier Bay. **Type:** Salt water bait casting. **How:** Charter boat. **Species:** Halibut; king salmon; coho salmon; pink salmon; chum salmon, ling cod. **Guides:** Local charters ($210 per person/ per day.) Includes rods; tackle and bait. **Equipment :** All saltwater gear included. **Insider's Tip:** Enjoy whale watching while halibut fishing. King Salmon fishing is best in May and June.

ACCOMMODATIONS: Lodge rooms ($135 per person/day) include 3 meals and use of lodge's bikes and fishing poles. Charter fishing packages (start at $875 per person for 3 days, 2 nights) includes lodging, meals, fishing charter, tackle, bait and rods. Children under 12 are half price.

AMENITIES AND ACTIVITIES: Wine available with dinner. Kayaking; whale watching; hiking; photography; naturalist walks; flight seeing. **Places to Visit:** Glacier Bay National Park.

PAYMENT: MasterCard; Visa; American Express; personal checks; cash.

GUEST COMMENTS: "Never bored, but never rushed either." "...variety of activities offered. " Fantastic, the Lesh family made excellent suggestions" Guest-recommended activities included "renting a kayak"; "the catamaran trip up Glacier Bay" and "evening bicycle rides." Fishing guide was "outstanding". "Friendly staff;" "fabulous location; " an "exceptional value..."

Guest Ratings

Room	🎣🎣🎣
Staff	🎣🎣🎣🎣
Meals	🎣🎣🎣🎣
Outside areas	🎣🎣🎣
Fishing Guides	NA
Fishing Equipment	NA
Children's Activities	NA

Resort Features

🐟	
👫	
🍳	✓
🎣	
♀	
▽	
⑤	

ISLAND POINT LODGE

(Petersburg; Alaska) • PO Box 929 • Westborough, MA 01581
Phone: 508-366-4522

PRICE CATEGORY: $$$$

SEASON: Early June-late September.

TRANSPORTATION: Petersburg; AK (shuttle to lodge).

FISHING: Where: Wrangell Narrows; Sumner Strait; Frederick Sound; Falls Creek; Bind Slough. **Type:** Troll; spin cast; bottom fish; fly fish. **How:** Boat. **Species:** King salmon; coho salmon; sockeye salmon; pink salmon; chum salmon; halibut; cutthroat trout; dolly varden; steelhead. **Guides:** Salmon; halibut and sightseeing charters are available for an additional $150 per person; per day. **Equipment:** Boat with motor; fuel; halibut rods; crab pot are included. **Insider's Tip:** Bring lots of red pixies; pink spoons; black krocodiles and daredevils 7/8 oz. or larger. Red; pink; orange and chartreuse imitation salmon eggs for salmon; arctic char and cutthroat trout fishing.

ACCOMMODATIONS: Basic cabins ($1425 per person for 7 day; 6 nights) includes bunk style beds furnished with pillow; sheets and blankets; shared bathroom. Hot breakfast and dinner; self serve sandwiches for lunch. Electricity provided by diesel generator.

AMENITIES AND ACTIVITIES: Lodge store; fish freezing space. Wildlife viewing.

PAYMENT: MasterCard; Visa; personal check; cash.

GUEST COMMENTS: Accommodations are "not plush but comfortable. Just fine for the average person who wants to go fishing..." "The staff takes a lot of time making sure the guests understand the maps and can find their way around." Fishing got extremely good ratings both for quantity and variety. "It's not a "gimme" fishing trip; you have to put your time in; but if you fish; and fish right; you'll be amply rewarded." "It's a heck of a bargain." "You'd be hard pressed to find the scenery, fishing, friendly staff and comfortable accommodations for a lower price."

KENAI MAGIC LODGE

2440 East Tudor #205 • Anchorage, AK 99507
Phone: 907-248-9889 • Fax: 888-262-6466
Email: KenaiMagicLodge@compuserve.com

PRICE CATEGORY: $$$$

SEASON: May 1 through October 15; various discounts offered; call for details.

TRANSPORTATION: Anchorage; AK (2 1/2 hour drive). Kenai; AK (complimentary shuttle to lodge).

FISHING: Where: Kenai River; Kasilof River; Moose River; Deep Creek; Ninilchik River; Kachemak Bay; Prince William sound. **Type:** Bait casting; spin casting; fly casting; salt water charters. **How:** Boat; shore. **Species:** King salmon; red salmon; silver salmon; pink salmon; rainbow trout; dolly varden; grayling; pike; lake trout; char; halibut. **Guides:** Alaska licensed guides included. **Equipment:** All gear provided with guided fishing trips. **Insider's Tip:** Fly fishers should bring own equipment. 8 wt. fly rod is recommended. For those bringing own spin casting equipment; a 7 - 71/2 ft. spin rod with 20 lb. test line is recommended.

ACCOMMODATIONS: Log cabins ($995 for three nights - two days) includes meals; guided fishing; equipment. Log cabin only ($1000-$1200 per week).

AMENITIES AND ACTIVITIES: Flight see Denali; Katmai bear viewing; Kenai Fjords; sea kayaking and sailing; backcountry Kenai guided wilderness trips; canoe trips; hiking; river rafting; fly out fishing; horseback riding. **Insider's Tip:** Guests suggest trying bear watching; flight seeing and the Kenai Fjords cruise.

PAYMENT: Visa; MasterCard; American Express; cash; (personal checks for deposits).

GUEST COMMENTS: "We thought Alaska was supposed to be wilderness; but Kenai Magic is a five star resort." "Different; quality fishing opportunities as well as interesting side trips." "Meals are absolutely fabulous;" "The food is excellent; the ambiance perfect." "Wonderful experience for both children and adults." "Fishing was great 70; 50 and 45 pound salmon." "Caught a lot of fish." Guides were "experts at their craft." "Great food; great people; great bears."

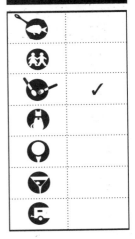

Guest Ratings

Room	🐟🐟🐟🐟
Staff	🐟🐟🐟🐟
Meals	🐟🐟🐟🐟
Outside areas	🐟🐟🐟🐟
Fishing Guides	🐟🐟🐟
Fishing Equipment	NA
Children's Activities	NA

Resort Features

🐟	
🧑‍🤝‍🧑	
🍳	✓
🍾	
☕	
🍸	
⛽	

Guest Ratings

Room	🐟🐟🐟🐟
Staff	🐟🐟🐟
Meals	🐟🐟🐟
Outside areas	🐟🐟🐟
Fishing Guides	🐟🐟🐟
Fishing Equipment	NA
Children's Activities	NA

Resort Features

🐟	
👨‍👩‍👧	
🍳	✓
🍸	
🔦	✓
▽	
🚲	

ORCA LODGE

PO Box 4653 • Soldotna, AK 99669
Phone: 907-262-5649 • Fax: 907-262-9516
www.alaskaone.com/orcalodge • Email: fishorca@alaska.net

PRICE CATEGORY: $$$$

SEASON: May 1 through October 1.

TRANSPORTATION: Anchorage (3 hours by car), Kenai (10 miles).

FISHING: Where: Kenai River; Kachemak Bay; Kasilof River; Alaska Peninsula streams and lakes **Type:** Bait casting; fly casting. **How:** Wade; fishing boat; shore. **Species:** King salmon; red salmon; silver salmon; pink salmon; rainbow trout; halibut. **Guides:** Coast Guard licensed guides as part of package or separately ($135 half day; $225 full day) **Instruction:** Fly fishing instruction on request.

ACCOMMODATIONS: Private river front cabins (1 to 3 bedrooms) equipped with full kitchens; loft; full bath cathedral ceiling; Kenai River View. (Lodging/Fishing packages start at $725. Daily rates start at $150 double occupancy).

AMENITIES AND ACTIVITIES: Barbecue facilities; campfire area; dock; bank fishing area; hot tub. Golf course in area. Hiking; Kenai Fjords Glacier/ Wildlife Cruise; Kenai Canyon Wilderness Float; floatplane flightseeing; golf.

PAYMENT: MasterCard; Visa; American Express; personal checks; cash.

GUEST COMMENTS: Staff is "helpful; accommodating; willing to go out of their way to help." "Good meals; well presented." "Perfect cabins comfortable; spacious; inviting after a long day on the water." "Best freshwater fishing anywhere." "Lots of freshwater and saltwater fishing from the same lodge." "Beautiful place; fantastic fishing; great people."

REEL M INN – KATMAI FISHING ADVENTURES

PO Box 221 • King Salmon, AK 99613
Phone: 907-246-8322 • Fax: 907-246-8322

Guest Ratings

Room	🐟🐟🐟🐟
Staff	🐟🐟🐟🐟
Meals	🐟🐟🐟🐟
Outside areas	🐟🐟🐟
Fishing Guides	🐟🐟🐟🐟
Fishing Equipment	🐟🐟🐟
Children's Activities	NA

PRICE CATEGORY: $$$$

SEASON: Open all year.

TRANSPORTATION: King Salmon, AK. (lodge pick up from King Salmon).

FISHING: Where: Naknek River; Iliamna drainage; Becharof drainage. **Type:** Fly casting; bait casting; spin casting. **How:** Boat; shore. **Species:** King salmon; pink salmon; red salmon; silver salmon; chum salmon; rainbow trout; arctic char; grayling. **Guides:** Guide service included in package. **Equipment:** All fishing equipment provided. King salmon fishing is available June 15th through July 31. Silver salmon is available August 1st through September 5. **Insider's Tip:** Bring warm layered clothing and comfortable waders.

ACCOMMODATIONS: Private lodge rooms ($1365 for 3 nights, 4 days) includes meals; guided river and fly out fishing; all tackle except for waders; round trip transfers from King Salmon Airport.

AMENITIES AND ACTIVITIES: Bear viewing; fly-tying clinics; fly casting clinics; nature hikes.

PAYMENT: Personal check; cash.

GUEST COMMENTS: "I enjoyed the personal service and the one on one attention provided by the small guest list." Meals were "hearty; home cooking." "Our cook did a good job of accommodating personal preferences;" "quantity was never a problem." Rooms were "basic;" "clean and comfortable." Fishing guides were "outstanding," "extensive knowledge and expertise during river fishing trips." "We were impressed with the level of personalized attention during fishing trips...most often the ratio was 2 guests to 1 guide." "This lodge is for die-hard fisherman. My guide never cut corners on our fishing time." " We got a good full day of fishing—every day." "Long days on the water—quiet; easy-going evenings."

Resort Features

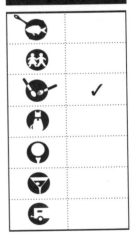

🍳	
👥	
🍳	✓
👕	
🔍	
🍸	
⛽	

Guest Ratings

Room	🐟🐟🐟🐟
Staff	🐟🐟🐟🐟
Meals	NA
Outside areas	🐟🐟🐟🐟
Fishing Guides	🐟🐟🐟
Fishing Equipment	NA
Children's Activities	NA

Resort Features

🐟	✓
👪	
🍳	✓

SILVER SALMON CREEK LODGE

PO Box 3234 • Soldotna, AK 99669
Phone: 907-262-4839 • Reservations: 888-8SALMON
www.alaskan.com/silversalmon

PRICE CATEGORY: $$ – $$$$

SEASON: Mid-May through September.

TRANSPORTATION: From Anchorage, parties of 3 or more can fly directly to lodge. Others fly to Kenai, then to lodge. Or from Anchorage drive to Soldotna (3 hours); fly to lodge.

FISHING: Where: Silver Salmon Creek; Shelter Creek; Johnson River; Cook Inlet. **Type:** Spin casting; fly casting; deep sea fishing. **How:** Walk and wade; shore; boat. **Species:** Silver salmon; king salmon; pink salmon; chum salmon; dolly varden; halibut. **Guides:** Included in package or $100 per person/day. **Equipment:** Spinning rods/reel rentals; fishing licenses. All deep sea fishing tackle provided. **Insider's Tip:** "...if you're a serious or particular fisherman bring your own freshwater gear."

ACCOMMODATIONS: Full service lodge rooms ($1140 for 3 days/2 nights); private cabin with fully equipped kitchen; linens. Rest room and refrigerator in main lodge; tents equipped with wood stove; cook stove; lantern; sleeping bags, inflatable canoe ($600 for 3 days/2 nights). Deluxe accommodations include guides/meals.

AMENITIES AND ACTIVITIES: Sauna; great room. Hiking; beach combing for fossils; clamming; bear watching; bird watching; sea kayaking; photography. **Places to Visit:** Tuxedni Bay; Chisik Island Bird Sanctuary; Lake Iliamna.

PAYMENT: MasterCard; Visa; American Express; personal check; cash.

GUEST COMMENTS: "The tent site is the most scenic..." "Lodge was rustic; but clean." Food was "plentiful and outstanding." Guides were "knowledgeable," "willing to stay as long as we wanted." "The salmon/freshwater gear used by lots of guests is more difficult to maintain..." "Great silver salmon fishing;" "averaged 100 fish a week," "able to experience the "bush" of Alaska...in a safe, comfortable environment."

WOODEN WHEEL COVE LODGE

PO Box 118 • Point Baker, AK 99927
Phone: 907-489-2288 • Reservations: 888-489-9288
www.pws.net/wwcl • Email: wwclodge@aol.com

Guest Ratings

Room	🐟🐟🐟🐟
Staff	🐟🐟🐟🐟
Meals	🐟🐟🐟🐟
Outside areas	🐟🐟🐟🐟
Fishing Guides	🐟🐟🐟🐟
Fishing Equipment	🐟🐟🐟🐟
Children's Activities	NA

Resort Features

🍳	
👨‍👩‍👧	
🍳	✓

PRICE CATEGORY: $$$$

SEASON: Mid April through mid-September.

TRANSPORTATION: Ketchikan; AK (One hour float plane ride to the lodge).

FISHING: Where: Sumner Strait; west coast of Prince of Wales Island; Flicker Creek; Alder Creek and Staney Creek. **Type:** Salt water and fresh water fishing **Species:** Halibut; various bottom species; steelhead; cutthroat trout; dolly varden; coho salmon; pink salmon; king salmon and sockeye salmon. **Guides:** Coast Guard licensed; CPR certified guide included. **Equipment:** Salt water fishing tackle and an Alaskan fishing license with king salmon stamp are included in the trip price. **Insider's Tip:** Guests must bring their own fresh water fishing gear. No live bait is allowed; be sure to bring flies; spinners and spoons.

ACCOMMODATIONS: Two-story hand-crafted cedar lodge accommodates up to 8 people (four night/five day fishing package is $2,275) includes guided fishing, lodging; float plane and meals.

AMENITIES AND ACTIVITIES: Dining room; lounge and sitting room with stone fireplace; wraparound deck. Cave tours; wildlife viewing. **Insider's Tip:** Bring warm; layered clothing; a deck of cards; a good book for the evenings and lots of film.

PAYMENT: MasterCard, Visa, personal checks and cash.

GUEST COMMENTS: The lodge is "modern; comfortable and clean," "even though some rooms share bathrooms they are all kept very clean." The "staff was very accommodating in every way." "Well prepared seafood meals and customized lunches were made even better by wonderful hospitality." "Our guide and the owners worked very hard to get us on fish." "The equipment was excellent." "The nicest; most enjoyable part is—there's nobody around." "...the scenery is absolutely incredible and if you don't take pictures of all the fish you catch nobody at home will believe your stories."

107

ARIZONA · ARKANSAS

Guest Ratings

Room	🐟🐟🐟
Staff	🐟🐟🐟🐟
Meals	NA
Outside areas	🐟🐟🐟🐟
Fishing Guides	NA
Fishing Equipment	🐟🐟🐟
Children's Activities	NA

Resort Features

🐟	✓
👥	
🍳	
🎣	✓
🔦	
⛵	
🚐	✓

HAWLEY LAKE RESORT

White Mountain Apache Reservation • PO Box 448 • McNary, AZ 85930
Phone: 520-335-7511

PRICE CATEGORY: $

SEASON: May through October.

TRANSPORTATION: Phoenix (5 hours).

FISHING: Where: Hawley Lake. **Type:** Bait casting; spin casting; fly casting. **How:** Boat; shore. **Species:** Apache; brown; brook; lake; rainbow trout. **Equipment:** Boat and motor rental; boat dock.

ACCOMMODATIONS: Lodge rooms (start at $60 double occupancy); RV sites (start at $20 double occupancy); Lakeside cabins with kitchenettes (start at $80 double occupancy).

AMENITIES AND ACTIVITIES: Laundry; convenience store. Hiking; bird watching; backpacking; mountain biking.

PAYMENT: MasterCard; Visa; personal checks (Arizona only); cash.

GUEST COMMENTS: "Hawley Lake is...no frills but functional." "...minimal human impact makes fishing for native trout fun and exciting." "As far as I know...the only place in the country where you can catch Apache trout." "We liked the RV camp...the sites offer some privacy." "Dock and boat rentals are showing their age but well maintained."

CRYSTAL SPRINGS RESORT

1647 Crystal Springs Rd. • Royal, AR 71968
Phone: 501-991-3361 • Fax: 501-991-3806

Guest Ratings

Room	♦♦♦♦
Staff	♦♦♦♦
Meals	NA
Outside areas	♦♦♦♦
Fishing Guides	♦♦♦♦
Fishing Equipment	♦♦♦♦
Children's Activities	NA

Resort Features

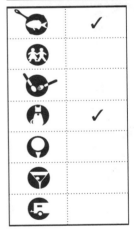

🐟	✓
👥	
🍳	
🔧	✓
⚑	
▽	
⛺	

PRICE CATEGORY: $

SEASON: Open all year.

TRANSPORTATION: Little Rock; AR (1 hour drive).

FISHING: Where: Lake Ouachita; Lake Hamilton; Lake Catherine; Arkansas River; Ouachita River. **Type:** Fly casting; bait casting; spin casting; bobber; trolling; scuba divers can spear fish. **How:** Boat; shore. **Species:** Smallmouth bass; largemouth bass; black bass; white bass; striped bass; walleye; catfish; bream; crappie. **Guides:** Local guides ($200 per day for 1 or 2 people) includes boat; tackle; guide. **Equipment:** Boat and motor rentals; tackle shop; full service marina; spearfishing dive shop; covered and padded boat slips. **Insider's Tip:** Best fishing March and April.

ACCOMMODATIONS: Kitchenettes ($64.95 per day double occupancy); Cabins equipped with kitchen; deck; grill; linens ($69.95 double occupancy); Lodge suites ($64.95 double occupancy); Duplex with full kitchen; linens ($69.95 double occupancy). Extra guests in any unit are $5 per night.

AMENITIES AND ACTIVITIES: Restaurant (open April through October); meeting facilities; rentals (jet skis; houseboat; pontoon). Horseback riding; canoeing; scuba diving; sailing; go carts; mini golf. **Places to Visit:** Crystal Mines; Hot Springs thermal baths; Ouachita National Park.

PAYMENT: MasterCard; Visa; cash.

GUEST COMMENTS: "Lovely rooms;" "clean; well equipped kitchen" "Meeting facilities were...attractively furnished and conveniently located." Staff was "...professional without being hurried;" "Lake Ouachita in the spring is hard to beat; big stripers and lots of crappie..." "Boats looked brand new..." "Well stocked tackle shop." Guide "...knew where the fish liked to be and how to catch them." "Turn in early...or go to town..."

Guest Ratings

Room	🎣🎣🎣
Staff	🎣🎣🎣
Meals	NA
Outside areas	🎣🎣🎣🎣
Fishing Guides	NA
Fishing Equipment	🎣🎣🎣🎣
Children's Activities	NA

Resort Features

🐟	
👫	✓
🍳	
🎣	
🏊	✓
🚐	
🚲	✓

DEGRAY LAKE RESORT

State Park Rt. 3 • Box 490 • Bismarck, AR 71929-8194
Phone: 501-865-2801 • Reservations: 800-737-8355 • Fax: 501-865-2880

PRICE CATEGORY: $-$$

SEASON: Open all year. Discounts offered December through February.

TRANSPORTATION: Little Rock, AR (1 hour drive).

FISHING: Where: DeGray Lake. **Type:** Bait casting; spin casting; fly casting. **How:** Wade; boat; shore. **Species:** Black bass; hybrid bass; crappie; catfish; bream. **Guides:** Local guides; start at $150 per day for 1 or 2 people; includes boat; bait and beverages. **Equipment:** Tackle shop; covered boat slips; open boat slips; fishing boat rentals; boat ramp; full service marina.

ACCOMODATIONS: Lodge rooms; start at $62 for up to 4 people. Tent camp sites ($7); RV hook-up sites ($13-$15 depending on location).

AMENITIES AND ACTIVITIES: Baby-sitting available with prior notice. Golf course; conference center; restaurant; swimming pool; playground; birding; beach; laundry; tennis courts; hiking trails; picnic areas; rentals (party barge; personal water craft; canoes); horseback riding; biking; lake cruises; square dancing; campfires.

PAYMENT: MasterCard; Visa; American Express; personal checks; cash.

GUEST COMMENTS: "Lodge rooms...looked like most other hotel rooms." "The park is very clean and facilities well maintained for the level of use." "Good boat rentals." "...the dock help put me on to a really hot crappie bed...couldn't bait my hook fast enough!" "Naturalist programs are outstanding." "A family can stay for a week at the campground and enjoy...many amenities; such as the golf course and marina...usually only found at more expensive places."

LINDSEY'S RAINBOW RESORT

350 Rainbow Loop • Heber Springs, AR 72543
Phone: 501-362-3139 • Reservations: 800-305-8790 • Fax: 501-362-3824

Guest Ratings

Room	🐟🐟🐟
Staff	🐟🐟🐟
Meals	🐟🐟🐟
Outside areas	🐟🐟🐟🐟
Fishing Guides	🐟🐟🐟
Fishing Equipment	🐟🐟🐟
Children's Activities	NA

Resort Features

🍳	✓
👫	
🍴	
🍸	
⭕	
▼	
⑤	✓

PRICE CATEGORY: $

SEASON: Open year round; discounts offered December through February.

TRANSPORTATION: Little Rock, AR (1 hour drive); Heber Springs (small aircraft).

FISHING: Where: Greers Ferry Lake; Little Red River. **Type:** Bait casting; fly casting. **How:** Shore; boat; wade. **Species:** Rainbow trout; brook trout; brown trout; cutthroat trout. **Guides:** Professional guides (start at $140 per day for 1 or 2 people) includes boat, motor, guide. **Equipment:** Boat & motor rentals; tackle shop; trout dock. **Instruction:** Weekend fly fishing seminars.

ACCOMMODATIONS: Log motel rooms with kitchenettes or 1 and 2 bedroom log cabins with fully equipped kitchens; color TV; charcoal grill; linens; some with Jacuzzi (start at $58 for 1 or 2 people). RV hook-ups ($20 per day double occupancy); tent camping sites ($14 per day double occupancy). Children under 6 stay free.

AMENITIES AND ACTIVITIES: Swimming pool; picnic area; play area; restaurant; 2100 sq. ft. conference lodge. Golf; antique shopping; water skiing; canoeing; hiking; biking. **Places to Visit:** Federal Trout Hatchery; Mossy Bluff Nature Trail; Heber Springs; Ozark Folk Center; Blanchard Springs Caverns.

PAYMENT: Visa; MasterCard; Discover; American Express; Personal checks; cash.

GUEST COMMENTS: "Peaceful; natural setting," "no phones to disturb the quiet." Cabins have a pleasant "cedar smell," "exceptionally clean." Staff were praised for "making me feel like family." Guides were "good; patient teacher(s)." "Safe and well maintained dock area; large lake that provides enough variety for the advanced angler." Fishing is "well above average." "Quiet; serene; refreshing."

Guest Ratings

Room	🎣🎣🎣🎣
Staff	🎣🎣🎣🎣
Meals	NA
Outside areas	🎣🎣🎣
Fishing Guides	🎣🎣🎣
Fishing Equipment	🎣🎣🎣🎣
Children's Activities	NA

Resort Features

🐟	✓
👥	
🍳	
🎣	
🔍	
🛶	
⛽	

NORTH SHORE RESORT

1462 C. R.. 19 • Mountain Home, AR 72653
Phone: 870-431-5564 • www.bullshoalslake.com/northshore
Email: northshore@centuryinter.net

PRICE CATEGORY: $

SEASON: March 1st through December 1st. Discounted rates early spring and late fall.

TRANSPORTATION: Springfield - Branson, MO (1 hour drive). Baxter County Regional Airport (small aircraft).

FISHING: Where: Bull Shoals Lake; White River; Crooked Creek. **Type:** Bait casting; fly casting; spin casting. **How:** Boat; shore. **Species:** Bass (smallmouth; spotted; largemouth; white; striped); trout (rainbow; lake; brown); walleye; crappie; catfish. **Guides:** State licensed guides ($180 plus fuel per day for 1 or 2 people.) **Equipment:** Aluminum fishing boat is free with cottage rental. Fully rigged bass boat rentals; motor rentals; freezer facilities for fish.

ACCOMMODATIONS: 1 and 2 bedroom cottages ($53 per day double occupancy) with linens; fully equipped kitchen; microwave; toaster; coffee make; color TV; outdoor grill; heat; air conditioning; some with whirlpool and fireplace.

AMENITIES AND ACTIVITIES: Water-skiing; scuba diving; river float trips; hiking canoeing; golf in area; horseback riding; spelunking; railroad sightseeing tours, horseshoes; shuffleboard; swimming pool; private dock; swim platform; pontoon rentals. **Places to Visit:** 1890's Village; Trout Hatchery; Bull Shoals Dam; Ozark Folk Center; Blanchard Springs Caverns. **Insider's Tips:** Guests especially recommend cave tours; the fish hatchery; fishing the white river; and boating.

PAYMENT: MasterCard; Visa; Discover; personal checks; cash.

GUEST COMMENTS: Cabins were "pretty; with a great view of the lake." Staff was "very helpful;" able to "point me in the direction of some real hotspots and recommend the right lures." "We caught good-sized fish." One guest suggested "a guide for at least 1 day; as fishing the lake can be difficult for first timers." "Plenty to do in area besides fishing."

OAK RIDGE RESORT

275 C.R. 106 • Mountain Home, AR 72653
Phone: 870-431-5575
www.mtncom.com/oakridge • Email: oakridge@centuryinter.net

PRICE CATEGORY: $

SEASON: Year round; discounts offered October through March.

TRANSPORTATION: Springfield - Branson (1 hour drive).

FISHING: Where: White River; Bull Shoals Lake. **Type:** Bait casting; fly casting. **How:** Shore; boat. **Species**: Largemouth bass; smallmouth bass; Kentucky bass; walleye; crappie; lake trout; catfish. **Guides:** Professional guides (full day $150 including boat; $115 using customer's boat.) **Equipment:** 16' boat or boat slip free with cottage rental; fish cleaning table; lighted boat dock with electric outlets and individual lockers; motor rentals; fuel; small tackle shop.

ACCOMMODATIONS: 1 to 4 bedroom cottages (start at $42 per day double occupancy) including color TV; microwave; charcoal grill; air conditioning; heat; all linens; tableware; cooking utensils.

AMENITIES AND ACTIVITIES: Golf in area; pontoon boat rentals, swimming pool; playground; picnic area; swimming deck, scuba diving; canoe trips; fishing tournaments. **Places to Visit:** Mark Twain National Forest; Eureka Springs; Branson, MO; Silver Dollar City; Ozark Folk Center.

PAYMENT: MasterCard; Visa; personal checks; cash.

GUEST COMMENTS: The rooms were "good-sized and priced right." Staff got unanimous and hearty approval: " the "best of hosts..." Resort was "clean; well located on the lake;" "peaceful and secluded." "Bring your own food and plan for quiet nights." The lake is "full of bass; and provides a good supply of trophy walleye." "...a lot of different fish species. If one...isn't biting, another one is." "Our guide put us on fish even when it was slow."

Guest Ratings

Room	🐟🐟🐟
Staff	🐟🐟🐟
Meals	NA
Outside areas	🐟🐟🐟
Fishing Guides	🐟🐟🐟
Fishing Equipment	🐟🐟🐟
Children's Activities	NA

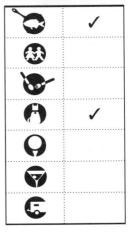

Resort Features

🍳	✓
👥	
🍴	
🎣	✓
🅴	

Guest Ratings

Room	🎣🎣🎣🎣
Staff	🎣🎣🎣🎣
Meals	NA
Outside areas	🎣🎣🎣🎣
Fishing Guides	🎣🎣🎣
Fishing Equipment	🎣🎣🎣🎣
Children's Activities	NA

Resort Features

🐟	✓
🏃	
🍴	
🎿	
⛳	
⛵	
🚐	

RAINBOW DRIVE RESORT

669 Rainbow Landing Dr. • Cotter, AR 72626
Phone: 870-430-5217 • Fax: 870-430-5686
www.whiteriver.net/rainbow • Email: rainbow@mtnhome.com

PRICE CATEGORY: $

SEASON: February through November.

TRANSPORTATION: Baxter County Regional Airport (complimentary shuttle to resort).

FISHING: Where: Bull Shoals Lake; White River; Lake Norfork; North Fork River; Buffalo National River. **Type:** Spin casting; fly casting. **How:** Wade; boat; shore. **Species:** Rainbow trout; brown trout; cutthroat trout. **Guides:** Full day float trip ($90 per person) includes guide; lunch boat; gas; bait/tackle. **Equipment:** Rod/reel rentals; boat ramp; tackle shop; boat and motor rentals. **Instruction:** Fly fishing lessons available. **Insider's Tip:** "Try the area in front of the lodge for excellent fly fishing."

ACCOMMODATIONS: Cabins with fully equipped kitchens; linens; screened porch; grill; boat; some with Jacuzzi tubs. ($488 per week for 1-4 people).

AMENITIES AND ACTIVITIES: Fire pits; picnic tables; grill; meeting facilities; catering services. Boating; scuba diving; bowling; golf in area; spelunking; mini-golf. **Places to Visit:** Historical sites; Norfork National Fish Hatchery; Wolf House.

PAYMENT: MasterCard; Visa; American Express; personal checks; cash.

GUEST COMMENTS: "...a very well run; family oriented resort...sleep; eat and fish." "No phones or TV's." "The fishing is generally good year round." "...needs in a guide well matched by the resort owner." "enjoyed the fresh cinnamon rolls and coffee waiting at the dock each morning." "Motors always start." "...relaxing getaway for those who fish and those who don't."

SCOTT VALLEY RESORT AND GUEST RANCH

PO Box 1447 • Mountain Home, AR 72653
Phone: 870-425-5136 • Reservations: 888-855-7747 • Fax: 870-424-5800
www.scottvalley.com • Email: svr@mail.ot.centuryinter.net

Guest Ratings

Room	🐟🐟🐟🐟
Staff	🐟🐟🐟🐟
Meals	🐟🐟🐟🐟
Outside areas	🐟🐟🐟🐟
Fishing Guides	NA
Fishing Equipment	NA
Children's Activities	NA

Resort Features

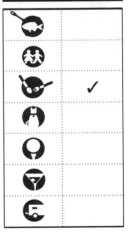

🐟	
👪	
🍳	✓

PRICE CATEGORY: $$

SEASON: March to November.

TRANSPORTATION: Little Rock; AR (3 hour drive).

FISHING: Where: White River; North Fork River. **Type:** Spin casting; bait casting; fly casting. **How:** Shore; boat; walk and wade. **Species:** Rainbow trout; brown trout; cutthroat trout; bass. **Guides:** Local guide ($155 per person/day) includes lunch; guide; boat; fishing tackle. **Equipment:** Trout dock; fishing equipment available.

ACCOMMODATIONS: 1, 2 bedroom units with private bath (Adult $130 per night; ages 2-5 $65; children under 2 are free.)

AMENITIES AND ACTIVITIES: Swimming pool; whirlpool spa; game room; volleyball; tennis; playground; petting zoo. Horseback riding; hiking; trail ride camp out; canoeing; cookouts; hiking. **Places to Visit:** Wolf House; Blanchard Springs Caverns; 1890's village.

PAYMENT: Visa; MasterCard; personal check; cash.

GUEST COMMENTS: "Not really a fishing destination...but a perfect place to go...if only one or two people really love fishing." "Exceptionally clean rooms; comfortable." "Hearty meals; basic and well prepared." "Tremendous staff in every way; great with kids; safety conscious." Guides "provided everything we needed from boat to bait; and we caught fish." "Great variety of activities;" "something for everyone;" "Hayrides; canoeing, we were never bored."

Guest Ratings

Room	🐟🐟🐟
Staff	🐟🐟🐟🐟
Meals	🐟🐟🐟🐟
Outside areas	🐟🐟🐟🐟
Fishing Guides	NA
Fishing Equipment	🐟🐟🐟🐟
Children's Activities	NA

Resort Features

🐟	✓
👥	✓
🍳	
🎣	✓
⚲	
🍸	
🚐	

SHADY OAKS RESORT

HC 62, Box 128 • Flippin, AR 72634
Phone: 870-453-8420 • Fax: 870-453-7813
www.bullshoalslake.com/shadyoaks • Email: shdyoaks@southshore.com

PRICE CATEGORY: $

SEASON: Open all year, seasonal discounts November 1 - February 28.

TRANSPORTATION: Mountain Home, AR; Springfield, MO; Little Rock, AR.

FISHING: Where: Bull Shoals Lake; Norfork Lake; Buffalo River; White River; Norfork River. **Type:** Bait casting; fly casting; spin casting; trolling; down rigging. **How:** Wade; fishing boat; shore; float. **Species:** Bass; crappie; walleye; trout; catfish. **Guides:** Licensed, insured, professional guides ($150 to $250 per day for up to 2 people). **Equipment:** Some equipment provided but best to bring own. Recommend camouflage 8# test (max) line.

ACCOMMODATIONS: Individual housekeeping cottages; 1 bedroom (start at $40/day and $240/wk); 2 bedrooms (start at $50/day and $300/wk); 4 bedrooms (start at $100/day or $300/wk). Rates are dependent on season. Spring and fall fishing specials are available.

AMENITIES AND ACTIVITIES: Swimming pool. Baby-sitting available upon request. Golf in area; hunting; canoeing; historic tours. **Places to Visit:** Bass Pro Shop, Branson, Eureka Springs, Ozark Folk Center.

PAYMENT: MasterCard; Visa; Discover; personal checks; cash.

GUEST COMMENTS: Cabins were: "clean; very modern and well equipped." "The only thing lacking is good TV reception." Staff was "very friendly; helpful," "Fishing is great in the spring," "somewhat slow during really hot weather." "Fishing above average. Great location..." "...close to town; Lake Norfork and many other superb fishing lakes."

SISTER CREEK RESORT

9833 Promise Land Rd. • Mountain Home, AR 72653
Phone: 870-431-5587
www.sistercreekresort.com • Email: scr@mtnhome.com

Guest Ratings

Room	♦♦♦♦
Staff	♦♦♦♦
Meals	NA
Outside areas	♦♦♦♦
Fishing Guides	NA
Fishing Equipment	♦♦♦♦
Children's Activities	NA

PRICE CATEGORY: $

SEASON: All year, discounts offered October through April 15.

TRANSPORTATION: Memphis, TN (4 hour drive).

FISHING: Where: Bull Shoals Lake. **Type:** Spin casting; bait casting. **How:** Boat; shore. **Species:** Largemouth bass; smallmouth bass; trout; walleye; crappie; catfish; bluegill. **Guides:** Local guides available ($187 per day) includes boat; bait; tackle; fish cleaning. **Equipment:** Free boat or slip with each unit; fish cleaning station; covered boat dock; fishing license; fuel; bait; ice.

ACCOMMODATIONS: 2 bedroom cottages or condominium units with kitchens, air conditioning; color TV; all linens ($65 per day for 4 to 8 people).

AMENITIES AND ACTIVITIES: Hiking; golf in area; mini golf; tennis; bowling; scuba diving; swimming. Playground; pool; recreation room; volleyball court; horse shoe pit; barbecue grills; laundry facilities. **Places to Visit**: Branson, MO; Old Wolf House; Norfork Trout Hatchery; Ozark Folk center; Blanchard Springs Cavern.

PAYMENT: MasterCard; Visa; cash; personal check.

GUEST COMMENTS: "Accommodations are always clean and comfortable." "Great view of lake..." "Spacious covered boat dock..." "lights on the dock for night fishing." "Owners add a personal and caring touch..." "light the grill each evening and everyone gathers to barbecue and socialize."

Resort Features

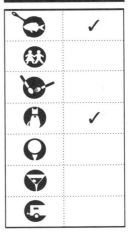

🐟	✓
👫	
🍴	
🎣	✓

Guest Ratings

Room	🐟🐟🐟
Staff	🐟🐟🐟🐟
Meals	NA
Outside areas	🐟🐟🐟🐟
Fishing Guides	NA
Fishing Equipment	🐟🐟🐟🐟
Children's Activities	NA

Resort Features

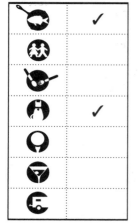

🐟	✓
👪	
🍳	
🎣	✓
♀	
▼	
⑤	

BIG ROCK RESORT

PO Box 126 • 120 Big Rock Rd • June Lake, CA 93529
Phone: 706-648-1067 • Fax: 760-648-1067

PRICE CATEGORY: $

SEASON: Open all year.

TRANSPORTATION: Reno-Tahoe International Airport (3 hour drive). Private planes; commuter flights land at Mammoth Lakes Airport (30 minute drive).

FISHING: Where: June Lake; Gull Lake; Silver Lake; Grant Lake; Rush Creek. **Type:** Bait casting; fly casting. **How:** Shore; boat; walk and wade. **Species:** Rainbow trout; brown trout; cutthroat trout. **Equipment:** Boat ramp; dock; tackle shop; boat rentals. **Instruction**: Personalized fishing instruction available. **Insider's Tip:** "Try salmon eggs for rainbow trout."

ACCOMMODATIONS: 1, 2 or 3 bedroom cabins with fully equipped kitchens; color TV; linens; some with microwaves and fireplaces (start at $70 per night).

AMENITIES AND ACTIVITIES: Horseback riding; paddle boats; mountain biking; hiking. **Places to Visit:** Mono Lake; Bodie (ghost town); Mammoth Lakes; Devil's Postpile National Monument; Yosemite National Park .

PAYMENT: MasterCard; Visa; American Express; personal checks and cash.

GUEST COMMENTS: Cabins are "basic but clean; rustic." "Terrific area for families and fishermen." Staff will "share the good fishing spots; best baits..." "Lots of secluded fishing spots..." "Bodie and Mono Lake are truly unique attractions..." "Reasonably priced...great area."

JIM'S SODA BAY RESORT

6380 Soda Bay Rd. • Kelseyville, CA 95451
Phone: 707-279-4837 • www.webwave.com/jimsresort

Guest Ratings

Room	🐟🐟🐟
Staff	🐟🐟🐟🐟
Meals	NA
Outside areas	🐟🐟🐟🐟
Fishing Guides	🐟🐟🐟🐟
Fishing Equipment	🐟🐟🐟
Children's Activities	NA

PRICE CATEGORY: $

SEASON: Open all year.

TRANSPORTATION: San Francisco, CA (3 hour drive).

FISHING: Where: Clear Lake **Type:** Bait casting; spin casting; fly casting. **How:** Boat; shore; dock. **Species:** Bass; bluegill; catfish; crappie. **Guides:** Licensed, insured guides start at $150 per person per day and includes lunch and some equipment. **Equipment:** Boat and motor rentals; boat ramps, dock.

ACCOMMODATIONS: Cabins with fully equipped kitchens; heat; air conditioning; TV; patio; picnic table; linens. $52 and up per family (2 adults and 2 children).

AMENITIES AND ACTIVITIES: Small beach; swimming area; rentals (pontoons; fishing boats; sailboat; peddle boat. Golf; bowling; movies; summer concerts in the park. **Places to Visit:** Museum, observatory.

PAYMENT: MasterCard; Visa; American Express; cash; personal checks.

GUEST COMMENTS: "Older buildings and facilities but well maintained and functional," "neat and tidy." "You can tell that the owners care about the resort and its visitors." "Gorgeous view of the lake." "Great fishing for big cats." "hard to beat, very homey and laid back." "A lot like visiting old friends." "Economical way to get the family out...for some good together time. Good lake for instructing young fishermen." "can fish just about any way you want to here."

Resort Features

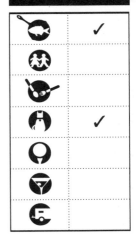

🐟	✓
👥	
🍳	
🛶	✓
⛵	
⛳	
🎳	

Guest Ratings

Room	🐟🐟🐟🐟
Staff	🐟🐟🐟🐟
Meals	🐟🐟🐟🐟
Outside areas	🐟🐟🐟🐟
Fishing Guides	🐟🐟🐟
Fishing Equipment	🐟🐟🐟
Children's Activities	NA

Resort Features

🐟	
👥	
🍴	✓
🔥	
♀	
▽	
€	

OASIS SPRINGS LODGE

PO Box 20368 • Oakland, CA 94620
Phone: 510-653-7630 • Reservations: 800-642-4150 • Fax: 510-653-6754
www.oasisflyfishing.com • Email: fish4fun@pacbell.net

PRICE CATEGORY: $$

SEASON: Open all year.

TRANSPORTATION: San Francisco; CA (3 1/2 hour drive).

FISHING: Where: South Fork of Battle Creek. **Type:** Fly fishing (catch and release). **How:** Walk and wade. **Species:** Rainbow trout; brown trout. **Guides:** Local guides ($250 per day for 1-4 people). **Equipment:** Rod; reel and wader rentals. **Instruction:** 3 hours instruction ($85).

ACCOMMODATIONS: Lodge rooms; some with fireplaces ($75 per person.) Meal package available.

AMENITIES AND ACTIVITIES: Hot tub; swimming pool; clay tennis court. Horseback riding; hiking; wildlife viewing; photography. **Places to Visit:** Lassen National Park. **Insider's Tip:** "Great fishing at Manzamita Lake in Lassen National Park."

PAYMENT: MasterCard; Visa; American Express; personal check; cash.

GUEST COMMENTS: "Exceptionally clean...well maintained." "...One phone on the property and no TV; we love it!" "...Caught and released 12"; 16" and 22" rainbows." "...Some hiking...to get to pools not frequented by the majority..." "Lodgers gather in the main hall to...tie flies and lie about their fishing prowess."

TENAYA LODGE AT YOSEMITE

1122 Hwy. 41 • Fish Camp, CA 93623
Phone: 209-683-6555
www. tenayalodge.com • Email: tenaya@tenayalodge.com

PRICE CATEGORY: $$

SEASON: Open all year.

TRANSPORTATION: San Francisco; CA (3 hours).

FISHING: Where: Sierra National Forest; Yosemite National Park lakes; rivers and streams. **Type:** Fly casting; spin casting; bobber. **How:** Shore; walk and wade. **Species:** Golden trout; brook trout; brown trout; rainbow trout. **Guides:** Local guides ($150 per person/day) includes tackle.

ACCOMMODATIONS: Lodge rooms ($69 mid week off season to $239 during peak season).

AMENITIES AND ACTIVITIES: Swimming pool; hot tub; spa; fitness center; meeting rooms; outdoor concert area; sauna; restaurant; kid's play area. Horseback riding; high country tours; mountain biking; hiking; nature walks; flashlight hikes; photography; golf; rock climbing. Camp Tenaya; structured kid's day camp.

PAYMENT: MasterCard; Visa; Discover; American Express; Diner's Club.

GUEST COMMENTS: Rooms were : "very well decorated." Staff: "knowledgeable about area flora and fauna." "My kids really liked Camp Tenaya". "Dry fly fishing for rainbows was outstanding." "...challenge anglers with different ability levels." "Our guide was...a good teacher." "many opportunities for outdoor recreation."

Guest Ratings

Room	🐟🐟🐟🐟
Staff	🐟🐟🐟🐟
Meals	NA
Outside areas	🐟🐟🐟🐟
Fishing Guides	🐟🐟🐟🐟
Fishing Equipment	NA
Children's Activities	🐟🐟🐟🐟

Resort Features

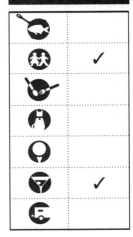

Guest Ratings

Room	♦♦♦♦
Staff	♦♦♦♦
Meals	NA
Outside areas	♦♦♦♦
Fishing Guides	♦♦♦♦
Fishing Equipment	♦♦♦♦
Children's Activities	NA

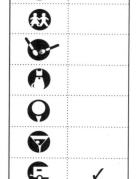

Resort Features

🐟	
👥	
🍳	
♿	✓

CROSS D BAR TROUT RANCH

2299 County Road 328 • Westcliffe, CO 81252
Phone: 719-783-2007 • Fax: 303-733-8859
www.coloradovacation.com • Email: dickm@csn.net

PRICE CATEGORY: $

SEASON: Open from May 1st through mid-October.

TRANSPORTATION: Colorado Springs, CO (2 hour drive).

FISHING: Where: 4 private, spring fed lakes, some equipped for wheelchair access. **Type:** Fly casting; bait casting. **How:** Shore. **Species:** Trout (rainbow, cutthroat, brown, golden, brook). **Equipment:** Custom made graphite rods, fly reels, waders for rent. **Instruction:** Full/half day fishing schools, instructors Trout Unlimited and/or Federation of Fly Fishers certified.

ACCOMMODATIONS: Ranch guest house with 3 bedrooms and two baths ($80 per night), deluxe Sioux tipi; heated; sleeps six ($50 per night), tent camping sites ($8); full RV hookups ($14).

AMENITIES AND ACTIVITIES: Tackle shop. Barbecue and wagon ride through Custer County's largest bison herd, horseback riding, pack trips; Jeep tours; community campfires, barbecues; fly-tying lessons. The Cross D Bar Recreation Foundation, based on the ranch, is a non-profit organization dedicated to providing the disabled and elderly with fishing and other outdoor recreation opportunities. The foundation is trying to make all fishing areas easily accessible to handicapped individuals and offers several free fishing days for nursing homes and physically challenged people.

PAYMENT: MasterCard, Visa, American Express, personal checks and cash.

GUEST COMMENTS: "Really unique place. Perfect for families." "The tipi was super comfortable...we caught a bunch of trout." Staff is..."incredible; caring; accommodating..." "one of this ranch's greatest assets." "Very healthy fish; well maintained fishery that offers a shot at trophy sized trout."

SYLVAN DALE GUEST RANCH

2939 North County Rd. 31D • Loveland, CO 80538
Phone: 970-667-3915
www.sylvandale.com • Email: ranch@sylvandale.com

Guest Ratings

Room	🐟🐟🐟🐟
Staff	🐟🐟🐟🐟
Meals	🐟🐟🐟
Outside areas	🐟🐟🐟
Fishing Guides	🐟🐟🐟
Fishing Equipment	🐟🐟🐟
Children's Activities	NA

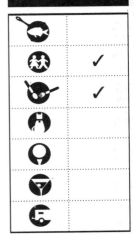

Resort Features

🍳🐟	
👨‍👩‍👧	✓
🍳	✓
🎯	
♀	
🏹	
ⒻⒺ	

PRICE CATEGORY: $

SEASON: Open all year for fishing and group events. Summer guest ranch season is mid-June through August 31.

TRANSPORTATION: Denver, CO (1 hour; 15 minute drive).

FISHING: Where: Big Thompson River; 12 private lakes. **Type:** Trophy trout fly fishing; catch and release; catch and keep. **How:** Shore; float tubes. **Species:** Trout (rainbow; brown; brook; cutthroat); steelhead. **Guides:** Ranch and local guides ($50 per half-day + access fee). **Equipment**: Rods; waders; etc. for rent; flies/equipment for sale. **Instruction:** Private/group lessons.

ACCOMMODATIONS: Cabins or lodge units (weekly rates for adults start at $838); includes all meals.

AMENITIES AND ACTIVITIES: Kids program, babysitting. Pool; tennis; picnic area; meeting facilities; game room. Horseback riding; cattle drives; overnight pack trips; western dancing; hayrides; golf; hiking; mountain biking; white water rafting. **Places to Visit:** Rocky Mountain National Park; Estes Park.

PAYMENT: Personal checks; cash.

GUEST COMMENTS: "Ranch activities for non-anglers are varied..." "Excellent for ...trying to learn fly fishing for trout." Guide: "outstanding streamside knowledge." "...18"-24" rainbows...eagerly took dries and nymphs." Some guests said lakes were "smaller than expected..."; "small lakes; big trout."

Guest Ratings

Room	🐟🐟🐟
Staff	🐟🐟🐟🐟
Meals	NA
Outside areas	🐟🐟🐟🐟
Fishing Guides	🐟🐟🐟🐟
Fishing Equipment	🐟🐟🐟🐟
Children's Activities	NA

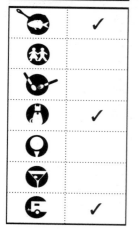

Resort Features

🐟	✓
👥	
🍳	
🎣	✓
♀	
▼	
🚐	✓

THREE RIVERS RESORT

130 Cty. Rd. 742 • Almont, CO 81210
Phone: 970-641-1303 • Reservations: 888-761-FISH • Fax: 970-641-1317
Email: tralmont@rmi.net

PRICE CATEGORY: $

SEASON: May through November

TRANSPORTATION: Colorado Springs (3 hour drive).

FISHING: Where: East River; Taylor River; Gunnison River; Taylor Reservoir; Spring Creek Reservoir. **Type:** Fly casting; spin casting. **How:** Walk and wade; float. **Species:** Trout (Makinaw; rainbow; cutthroat; brook; brown); pike. **Guides:** Local guides (walk/wade $150 per person/day); includes lunch/ equipment. **Equipment:** Fly rod/reel; wader and boat rentals. **Instruction:** Introduction to fly fishing; covers casting; gear; basic entomology.

ACCOMMODATIONS: Cabins ($30 double occupancy) includes fully equipped kitchen and linens. RV sites ($16); tent sites ($14).

AMENITIES AND ACTIVITIES: General store (fly shop; deli; gifts; groceries); table games; horseshoes; volleyball; playground. Rafting; kayaking; four wheeling; backpacking; hiking; mountain biking; horseback riding; golf; tennis; boating; ballooning.

PAYMENT: MasterCard; Visa; American Express; cash; personal checks.

GUEST COMMENTS: Cabins: "Basic but...had everything we needed." "Great staff." "RV and tent sites near river are really great." "...a nice place for family reunions...very reasonably priced." "I learned a lot from the guide." "Beautiful area with lots of hungry fish to catch." "Everything you need...in one spot."

OLD RIVERTON INN

Rt. 20 Box 6 • Riverton, CT 06065
Phone: 860-379-8678 • Fax: 860-379-1006
Email: mark.telford@snet.net

Guest Ratings

Room	🐟🐟🐟
Staff	🐟🐟🐟🐟
Meals	🐟🐟🐟🐟
Outside areas	🐟🐟🐟🐟
Fishing Guides	NA
Fishing Equipment	NA
Children's Activities	NA

Resort Features

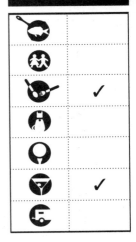

🍳	
👥	
🍳	✓
🎣	
🔆	
🍷	✓
⛽	

PRICE CATEGORY: $

SEASON: Open all year.

TRANSPORTATION: Hartford, CT (40 minute drive).

FISHING: Where: West Branch of Farmington River (designated: Wild and Scenic); Sandy Brook. **Type:** Bait casting; spin casting; fly casting. **How:** Walk and wade; boat; shore. **Species:** Trout. **Guides:** Available ($150 per person/day) includes tackle.

ACCOMMODATIONS : Bed and breakfast; on National Register of Historic Places (starts at $50 per person) Hobby Horse Bar; dining room; cable TV; private baths.

AMENITIES AND ACTIVITIES: Hiking; swimming; picnics; canoeing; golf; antiquing; shopping; skiing. **Places to Visit:** Peoples State Forest; Hitchcock Chair Company and Museum.

PAYMENT: MasterCard; Visa; American Express; cash.

GUEST COMMENTS: "The right blend of old New England charm..." Meals were "appetizing and well served." Guides "knew the right holes on the Farmington." "This is not a fishing lodge. It's a country inn...on a truly beautiful stream with guaranteed great trout fishing. No night life beyond...swapping lies with other fishermen. Better than many dedicated fishing lodges; friendlier, unpretentious."

FLORIDA

Guest Ratings

Room	🐟🐟🐟
Staff	🐟🐟🐟🐟
Meals	NA
Outside areas	🐟🐟🐟
Fishing Guides	🐟🐟🐟🐟
Fishing Equipment	🐟🐟🐟🐟
Children's Activities	NA

Resort Features

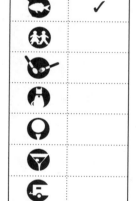

🐟	✓
👫	
🍴	
🎣	
♀	
🍸	
🎱	

ANGLER'S MARINA

910 Okeechobee Blvd. • Clewiston, FL 33440
Phone: 941-983-4613 • Reservations: 800-741-3141 • Fax: 941-983-4613
www.biglakearea.com/main/anglers.htm

PRICE CATEGORY: $

SEASON: Open all year.

TRANSPORTATION: Fort Myers; FL (90 minute drive).

FISHING: Where: Lake Okeechobee. **Type:** Bait casting; spinning; fly casting. **How:** Mostly from boats; shore. **Species:** Largemouth bass, crappie, bluegill and shellcracker. **Guides:** US Coast Guard certified guides start at $150 per half day for up to 2 people. Guide service includes full size bass boat, rod and reel. Guests must provide their own bait; lures; fishing license; food and drinks. **Equipment:** Covered and open boat slips; full service marina; fuel; boat sales and service; large tackle shop; boat rentals.

ACCOMMODATIONS: Efficiency motel rooms ($45 double occupancy) or fully furnished condominiums ($85 double occupancy) with fully equipped kitchens; cable TV; air conditioning.

AMENITIES AND ACTIVITIES: Swimming pool. Hiking/Biking trail on top of the levee that surrounds the lake allows wildlife viewing of alligators; eagles; manatees; herons and egrets. **Places to Visit:** Gulf coast (1 1/2 hours); Atlantic coast (1 /2 hours).

PAYMENT: MasterCard; Visa; personal checks; cash.

GUEST COMMENTS: "Good value." "Prices for guides; bait and fishing accessories were competitive with larger area stores." The staff and guides were "helpful;" "hard working;" and "accommodating;" "took the time to explain everything...showed us videos on how to fish shiners..." "Expert guides with great bass boats."

BIENVILLE PLANTATION

PO Box 241 • White Springs, FL 32096
Phone: 904-397-4215

Guest Ratings

Room	🐟🐟🐟🐟
Staff	🐟🐟🐟▸
Meals	🐟🐟🐟🐟
Outside areas	🐟🐟🐟🐟
Fishing Guides	🐟🐟🐟🐟
Fishing Equipment	NA
Children's Activities	NA

PRICE CATEGORY: $$$$

SEASON: Open all year.

FISHING: Where: 6000 acres of private phosphate pit lakes. **Type:** Fly fishing; artificial lures. **How:** Boat; walk and wade. **Species:** Largemouth bass (catch and release); crappie (2 lb. average); bluegill. **Guides:** Guides ($300 per person per day) includes boat. **Insider's Tip:** Suggest 14-17 lb. test line.

ACCOMODATIONS: 5 bedroom log cabins with kitchen ($475 per person/per day includes guided fishing; accomodations; meals; open bar; field transportation); TV; private bath for each room.

AMENITIES AND ACTIVITIES: Restaurant; bar; recreation room; meeting facilities; tackle shop; lighted skeet/trap range. Hunting (quail; duck; deer; gator; pheasant/chuckar); golf in area.

PAYMENT: MasterCard; Visa; personal check; cash.

GUEST COMMENTS: "Grounds, main facility and lodges very nice." "Large portions of gourmet class cuisine perfectly presented." Staff: "polite; yet personal." Guides: "excellent in every way." "Might be the best in the US for bass fishing." "A fisherman's wonderland. Abundant wildlife made the visit extra special..." "Pastoral bliss with serious piscatorial purpose."

Resort Features

🐟	✓
👥	
🍳	✓
🔫	
⛳	
▼	✓
⛽	

133

Guest Ratings

Room	♦♦♦
Staff	♦♦♦♦
Meals	NA
Outside areas	♦♦♦♦
Fishing Guides	NA
Fishing Equipment	♦♦♦♦
Children's Activities	NA

Resort Features

🐟	✓
👥	
🍳	
🎣	
⚓	
⛵	
🔥	✓

CAMP HENRY RESORT AND MARINA

HC 1, Box 522 • Georgetown, FL 32139
Phone: 904-467-2282

PRICE CATEGORY: $

SEASON: Open all year.

TRANSPORTATION: Orlando (1 1/2 hour drive).

FISHING: Where: St. John's River; Lake George; Little Lake George or the Oklawaha River. **Type:** Bait casting; fly casting; spin casting; trolling; bobber. **How:** Boat; shore. **Species:** Largemouth bass; striped bass; crappie; bluegill; sunfish and catfish. **Guides:** Guides available. **Equipment:** Marina store (bait; tackle; groceries); lighted; covered boat stalls with electricity; boat ramp; fuel; boat rentals; boat service.

ACCOMMODATIONS: Motel efficiencies with fully equipped kitchenettes ($40 double occupancy); 1 and 2 room cabins ($45 double occupancy); 2 bedroom trailers ($55 double occupancy); full RV hook-ups ($15 double occupancy). Weekly guests receive 7th night free.

AMENITIES AND ACTIVITIES: Picnic tables; grills. **Places to Visit:** Disney World; Epcot Center; MGM Studios; Seaworld.

PAYMENT: MasterCard; Visa; personal checks and cash.

GUEST COMMENTS: "Great location for a variety of fishing." Cabins: "very clean" "The RV area is very well maintained...good layout" "...quiet; natural setting" Staff: "efficient;" "courteous and helpful." Guides were: "knowledgeable; friendly," "went out of their way to help us catch fish." "At least one species is usually biting."

FISH HAVEN LODGE

1 Fish Haven Road • Auburndale, FL 33823
Phone: 941-984-1183

Guest Ratings

Room	🐟🐟🐟
Staff	🐟🐟🐟🐟
Meals	NA
Outside areas	🐟🐟🐟
Fishing Guides	NA
Fishing Equipment	🐟🐟🐟🐟
Children's Activities	NA

Resort Features

🍳	✓
👥	
🍽	
🔧	
🎯	
🍸	
🎣	✓

PRICE CATEGORY: $

SEASON: Year around.

TRANSPORTATION: Tampa; Orlando.

FISHING: Where: Lake Julianna. **Type:** Bait casting; fly casting; trolling. **How:** Boat; shore. **Species:** Bass; bluegill; speckled perch; bream; catfish. **Equipment:** 14' fiberglass fishing boat free with cottage rental, motors $30 per day plus gas; lighted fishing pier; boat rentals; boat ramp; bait and tackle shop.

ACCOMMODATIONS: Cottages include TV; heat; air conditioning; linens; fully equipped kitchen (start at $45 per night for 2 adults, $270 per week. First two children under 16 are free.) Fully equipped RV hook-ups ($20).

AMENITIES AND ACTIVITIES: Recreation building; shuffleboard. Water skiing; shopping. **Places to Visit:** Disney World; Sea World; Boardwalk and Baseball; Busch Gardens; Cypress Gardens; Bok Tower; Gator Land.

PAYMENT: Personal checks; cash.

GUEST COMMENTS: Cottages are "Clean and tidy; functional." Staff is "agreeable" and "helpful; hard working." "Fishing is really fun here." "Catch big fish all year. "Well maintained; conveniently situated dock area." "Nice; neighborly little resort." "Good people; great fishing; decent facilities—a better than average value for your money."

135

Guest Ratings

Room	🐟🐟🐟🐟
Staff	🐟🐟🐟🐟
Meals	🐟🐟🐟◗
Outside areas	🐟🐟🐟🐟
Fishing Guides	🐟🐟🐟🐟
Fishing Equipment	🐟🐟🐟🐟
Children's Activities	🐟🐟🐟🐟

Resort Features

🍳	
👫	✓
🥘	
🔧	
⚓	
🍸	✓
🅕	

HAWK'S CAY RESORT

61 Hawk's Cay Blvd. • Duck Key, FL 33050
Phone: 305-743-9000 • Fax: 305-743-3198
Email: hawk'scay@fla-keys.com

PRICE CATEGORY: $$$

SEASON: Open all year.

TRANSPORTATION: Miami, FL (2 hour drive).

FISHING: Where: Atlantic Ocean; Florida Bay; Florida Everglades National Park. **Type:** Deep sea; back country; reef fishing; offshore trolling; sight fishing. **Species:** Dolphin; tuna; wahoo; kingfish; snapper; grouper; shark; tarpon; bonefish; permit; marlin; barracuda; trout; snook; redfish. **Guides:** US Coast Guard Licensed Guides ($275 and up per half day) includes fishing license; appropriate tackle; bait; fish cleaning. **Equipment:** Fishing pole rentals; marina store; boat slips with fresh water hook-up; cable TV; electricity; telephone service (BOAT US and NBOA discounts available).

ACCOMMODATIONS: Hotel rooms with island motif (start at $175 per night double occupancy); suites ($350 and up).

AMENITIES AND ACTIVITIES: All-day kids program, 5-13. Babysitting. 2 swimming pools; lagoon beach; tennis; playground; fitness center; volleyball; dolphin discovery program; restaurants; lounge; boat rentals. Scuba diving; snorkeling; parasailing; biking; sea kayaking; nature walks. **Places to Visit:** Florida Key's Children's Museum; Dolphin Research Center; Long Key State Recreation Area; Florida Keys Wild Bird Center.

PAYMENT: MasterCard; Visa; American Express; personal checks; cash.

GUEST COMMENTS: "Glamorous but family-friendly." "Fishing is some of the best in the Keys..." "My guide was absolutely outstanding..." "Plenty to do for those who don't fish..." "great beach for kids." "...counselors were both fun and responsible." "We really enjoyed...deep sea and back country fishing from the same location." "Good place to do a little bit of everything."

HOWARD JOHNSON RIVERSIDE INN RESORT

5297 South Cherokee Way • Homosassa, FL 34448
Phone: 352-628-2474 • Reservations: 800-442-5020

Guest Ratings

Room	🎣🎣🎣
Staff	🎣🎣🎣🎣
Meals	🎣🎣
Outside areas	🎣🎣🎣🎣
Fishing Guides	🎣🎣🎣
Fishing Equipment	🎣🎣🎣🎣
Children's Activities	NA

Resort Features

🐟	
👥	
🍳	
🎯	✓
⛳	
🚤	✓
🚐	

PRICE CATEGORY: $

SEASON: Open all year.

TRANSPORTATION: Tampa, FL (1 1/2 hour drive). Orlando, FL (2 hour drive).

FISHING: Where: Homosassa River; Gulf of Mexico; Crystal River. **Type:** Bait casting; spin casting; fly casting; deep sea. **How:** Boat; shore (very limited). **Species:** Black bass; trout; bream; tarpon; sheepshead; grouper; red fish; speckled trout; snapper; shark; cobia. **Guides:** Licensed; insured guides (start at $250 per person/day) includes boat; bait; tackle; guide. **Equipment:** Boat and motor rentals; tackle shop. **Instruction:** Fishing classes and seminars are available with 30 days notice.

ACCOMMODATIONS: Standard hotel rooms ($50 double occupancy).

AMENITIES AND ACTIVITIES: Playground; swimming pool; recreation room; boat ramp; canoe and kayak trails; marina; volleyball court; restaurant; lounge; horseshoe pit; meeting rooms; basketball court; boat rentals. Cookouts and barbecues; manatee discovery safaris; airboat tours; scuba diving; golf; bird-watching; canoeing; river tours. **Places to Visit:** Sugarmill ruins; Ted Williams Baseball Museum; Antique Automobile and Boat Museum; Homosassa Springs Wildlife Park.

PAYMENT: Visa; MasterCard; American Express; Discover; cash.

GUEST COMMENTS: "I like to save money on the room so that I can afford a deep sea charter. Besides they've got a nice restaurant; good boats to rent..." "...accessible to everything fishy: freshwater creeks; saltwater flats; deep sea fishing." "Got good fishing tips from the marina..." "I've visited winter; spring; summer and fall—something is always biting." "Nice tackle shop with all of the necessities."

137

Guest Ratings

Room	🎣🎣🎣
Staff	🎣🎣🎣🎣
Meals	NA
Outside areas	🎣🎣🎣🎣
Fishing Guides	NA
Fishing Equipment	🎣🎣🎣🎣
Children's Activities	NA

Resort Features

🐟	✓
🚻	
🍳	
♒	
⚑	
☯	
♿	✓

MOONRISE RESORT

8801-18 East Moonrise Lane • Floral City, • FL 34436
Phone: 352-726-2553 • Reservations: 800-665-6701
E-mail: moonriz@citrus.infi.net

PRICE CATEGORY: $

SEASON: Open all year.

TRANSPORTATION: Orlando; Tampa; St. Petersburg.

FISHING: Where: Tsala Apopka Lake; Withlacoochee River. **Type:** Bait casting; fly casting; trolling. **How:** Wade; boat; shore. **Species:** Black bass; pickerel; bluegill; crappie; shellcracker; catfish. **Equipment:** Boat & motor rental.

ACCOMMODATIONS: 1 and 2 bedroom cabins (1 bedroom, up to 2 people—start at $42 day, $250 week) includes color TV; fully equipped kitchen; linens; toaster; coffee maker; microwave; screened porch; picnic table; air conditioning and heat. RV hook-ups.

AMENITIES AND ACTIVITIES: Bath house; laundry; shuffleboard; boat dock; boat & motor rental; canoe rental; paddleboat rental. Golf; boating; shopping. **Places to Visit:** Ted Williams Baseball Museum; Homosassa Springs State Park.

PAYMENT: Personal checks; cash.

GUEST COMMENTS: "Lovely little resort." "Extremely clean;" "well kept." "Cabins are always immaculate when we arrive—the grounds also." "Owners work real hard to keep everything nice." "Boat area is...easy to get to." "The fishing is mostly good and the owners will give you good advice to get your tackle set up right and also point you toward the hot fishing spots." "Peaceful; quiet at night and relaxing."

PARRAMORE'S CAMPGROUND

1675 South Moon Road • Astor, FL 32102
Phone: 904-749-2721 • Reservations: 800-516-2386 • Fax: 904-749-9744
Email: parramore@aol.com

PRICE CATEGORY: $

SEASON: Open all year.

TRANSPORTATION: Orlando, FL (1 hour 45 minute drive).

FISHING: Where: St. John's River; Lake Dexter; Lake George; Lake Woodruff. **Type:** Bait casting; spin casting; fly casting. **How:** Shore; boat. **Species:** Speckled perch; bream; bluegill; bass; catfish. **Equipment:** Small tackle shop; boat ramp.

ACCOMMODATIONS: Tent sites ($16 for 1 or 2 people); RV sites ($19.50 for 1 or 2 people); Cabins with fully equipped kitchens ($65 for 1-4 people).

AMENITIES AND ACTIVITIES: Swimming pool; playground; basketball court; tennis courts. Bird watching; hiking; biking. **Places to Visit:** Pioneer Arts Festival; Walt Disney World; Silver Springs; Ormond Beach.

PAYMENT: MasterCard; Visa; Discover; cash.

GUEST COMMENTS: Staff is "pleasant and amiable." "The cabins; and resort in general; is orderly; conveniently arranged and attractive." "Ideally located on the river between Lake George and Lake Dexter." "Lots of different places to fish; lots of fish to catch all year long." "Lot of things for non-fishing folks to do; lots of places to explore and very accessible fishing areas that are great for kids." "A bargain."

Guest Ratings

Room	♦♦♦
Staff	♦♦♦♦
Meals	NA
Outside areas	♦♦♦
Fishing Guides	NA
Fishing Equipment	♦♦♦♦
Children's Activities	♦♦♦♦

Resort Features

🐟	✓
👥	
🍳	
⚓	✓
◉	
▽	
🔥	✓

Guest Ratings

Room	🎣🎣🎣
Staff	🎣🎣🎣
Meals	NA
Outside areas	🎣🎣🎣🎣
Fishing Guides	🎣🎣🎣🎣
Fishing Equipment	NA
Children's Activities	NA

Resort Features

🐟	✓
👥	
🍳	
🦞	
⚓	
🚤	
🎣	

PELICAN COVE RESORT

PO Box 633, 84457 Old Overseas Hwy. • Islamorada, FL 33036
Phone: 305-664-4435 • Reservations: 800-445-4690 • Fax: 305-664-5134
www.pcove.com

PRICE CATEGORY: $$$

SEASON: Open all year. Discounts offered September through December.

TRANSPORTATION: Miami, FL (1 1/2 hour drive).

FISHING: Where: Atlantic Ocean; Gulf of Mexico. **Type:** Fly or spin cast; deep sea fishing; back country fishing. **How:** Boat; shore. **Species:** Sailfish; marlin; permit; bonefish; tarpon; snook. **Guides:** US Coast Guard Licensed guides ($350 per day) includes rods; reels; license; bait; fuel; rain gear. **Equipment :** Rentals; marina.

ACCOMMODATIONS: Standard hotel style rooms ($165 double occupancy); equipped with coffee makers; cable TV; refrigerators; free continental breakfast; some with fully equipped kitchens.

AMENITIES AND ACTIVITIES: 770 sq. ft. "meeting boat"; tennis; rentals (wave runners; jets skis; fun islands); pool; Jacuzzi; restaurant; swimming pool; hot tub. Snorkeling; swimming; sailing; windsurfing; scuba diving; shopping. **Places to Visit:** Theater of the Sea; World Wide Sportsman; Rain Barrel; Pennekamp Coral Reef State Park

PAYMENT: MasterCard; Visa; American Express; ATM; Diners Club; Carte Blanche; cash; personal check (for advance deposit only).

GUEST COMMENTS: "Rooms would be comfortable for 2; but are too small for a party of 4." "The scenery; entertainment and beach are wonderful!" Guides were: "helpful;" "professionals." "Great guys to go fishing with."

PIRATES COVE RESORT AND MARINA

4307 S.E. Bayview St. • Stuart, FL 34997
Phone: 561-287-2500 • Reservations: 800-332-1414 • Fax: 561-286-5126

Guest Ratings

Room	🐟🐟🐟🐟
Staff	🐟🐟🐟🐟
Meals	🐟🐟🐟🐟
Outside areas	🐟🐟🐟🐟
Fishing Guides	🐟🐟🐟
Fishing Equipment	🐟🐟🐟
Children's Activities	NA

Resort Features

PRICE CATEGORY: $$

SEASON: Open year round, off-season rates June 1-November 30.

TRANSPORTATION: Palm Beach International Airport (1 hour by car).

FISHING: Where: Gulf Stream; Indian River Lagoon; St. Lucie River. **Type:** Saltwater; freshwater; bait casting; fly casting; trolling; bottom fishing; wreck fishing. **How:** Boat; shore; wade. **Species:** Dolphin; wahoo; kingfish; sailfish; marlin; trout; snook; tarpon; redfish; grouper; tuna; shark; barracuda; cobia. **Guides:** Coast Guard Licensed, off-shore and inshore charters (start at $375 half day, $650 full day) includes bait and tackle.

ACCOMMODATIONS: Standard hotel rooms and mini-suites (start at $100 double occupancy).

AMENITIES AND ACTIVITIES: Baby-sitting arranged upon request. Restaurant; lounge, full service marina; rack storage; tackle shop; conference facilities; covered parking; laundry service; swimming pool. Fishing tournaments; golf; tennis; nature cruise; hot air balloon rides. **Places to Visit:** Dupuis Reserve; Elliot Museum; Harbor Branch Oceanographic Institution; Heathcote Botanical Gardens; Jupiter Lighthouse; Old Jensen Village; Treasure Coast Wildlife Hospital; Maritime and Yachting Museum.

PAYMENT: MasterCard; Visa; American Express; personal checks; cash.

GUEST COMMENTS: "Sparkling clean; beautiful facility." Staff "provided exceptional service and courtesy." "Great guide; patient teacher...didn't spend the entire day watching the clock." "Close enough to the fishing hot spots that we didn't waste a lot of time getting to the fish." "We paid for fishing and we got great fishing; not just a nice boat ride." "The room, meals and guide were worth every penny."

141

Guest Ratings

Room	♦♦♦
Staff	♦♦♦♦
Meals	♦♦♦♦
Outside areas	♦♦♦♦
Fishing Guides	♦♦♦♦
Fishing Equipment	♦♦♦♦
Children's Activities	NA

Resort Features

🐟	
👨‍👩‍👧	✓
🍳	
🅷	
🏊	
🔻	✓
🎾	✓

PORT OF THE ISLANDS HOTEL RESORT AND MARINA

25000 Tamiami Trail • East Naples, FL 34114-9602
Phone: 941-394-3101 • Fax: 941-394-3101
www.portoftheislands.com • *Email: info@portoftheislands.com*

PRICE CATAGORY: $$

SEASON: Open all year. Discounts offered during summer months.

TRANSPORTATION: Ft. Myers, FL ; Everglades Airport (private planes).

FISHING: Where: Gulf of Mexico; 10,000 Islands Area. **Type:** Bait casting; spin casting; fly casting. **How:** Boat; shore. **Species:** Snook; redfish; tarpon; triple-tail; trout. **Guides:** Backcountry guides ($350 day 1 or 2 people) includes boat; guide; equipment. **Equipment:** Full service marina; boat rentals; rod and reel rentals; tackle shop.

ACCOMMODATIONS : Hotel rooms and suites ($95 double occupancy).

AMENITIES AND ACTIVITIES: Banquet facilities; 2 swimming pools; restaurants; lounge; canoe rentals; 6 tennis courts; fitness center; playground; volleyball court; horseshoe pit. Canoeing; Everglades nature cruises; golf; shelling; birding. **Places to Visit:** Everglades National Park; Fakahatchee Strand State Preserve; Old Marine Market Place at Tin City; Coral Isle Outlet factory; Collier Seminole State Park. Baby-sitting available with prior notice.

PAYMENT: MasterCard; Visa; Discover; American Express; cash.

GUEST COMMENTS: Rooms were: "comfortable and clean." Cooks "will prepare your catch your way—very well done." "My guide knew all about fishing and...area wildlife." "Marina staff very friendly and helpful." "...to see wildlife; Port of the Islands has the ultimate nature cruise." "Beautiful old style resort in the Everglades."

RAINBOW BEND FISHING RESORT

Guest Ratings

Room	🐟🐟🐟🐟
Staff	🐟🐟🐟🐟
Meals	🐟🐟🐟
Outside areas	🐟🐟🐟🐟
Fishing Guides	🐟🐟🐟🐟
Fishing Equipment	🐟🐟🐟🐟
Children's Activities	NA

57784 Overseas Hwy, MM 58 • Marathon, FL 33050
Phone: 800-929-1505 • fla-keys.com/marathon/accom/rainbow.htm
Email: rainbowbend@fla-keys.com

Resort Features

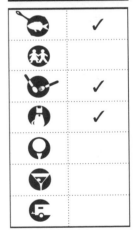

PRICE CATEGORY: $$

SEASON: Open all year.

TRANSPORTATION: Miami International Airport (1 1/2 hour drive). Marathon Airport (5 min.).

FISHING: Where: Atlantic Ocean; Gulf of Mexico. **Type:** Deep sea; fly casting; off shore reef; back country; flats. **How:** Walk and wade; boat. **Species:** Bone fish; snook; barracuda; tarpon; permit; lobster; shark; sailfish; yellowtail; dolphin; wahoo; red snapper; red mangrove; marlin. **Guides:** US Coast Guard licensed (start at $275 per 1/2 day) includes equipment and bait. **Equipment:** Bait and tackle shop; lighted dock; complimentary motor boat. **Insider's Tip:** "If you don't want to use a guide; or are put off by the cost; try fishing off the bridge (Seven Mile Bridge)."

ACCOMMODATIONS: Suites; cottages; efficiencies (start at $150 double occupancy) with fully equipped kitchens; includes 1/2 day motorboat; sailboat or canoe rental; complimentary breakfast.

AMENITIES AND ACTIVITIES: Jacuzzi; barbecue; gift shop; restaurant; cable color TV; swimming pool; beach. Scuba diving; swimming; snorkeling; biking; beach combing; birding; sand bar combing. **Places to Visit:** Sombrero Beach; Coco Plum Beach; Marathon Garden Club; Big Pine Key Flea Market.

PAYMENT: MasterCard; Visa; Discover; American Express; personal checks; cash.

GUEST COMMENTS: "Enjoyable and well managed." "Several different room options..." "...kept our room immaculately clean." Staff: "...helped us plan daily activities—fishing for my husband; snorkeling for the kids..." "Wide variety of fish species; both sport and eating..." "Guide; boat and equipment impeccable." "Good family place; tons to do both on the water and off." "Uncommon hospitality; quality service; varied fishing."

Guest Ratings

Room	🎣🎣🎣🎣
Staff	🎣🎣🎣🎣
Meals	🎣🎣🎣🎣
Outside areas	🎣🎣🎣🎣
Fishing Guides	🎣🎣🎣🎣
Fishing Equipment	🎣🎣🎣🎣
Children's Activities	🎣🎣🎣🎣

Resort Features

🐟	✓
👫	✓
🍴	✓
🎣	
🍷	✓
⚓	✓
🚐	

SOUTH SEAS PLANTATION

PO Box 194 • Captiva Island, FL 33924
Phone: 941-472-5111 • Reservations: 800-237-8482
www.ssrc.com

PRICE CATEGORY: $$

SEASON: Open all year, discounts offered May 26 - October 1.

TRANSPORTATION: Ft. Myers, FL (45 minute drive).

FISHING: Where: Pine Island Sound; Gulf of Mexico. **Type:** Spin casting; bait casting; fly casting. **How:** Boat; shore. **Species:** Snook; redfish; sea trout; snapper; grouper; shark; tarpon. **Guides:** Coast guard certified guides (start at $275 per half day) includes equipment. **Equipment:** Rod, reel rentals.

ACCOMMODATIONS: Hotel rooms; condominiums; private homes; villas (rates start at $145).

AMENITIES AND ACTIVITIES: 9 hole golf course; tennis courts; lounge; hot tub; 18 swimming pools; restaurants; full service marina; boat dockage. Sailing; snorkeling; golf; biking; family workshops; shelling; kayaking; canoeing. **Places to Visit:** Ding Darling Wildlife Refuge. All day structured "Kids Camp" featuring outdoor activities, crafts, games; baby-sitting available upon request.

PAYMENT: MasterCard; Visa; Discover; American Express; personal checks; cash.

GUEST COMMENTS: "Attractive; well appointed accommodations" "Most staff members are friendly but this is an absolutely huge resort. If you prefer small; intimate bed and breakfast type places—this isn't the place for you." "Every activity you could possibly imagine is available here; you'll never be bored." "Guide did a great job of teaching my wife; who was saltwater game fishing for the first time." "Phenomenal marina."

Guest Ratings

Room	🎣🎣🎣🎣
Staff	🎣🎣🎣🎣
Meals	🎣🎣🎣🎣
Outside areas	🎣🎣🎣🎣
Fishing Guides	🎣🎣🎣🎣
Fishing Equipment	🎣🎣🎣
Children's Activities	NA

Resort Features

🍳🐟	✓
👫	✓
🍴	
🏌	
🍸	✓
🍹	
🚐	

CALLAWAY GARDENS

PO Box 2000 • Pine Mountain, GA 31822-2000
Phone: 706-663-2281 • Reservations: 800 - CALLAWAY • Fax: 706-663-5068
www.callawaygardens.com • Email address: info@callawaygardens.com

PRICE CATEGORY: $$ – $$$$

SEASON: Open all year.

TRANSPORTATION: Atlanta's Hartsfield International Airport (1 hour).

FISHING: Where: Mountain Creek Lake and 12 smaller ponds. **Type:** Fly fishing; spin casting. **How:** Float tubes; boat; shore. **Species:** Bluegill, largemouth bass, shell cracker, rainbow trout, catfish and redbreast. **Guide:** Starts at $275 per day/one or two people (lunch)). **Equipment:** Fully equipped tackle bags, fishing boats, rods/reels available. **Instruction:** Two day fly fishing schools (starting at $150 per person, (lunch). Kids under 16 with an adult half price. Individual and group fly casting lessons (start at $40 per hour).

ACCOMMODATIONS: Standard hotel rooms (start at $96 double occupancy); 2-4 bedroom villas with fully equipped kitchen, washer, dryer, porch, patio, sundeck; separate bath for each bedroom ($280 per night 1-4 people).

AMENITIES AND ACTIVITIES: Baby-sitting arranged upon request. **Places to Visit:** Mr. Cason's Vegetable Garden (southern filming site for PBS's "The Victory Garden); Cecil B. Day Butterfly Center; Ida Cason Callaway Memorial Chapel.

PAYMENT: MasterCard, Visa, American Express, personal checks and cash.

GUEST COMMENTS: "Challenging fly fishing." "Guide was good; down to earth teacher..." "Rental boats in perfect condition..." "Tackle bags had most of the equipment we needed." " Where else can you go fishing before breakfast; play nine holes of golf and visit North America's largest collection of tropical butterflies all in one day?"

THE LODGE ON LITTLE ST. SIMON'S ISLAND

PO Box 21078 • Little St. Simon's Island, GA 31522
Phone: 912-638-7472 • Fax: 912-634-1881
www.pactel.com.au/lssi • Email: lssi@mindspring.com

Guest Ratings

Room	🎣🎣🎣
Staff	🎣🎣🎣
Meals	🎣🎣🎣
Outside areas	🎣🎣🎣
Fishing Guides	🎣🎣🎣
Fishing Equipment	🎣🎣🎣
Children's Activities	NA

Resort Features

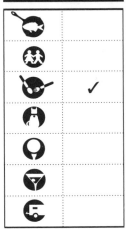

🐟	
🤼	
🍳	✓
🏇	
♀	
▽	
🎿	

PRICE CATEGORY: $$$$

SEASON: Open all year; discounts offered July through September.

TRANSPORTATION: Commercial flights Savannah, GA or Jacksonville, FL. Airport shuttle arrangements can be made through the lodge. Lodge accessible only by boat (complimentary transportation arranged through lodge).

FISHING: Where: Atlantic Ocean; Altamaha River; Hampton River. **Type:** Bait or spin casting; salt water fly fishing; surfcast. **How:** Wade; boat; shore. **Species:** Sea, speckled trout; amberjack; redfish; flounder; shark; tarpon. **Guides:** Orvis endorsed guides ($100 per person/per day.) **Equipment:** Bait and tackle complimentary to all guests. **Instruction:** Weekend fly fishing schools, fall. **Insider's Tip:** Fly fishing is best mid-August—early November. Peak time to surfcast for red fish is mid-September through mid-October

ACCOMMODATIONS: 13 private rooms w/baths in 5 cottages: fireplaces; air conditioning; screened porches ($385+ per night double occupancy, 3 meals).

AMENITIES AND ACTIVITIES: Swimming pool; washer; dryer; canoes; skiffs. Naturalist programs; "Summer Fun for Families" program; biking; hiking; guided nature walks; bird watching; horseback riding; fly tying classes; slide shows.

PAYMENT: MasterCard; Visa; personal check; cash.

GUEST COMMENTS: "Expertly operated..." "excellent staff and good mix of guests..." "Informative naturalist program" "...appreciate the off season rate that makes it possible for me..." "The beauty of the island is what I love; the live oaks; moss; magnolias; marshes and pines."

Guest Ratings

Room	♦♦♦♦
Staff	♦♦♦
Meals	♦♦♦♦
Outside areas	♦♦♦♦
Fishing Guides	♦♦♦♦
Fishing Equipment	NA
Children's Activities	♦♦♦♦

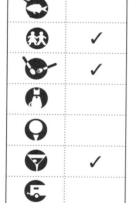

Resort Features

🐟	
👫	✓
🍴	✓
▽	✓
⑤	

KONA VILLAGE RESORT

PO Box 1299 • Kailua-Kona, HA 96745
Phone: 808-325-5555 • Fax: 808-325-0206
www.konavillage.com • Email: kvr@aloha.net

PRICE CATEGORY: $$$$

SEASON: Open all year.

TRANSPORTATION: Keahole International Airport. (10 minute drive).

FISHING: Where: Pacific Ocean. **Type:** Deep seas fishing; surfcasting. **How:** Boat. **Species:** Marlin; swordfish; tuna; dolphin; wahoo. **Guides:** US Coast Guard Licensed guides ($350 per half day/up to six people) includes bait; tackle; instruction. **Insider's Tip:** "Mild weather; wear sunscreen while fishing."

ACCOMMODATIONS : Individual thatched bungalows include meals and activities ($425 double occupancy).

AMENITIES AND ACTIVITIES: Hot tub; sauna; pool; restaurant; kayaks; fitness center; tennis courts. Supervised kids day camp: "Keikis in Paradise." Snorkeling; kayaking; sunfish sailing; boogie boarding; glass bottom boat tours; scuba diving; golf. **Places to Visit:** Volcano National Park; Waipio Valley; Coffee Plantations.

PAYMENT: MasterCard; Visa; American Express; personal checks; cash.

GUEST COMMENTS: "While sea kayaking I found myself in the middle of a pod of dolphin." "Large resort; personalized service is hard to accomplish." "For my money; snorkeling was better than the boat trip." "The excitement of hooking an occasional papio is equally matched by the serenity of just sitting on my rock."

Guest Ratings

Room	🐟🐟🐟🐟
Staff	🐟🐟🐟🐟
Meals	🐟🐟🐟🐟
Outside areas	🐟🐟🐟🐟
Fishing Guides	NA
Fishing Equipment	NA
Children's Activities	NA

Resort Features

🐟	✓
👫	
🍴	
🎣	
⛏	
⛵	
🚐	✓

JARED'S WILD ROSE RANCH RESORT

HC 66, Box 140 • Island Park, ID 83429
Phone: 208-558-7201 • Fax: 208-558-7083
www.wildrose.com

PRICE CATEGORY: $

SEASON: Open all year. Fishing season is Memorial Day through October 31.

TRANSPORTATION: Idaho Falls, ID (2 hour drive.) West Yellowstone, MT (15 minutes).

FISHING: Where: Henry's Lake; Henry's Fork River; Quake Lake; Hebgen Lake; Madison River; Snake River. **Type:** Bait, spin, fly casting; trolling with bait; fly rods and spinners. **How:** Walk and wade; boat; shore. **Guides:** Local guides ($125 per person/day). **Species:** Cutthroat, hybrid, brook trout. **Equipment:** Boat/motor rentals; tackle shop; boat slips; fish cleaning station. **Insider's Tip:** "Not much bank fishing; try fly casting into weed beds with fast sinking line." Peak fishing: late September and October.

ACCOMMODATIONS: Cabins ($55 and up double occupancy); Condominiums equipped with kitchens ($105 and up double occupancy); RV sites ($20 double occupancy); tent sites ($14 double occupancy).

AMENITIES AND ACTIVITIES: Banquet room; laundry; RV and camp bathrooms; restaurant; arcade; theater; hot tub; convenience store; gas; snowmobile rentals. Horseback riding; dinner theater; golf; hiking; wildlife viewing; photography; snowmobiling. **Places to Visit:** Yellowstone National Park; Henry's Lake Fish Hatchery.

PAYMENT: MasterCard; Visa; Discover; cash.

GUEST COMMENTS: "Centrally located...lot of different places to fish..." "Wonderful staff; management is working hard to upgrade...doing a great job." "Some rooms brand new...great view" "Boat dock basic but in good shape." "We keep coming back for the excellent location; wonderful fishing, relaxed atmosphere."

SOUTH FORK LODGE AND FLOAT TRIPS

PO Box 22 • Swan Valley, ID 83449
Phone: 208-483-2112
www.ohwy.com/id/s/southfkl.html • EMail: southforklodge@internetmci.com

PRICE CATEGORY: $ - $$$

SEASON: Memorial Day weekend through November 30th. 10% Discount October and November.

TRANSPORTATION: Idaho Falls, ID (1 hour drive); Jackson Hole, WY (1 1/2 hour drive).

FISHING: Where: South Fork of the Snake River. **Type:** Fly casting; spin casting. **How:** Walk and wade; boat; shore. **Species:** Brown; cutthroat; rainbow; cut-bow hybrid trout. **Guides:** IOGA guides included with package. Non-package guide service ($335 per day for 1 or 2 people) includes lunch. **Equipment:** Loaned to full package guests at no additional cost.

ACCOMMODATIONS: Lodge rooms (start at $675 for 3 nights/ 2 days) includes guided fishing; 3 meals; welcome drink.

AMENITIES AND ACTIVITIES: RV sites; tent sites. Lounge; fly shop; restaurant. Hiking; photography; river rafting; boating; hunting. **Places to Visit:** Palisades Reservoir.

PAYMENT: MasterCard; Visa; American Express; Discover; personal checks; cash.

GUEST COMMENTS: "Immaculate facility." "Everyone went out of their way to make sure we had a good time." "My guide took two greenhorns and had us fly fishing in no time...that I reeled in seven of those beauties attests to his skill." Another guide: "taught me at least five different casting techniques; three fishing styles...helped me get a "South Fork Slam—...one each brown; rainbow and cutthroat."

Guest Ratings

Room	🐟🐟🐟🐟
Staff	🐟🐟🐟🐟
Meals	🐟🐟🐟🐟
Outside areas	🐟🐟🐟
Fishing Guides	🐟🐟🐟🐟
Fishing Equipment	🐟🐟🐟🐟
Children's Activities	NA

Resort Features

🍳	
👪	
🍴	✓
🔧	
🎣	
⛵	✓
🚐	✓

151

Guest Ratings

Room	
Staff	
Meals	
Outside areas	
Fishing Guides	
Fishing Equipment	NA
Children's Activities	NA

ST. JOE HUNTING AND FISHING CAMP

HC 01, Box 109 A • St. Maries, ID 83861
Phone: 208-245-4002

Resort Features

	✓

PRICE CATEGORY: $$$

SEASON: Late June through September.

TRANSPORTATION: Missoula, MT (2 1/2 hour drive). Spokane; WA (3 1/2 hour drive.) The camp is accessible via horseback only (included).

FISHING: Where: St. Joe River. **Type:** fly casting; catch and release only; artificial flies or lures with single barbless hook. **How:** Walk and wade. **Guides:** Orvis endorsed fly fishing guides ($150 for 1-2 people). **Insider's tip:** Fishing guides must be hired in advance; bring sleeping bag; fishing equipment/ license.

ACCOMMODATIONS: 2 cabins; each with 4 single beds; wood stove ($800 per person for 4 days/3 nights) includes meals; lodging; transportation from and to trailhead (saddle horse and pack horse); trail guide. Guided fly fishing add $75 per day.

AMENITIES AND ACTIVITIES: Hunting (in season); hiking; wildlife viewing; overnight camping trips; pack trips.

PAYMENT: Personal checks; cash.

GUEST COMMENTS: "St. Joe Camp is rustic; but very comfortable. Fishing is very good...westslope cutthroats are outstanding fighters." "Not for those who seek Holiday Inns." "Food was great and plentiful." "One of the last wilderness experiences in the...US; along one of the last great rivers; with native trout in an uncorrupted state. Like stepping back in time."

THE LODGE AT PALISADES CREEK

PO Box 70 • Irwin, ID 83428
Phone: 208-483-2222 • Fax: 208-483-2227
www.webfactor.com/thelodge • E-mail: palisade@micron.net

PRICE CATEGORY: $$$ – $$$$

SEASON: June 7 through October 10.

TRANSPORTATION: Idaho Falls, ID (45 minute drive). Jackson Hole, WY (1 hour drive).

FISHING: Where: South Fork of the Snake River; Henry's Fork; Teton River. **Type:** Fly casting. **How:** Boat. **Species:** Rainbow trout; cutthroat trout; brown trout. **Guides:** Included in fishing packages or hired on daily basis ($350 per day for 1 or 2) includes boat; guide; lunch. **Equipment:** Fly casting equipment available for rent.

ACCOMMODATIONS: Private log cabins; 3 meals included. One week fishing package includes meals; accommodations and guided fishing ($2150 per person.) Non fishing guests $210 per day. Outside dining deck; dining room; lounge.

AMENITIES AND ACTIVITIES: Hiking; photography. **Places to Visit:** Caribou National Forest; Targhee National Forest; Grand Teton National Park; Yellowstone National Park.

PAYMENT: MasterCard; Visa; personal checks; cash.

GUEST COMMENTS: "Not much to say, the cabins, staff, fishing and meals were all perfect." "Comfortable cabins for privacy and lounge for socializing." "Staff was more than accomodating, they were professionals who knew how to honor my requests." "Guide really knew his stuff...read the water, explained the area's entomology and was very personable." "Scenery out of this world, the perfect backdrop for incredible fishing."

Guest Ratings

Room	🐟🐟🐟🐟
Staff	🐟🐟🐟🐟
Meals	🐟🐟🐟
Outside areas	🐟🐟🐟🐟
Fishing Guides	🐟🐟🐟
Fishing Equipment	🐟🐟🐟
Children's Activities	NA

Resort Features

153

Guest Ratings

Room	🐟🐟🐟
Staff	🐟🐟🐟🐟
Meals	🐟🐟🐟🐟
Outside areas	🐟🐟🐟🐟
Fishing Guides	🐟🐟🐟🐟
Fishing Equipment	🐟🐟🐟
Children's Activities	NA

Resort Features

🐟	
👪	
🍴	✓
🍼	
⚇	
🍸	
🚐	

WAPITI MEADOW RANCH

HC 72 • Cascade, ID 83611
Phone: 208-633-3217 • Fax: 208-633-3219
E-mail: wapitimr@aol.com

PRICE CATEGORY: $$ – $$$$

SEASON: Open year round

TRANSPORTATION: Boise, ID (2 1/2 hour drive).

FISHING: Where: Middle Fork Salmon River; South Fork Salmon River; Salmon River Watershed; high mountain lakes. **Type:** Fly casting; spin casting. **How:** Wade; walk; float tubes. **Species:** Cutthroat; rainbow; brook; bull trout. **Guides:** Orvis trained guides, instruction included with fishing packages or $125 per day add-on to riding packages. **Equipment:** Orvis rods/reels with fly casting package; spin casting equipment rentals.

ACCOMMODATIONS: 1 or 2 bedroom private cabins with full bath, baseboard heat, wood stove, stocked refrigerator, coffee maker. Fly fishing package; includes guided fishing; meals; lodging; horseback riding; equipment; $1980 for 6 nights. Lodging and meals only starts at $660 for 6 nights.

AMENITIES AND ACTIVITIES:. Hot tub; horseshoe pit; basketball court; tackle shop; campfire ring; trout pond; great room; library; board games; hiking; volleyball; cross country skiing; snowmobiling; horseback riding; gold panning; 4 x 4 sightseeing; wildlife viewing; pack trips; bird watching; river rafting; pine cone collecting; hunting. **Places to Visit:** Rainbow Lake; Riordan Lake; Rainbow Peak; Thunder Mountain Gold Mines; ghost town of Cinnabar.

PAYMENT: Personal checks; cash.

GUEST COMMENTS: On the resort survey, several guests drew extra boxes labeled "better than excellent" or "superb." Meals were "excellent and hearty," even "too much." "Guides made a great effort to get us into fish" and went "above and beyond the call of duty," "fantastic fishing."

ANTHONY ACRES RESORT

PO Box 1371 • Effingham, IL 62401
Phone: 217-868-2950

Guest Ratings

Room	♦♦♦♦
Staff	♦♦♦♦
Meals	NA
Outside areas	♦♦♦♦
Fishing Guides	NA
Fishing Equipment	NA
Children's Activities	NA

PRICE CATEGORY: $

SEASON: Open early April through early November.

TRANSPORTATION: St. Louis; MO (1 hour drive).

FISHING: Where: Lake Sara. **Type:** Bait casting; spin casting; trolling; bobber. **How:** Boat; shore. **Species:** Largemouth bass; walleye; crappie; bluegill; catfish. **Guide Service:** Unavailable. **Equipment:** Boat dock; fish cleaning room; boat and motor rentals; bait shop. **Insider's Tip:** "I'd recommend chicken livers for the channel cats."

ACCOMMODATIONS: Housekeeping units ($62 and up double occupancy; children under 6 free) includes fully equipped kitchen; all linens.

AMENITIES AND ACTIVITIES: Private gradual sand beach; playground; game room; convenience store. Golf; outlet shopping; movie theater. pontoon rentals; basketball; tetherball; badminton; horseshoes; shuffleboard; volleyball.

PAYMENT: MasterCard; Visa; personal checks; cash.

GUEST COMMENTS: "Lovely quiet area." "Rooms are neat and tidy." "..well stocked kitchen; all the appliances worked." Staff: "made me feel at home." "like to talk fish and fishing techniques." "The catfishing is extra good." "...dock area is...accessible...well maintained." "...reasonably priced...lots of extras for the whole family."

Resort Features

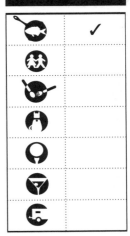

Guest Ratings

Room	🐟🐟🐟🐟
Staff	🐟🐟🐟🐟
Meals	🐟🐟🐟🐟
Outside areas	🐟🐟🐟🐟
Fishing Guides	NA
Fishing Equipment	🐟🐟🐟
Children's Activities	🐟🐟🐟🐟

Resort Features

🐟	✓
👪	✓
🍴	
🎣	
🍸	✓
⛵	✓
🎰	

EAGLE RIDGE INN AND RESORT

Box 777 • Galena, IL 61036
Phone: 815-777-2444 • Fax: 815-777-0445
www.eagleridge.com • Email: eri@galcuetink

PRICE CATEGORY: $$ – $$$$

SEASON: Open all year.

TRANSPORTATION: Chicago, IL (2 hour drive).

FISHING: Where: Galena Lake; Mississippi River. **Type:** Spin casting; bait casting. **How:** Boat; shore. **Species:** Smallmouth bass; perch; bluegill; catfish; crappie; rainbow trout; tiger muskie. **Guides:** Experienced guides ($125 per half day). **Equipment:** Fishing licenses; tackle; boat and motor rentals; marina. **Insider's Tip:** Recommended baits include nightcrawlers; wax worms; leeches; leaf worms; minnow and red worms.

ACCOMMODATIONS Inn rooms ($145 and up double occupancy); 1-3 bedroom villas ($170 and up); 3-5 bedroom homes ($290 and up).

AMENITIES AND ACTIVITIES Conference space; golf course; hiking/biking trails; 4 tennis courts; exercise room; massage therapist; sauna; stables. Extensive kids day camp program. Babysitting available. Hiking; biking; swimming; antiquing; horseback riding; golf; ice skating; cross country skiing. **Places to Visit:** Historic homes; Whistling Wings (largest mallard duck hatchery in the world); Galena Cellars Winery; Riverboat Casino.

PAYMENT: MasterCard; Visa; American Express; cash.

GUEST COMMENTS: "Eagle Ridge can't really be categorized as a fishing destination. However; Lake Galena...ideal...to get in some early morning fishing... while others in your party are happily occupied elsewhere at this exceptional resort." "Impressive..." "Great...hiking." "...never been so pampered." "Buffets; meals and snacks...excellent." "...well maintained dock area." "Outstanding variety of activities...quiet fishing."

Guest Ratings

Room	🐟🐟🐟🐟
Staff	🐟🐟🐟🐟
Meals	🐟🐟🐟🐟
Outside areas	🐟🐟🐟🐟
Fishing Guides	🐟🐟🐟🐟
Fishing Equipment	🐟🐟🐟
Children's Activities	NA

Resort Features

🍳🐟	✓
👪	✓
🍳	
⛄	
♀	
▽	
🅕	✓

BIG BEAR RESORT AND MARINA

30 Big Bear Resort Rd. • Benton, KY 42025
Phone: 502-354-6414 • Reservations: 800-922-BEAR • Fax: 502-354-9092
www.bigbearkentuckylake.com • Email: BigBearResort@Juno.com

PRICE CATEGORY: $-$$

SEASON: Open all year.

TRANSPORTATION: Nashville, TN (2-hour drive). Paducah, KY (30 minute drive).

FISHING: Where: Kentucky Lake; Lake Barkley; Ohio River. **Type:** Bait casting; fly casting; spin casting. **How:** Boat; shore. **Species:** Largemouth, smallmouth, white bass; crappie; bluegill; catfish; perch; sauger; rockfish. **Guides:** Licensed; insured guides ($125 per person/per day and up) includes tackle; gas; fish cleaning. **Equipment:** Covered boat slips; boat and motor rentals; tackle; fuel.

ACCOMMODATIONS: Condominiums ($338.31 per day/up to 8 people); town-houses ($158.63 double occupancy); standard motel rooms ($60 double occupancy); cottages ($102.12 per day/ up to 8 people); full RV hook-ups ($21.63 up to 4 people); camp site ($13.39 up to 4 people).

AMENITIES AND ACTIVITIES: Structured kids recreation program 7 days a week Memorial Day through Labor Day. Baby-sitting available. Grocery and gift shop; swimming pool; game room; laundromat; volleyball courts; basketball courts; rentals: pontoon; ski boat; paddle boat; skis; tube; ski chariot. Boating; biking; skiing; golf. **Places to Visit:** National Boy Scout Museum; Land Between the Lakes Wildlife Management Area; Riverboat Casino; Mammoth Cave; Nashville (2 hours).

PAYMENT: MasterCard; Visa; Discover; American Express; personal checks; cash.

GUEST COMMENTS : Overall: "...clean;" "very attractive;" "well managed." Staff: "always willing to satisfy." "While everything isn't perfect every minute this resort tries hard to make you feel at home." "Campground is well maintained ...toilets and showers are very clean," "marina is well equipped and staffed with an exceptionally knowledgeable staff..." "Always a relaxing and friendly atmosphere."

GREEN TURTLE BAY RESORT

PO Box 102 • Grand Rivers, KY 42045
Phone: 502-362-8364 • Reservations: 800-498-0428 • Fax: 502-362-4119
KentuckyLake.com/gtb/index.htm • Email: gtb@apex.net

Guest Ratings

Room	🎣🎣🎣🎣
Staff	🎣🎣🎣🎣
Meals	🎣🎣🎣🎣
Outside areas	🎣🎣🎣🎣
Fishing Guides	🎣🎣🎣
Fishing Equipment	🎣🎣🎣🎣
Children's Activities	NA

Resort Features

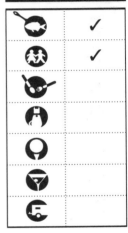

PRICE CATEGORY: $$

SEASON: Open all year; discounts offered November 1 through April 15.

TRANSPORTATION: Nashville, TN (2 hour drive).

FISHING: Where: Kentucky Lake; Tennessee River; Lake Barkley; Cumberland River. **Type:** Trolling; spin casting; bait casting; fly casting. **How:** Walk and wade; boat; shore. **Species:** Catfish; bass; striped bass; crappie; bluegill; spoonbill; sunfish. **Guides:** Local guides available including wheelchair accessible boat; ($150 per person for full day) includes boat; gas; tackle. **Equipment:** Full service marina; covered, padded dock; Yacht sales and service; dry stack storage; fish cleaning house; tackle shop; boat fuel; boat dockage to 70 feet.

ACCOMMODATIONS: Condominiums and townhouses with fully equipped kitchens ($110 per night; double occupancy).

AMENITIES AND ACTIVITIES: Swimming pool; tennis; activity center; picnic area; boat rentals; houseboat rentals; playground. Swimming; sailing lessons; golf course; boating. Baby-sitting available with advance notice. **Places to Visit:** Land Between the Lakes Recreation Area; Water Park; Hunter Moon Festival (2nd Weekend in October).

PAYMENT: MasterCard; Visa; American Express; cash.

GUEST COMMENTS: "Great all around resort...on a quiet bay that's perfect for fishermen." Condominiums: "exceptionally clean;" "picture perfect;" Staff "went all out to make our vacation great." "Incredible dock area." "...I didn't hesitate to trust my boat to these facilities." Guide: "knew where to find the fish." "Lot's of different activities." "Great place to enjoy the out of doors without roughing it."

159

Guest Ratings

Room	🐟🐟🐟🐟
Staff	🐟🐟🐟🐟
Meals	NA
Outside areas	🐟🐟🐟🐟
Fishing Guides	NA
Fishing Equipment	🐟🐟🐟🐟
Children's Activities	NA

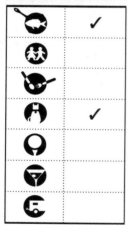

Resort Features

🍳	✓
🧒	
🥘	
🍸	✓
🎾	
⛳	
🎱	

HESTER'S SPOT IN THE SUN

3500 Hester's Rd. • Benton, KY 42025
Phone: 502-354-8280 Reservations: 800-455-7481

PRICE CATEGORY: $

SEASON: Open all year.

TRANSPORTATION: Nashville, TN (2 hour drive).

FISHING: Where: Kentucky Lake; Lake Barkley. **Type:** Fly casting; spin casting; bait casting. **How:** Boat; shore. **Species:** Largemouth, smallmouth, white bass; catfish; crappie; blue gill. **Guides:** Local guides (start at $175 per day, 1 or 2 people) w/boat; bait. **Equipment:** Small tackle shop; covered boat slips; boat and motor rental.

ACCOMMODATIONS 2 and 3 bedroom cottages ($90 and up) with fully equipped kitchen; linens; color TV; air conditioning; picnic table; grill.

AMENITIES AND ACTIVITIES: Pontoon rental; basketball court; tennis court; horseshoes; golf; boating; antiquing; horseback riding; hiking. **Places to Visit:** Land Between the Lakes National Park; Fort Donelson National Park; Home Place; Players Riverboat Casino; Kentucky Dam.

PAYMENT: MasterCard; Visa; personal check; cash.

GUEST COMMENTS: "Small; clean...well managed resort with very good fishing," "quiet' "no-nonsense" with a "good; convenient layout." Staff: "quietly efficient and helpful." "Just sign you in and leave you alone; but always available ...Exactly the kind of resort I like," "place to relax and get away from it all."

HICKORY HILL RESORT

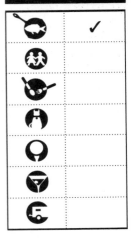

Guest Ratings

Room	🎣🎣🎣
Staff	🎣🎣🎣🎣
Meals	NA
Outside areas	🎣🎣🎣🎣
Fishing Guides	NA
Fishing Equipment	🎣🎣🎣🎣
Children's Activities	NA

90 Hickory Hill Lane • Benton, KY 42025
Phone: 502-354-8207 • Reservations: 800-280-4455
E-mail: kyresort@apex.net

PRICE CATEGORY: $-$$

SEASON: Open all year. 15% discount offered in March.

TRANSPORTATION: Nashville, TN (2 1/2 hour drive).

FISHING: Where: Kentucky Lake; Barkley Lake. **Type:** Spin casting; bait casting. **How:** Boat; shore. **Species:** Crappie; smallmouth, largemouth, white bass; catfish; bluegill; sauger. **Guides:** Professional, licensed guides (start at $145 per half day for 1 or 2 persons) w/ boat; bait; filleting. **Equipment:** Small tackle shop on premises.

ACCOMMODATIONS : 2, 3, 4 and 6 bedroom cottages with air conditioning; linens; fully equipped kitchen; (microwave; toaster; coffee pot) TV; VCR; radio; charcoal grill; picnic table (Start at $145 for 1 to 5 people).

ACTIVITIES AND EXTRAS: Basketball court; badminton; game room; horseshoes; shuffleboard; 2 playgrounds; swim float with slide; swimming pool; covered boat dock; freezer service; fish cleaning house; boat and motor rental; concrete launch ramp. Golf; boating; hiking; photography; wildlife viewing. **Places to Visit:** Land Between the Lakes; Woodlands Nature Center; Planetarium; Home Place.

PAYMENT: Visa; MasterCard; Discover; cash.

GUEST COMMENTS: Cabins: "very clean," kitchens "supplied all the necessities...". "...staff and owners will bend over backwards to make sure you have a good time." "Minnows and ice are available even after hours." "Great guide explained lake and fishing techniques..." "If you want to relax and fish and be treated like royalty this is the place..."

Resort Features

🐟	✓
👥	
🍴	
🔧	
🔍	
⛵	
🚐	

Guest Ratings

Room	♦♦♦♦
Staff	♦♦♦♦
Meals	NA
Outside areas	♦♦♦♦
Fishing Guides	NA
Fishing Equipment	♦♦♦♦
Children's Activities	NA

Resort Features

🐟	✓
👪	
🍳	
🍶	
◯	
▽	
🚐	

PARADISE RESORT

1024 Paradise Drive • Murray, KY 42071
Phone: 502-436-2767 • Reservations: 800-340-2767
www.angelfire.com/il/fotoz/valarie.html • Email: paradise@ldd.net

PRICE CATEGORY: $

SEASON: Open all year.

TRANSPORTATION: Nashville, TN (2 hour drive).

FISHING: Where: Kentucky Lake, Lake Barkley. **Type:** Bait, spin, fly casting; trolling. **How:** Boat; shore; dock; wade. **Species:** Largemouth, smallmouth, striped, white bass; crappie; sauger; channel catfish; red ear sunfish; bluegill. **Guides:** Local guides ($165 per person/day). **Equipment:** Tackle shop; covered dock; boat rentals; boat ramp; fuel; fishing licenses available. **Insider's Tip:** Crappie are taken on minnows and jigs along creek channels as they migrate; or around brush in shallow coves. Catch bass on crankbaits and spinnerbaits early in the spring. "Try fishing deep with chicken livers for catfish."

ACCOMMODATIONS: Cabins and condominiums with fully equipped kitchens; linens included (start at $60 per night double occupancy).

AMENITIES AND ACTIVITIES: Swimming pool; beach; playground; practice tennis court; horseshoes; badminton court; satellite TV; campfire pits; laundry. Boating; golf; hiking and biking trails; antiquing; sailing; skiing; bald eagle tours; horseback riding. **Places to Visit:** Land Between the Lakes; National Scouting Museum; Playhouse in the Park; Murray State University; Golden Pond Planetarium; 1880's Home Place.

PAYMENT: MasterCard; Visa; Discover; personal checks; cash.

GUEST COMMENTS: Cottage: "very clean;" with "well equipped kitchens." "Wonderful staff..." "...if one kind of fish isn't biting; another...is." "Crappie fishing is great in the spring; unbeatable." "The rental boats; dock area is clean; safe and well-maintained." "...Fish early in the morning or at night and go skiing and boating with your family during the day." "I always leave feeling refreshed and relaxed."

Guest Ratings

Room	🐟🐟🐟🐟
Staff	🐟🐟🐟🐟
Meals	🐟🐟🐟
Outside areas	🐟🐟🐟🐟
Fishing Guides	🐟🐟🐟🐟
Fishing Equipment	NA
Children's Activities	NA

Resort Features

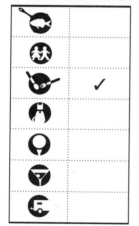

🐟	
👥	
🍳	✓
🔧	
⚓	
🍸	
🚐	

BOSEBUCK MOUNTAIN CAMPS

PO Box 1213 • Rangeley, ME 04970
Phone: 207-474-5903 • Fax: 207-474-5460

PRICE CATEGORY: $$

SEASON: May 15 through October 1.

TRANSPORTATION: Portland, ME (4 hour drive).

FISHING: Where: Megalloway River (designated trophy trout waters by state of Maine); Aziscohos Lake; Parmachenee Lake. **Type:** Fly casting; trolling. **How:** Walk and wade; boat. **Species:** Brook trout; landlocked salmon. **Guides:** Maine registered, $100 per person/day w/boat/tackle. **Insider's Tip:** Best streamer fishing May-September; dry fly fishing hatches peak, June. Recommend caddis; green drake, hoppers.

ACCOMMODATIONS: Rustic lakefront cabins that sleep from 2-6 people ($88 per person per day) includes 3 meals; private baths in cabins. Library and dining room in main lodge.

AMENITIES AND ACTIVITIES: Hunting packages; hiking; wildlife; canoeing.

PAYMENT: MasterCard; Visa; personal check; cash.

GUEST COMMENTS: "Incredible wilderness. Very remote but good vehicle access." "Many loons." "Clean; very basic cabins and accommodating staff." "Good photography opportunities during fall foliage times." "Fishing was very good." "Outstanding fly fishing for brook trout and landlocked salmon." "Caught a brook trout that measured in at 17 inches with brilliant spawning colors."

FROST POND CAMPS

Guest Ratings

Room	🐟🐟🐟
Staff	🐟🐟🐟🐟
Meals	NA
Outside areas	🐟🐟🐟
Fishing Guides	🐟🐟🐟
Fishing Equipment	NA
Children's Activities	NA

Box 620, Star Route 76 • Greenville, ME 04441
Phone: 207-723-6622 • Radio: 207-695-2821
www.maineguide.com/katahdin/frostpond

Resort Features

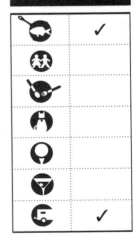

🐟	✔
👫	
🍳	
🔨	
💡	
🍸	
🔥	✔

PRICE CATEGORY: $

SEASON: May through November.

TRANSPORTATION: Bangor, ME (3 hour drive).

FISHING: Where: Frost Pond; Little Frost Pond; Chesuncook Lake; West Branch of the Penobscot River; Harrington Lake. **Type:** Fly casting; spin casting. **How:** Boat; shore. **Species:** Brook trout; landlocked salmon; lake trout. **Equipment:** Boat rentals; motor rentals; canoe rentals; dock. **Insider's Tip:** Best times: mid May through June or September; fly fishing best in June. "Try light colored Hendrickson dry flies size 12 or 14 and blue wing olives for trout." "Use streamers; Hendrickson and blue wing olive dry flies for land locked salmon."

ACCOMMODATIONS: Cabins with gas lights; full size stove/oven; wood stove; linens; hot showers available in separate building; with plumbing ($26 per person/night); without plumbing ($23.50 per person/night); campsite; primitive RV ($15 per night).

AMENITIES AND ACTIVITIES: Picnic table; swing set; sandbox; hunting; hiking; canoeing. **Places to Visit:** Baxter State Park.

PAYMENT: Personal checks; cash.

GUEST COMMENTS: "Cabins are very nice; warm." "Must bring own drinking water to some cabins...heat water on the stove to do dishes." "Outhouses very clean." "Shower houses...clean...lots of hot water." "Fishing on lake is great; no trash fish." "Hatches are tremendous," "Black flies can be a problem; Deep Woods OFF and/or netting works for us." "Just talk to fishing buddies and listen to the loons."

Guest Ratings

Room	♦♦♦
Staff	♦♦♦♦
Meals	NA
Outside areas	♦♦♦♦
Fishing Guides	♦♦♦♦
Fishing Equipment	♦♦♦
Children's Activities	NA

Resort Features

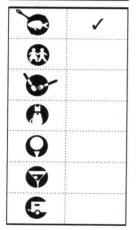

🍳	✓

GREAT POND WILDERNESS LODGE AND SPORTING CAMPS

RR 2, Box 482 • Eddington, ME 04428
Phone: 207-745-6728

PRICE CATEGORY: $

SEASON: Open all year.

TRANSPORTATION: Bangor, ME (1 hour drive).

FISHING: Where: Great Pond; Alligator Lake; Union River; Machias River; Penobscot River. **Type:** Bait casting; spin casting; fly casting; ice fishing. **How:** Boat; shore; walk and wade. **Species:** Smallmouth bass; brown trout; pickerel; brook trout; salmon. **Guides:** $100 per person per day, lunch. Canoe trips include all equipment. **Equipment:** Boat and motor rentals; small tackle shop. **Instruction:** Available. **Insider's Tip:** Bring daredevil and rapala lures; royal coachman and muddler minnow flies.

ACCOMMODATIONS: Cabins with gas cookstove; gas lights; cooking and eating utensils; central toilet and shower house (starts at $40 double occupancy); ice fishing shacks.

AMENITIES AND ACTIVITIES: Canoeing; private sand beach; hunting; cross country skiing; hiking; canoe camping. **Places to Visit:** Acadia National Park; Penobscot Indian Museum.

PAYMENT: Personal checks; cash.

GUEST COMMENTS: "Beautiful; quiet; serene and on top of that the fishing is good." "We were looking for rustic...deep in the woods and away from everything except nature. These cabins filled the bill; yet some...had modern conveniences." "Owners included us in their personal camp fire activities and made us feel like 'old' guests." "The fishing was amazing; caught a lot." "No noise; no hussle; no bussle. Just peace and fish."

HARRISON'S PIERCE POND SPORTING CAMPS

PO Box 315 • Bingham, ME 04920
Phone: 207-672-3625 • Winter: 603-524-0560 or 603-279-8424

Guest Ratings

Room	🎣🎣🎣🎣
Staff	🎣🎣🎣🎣
Meals	🎣🎣🎣🎣🎣
Outside areas	🎣🎣🎣
Fishing Guides	NA
Fishing Equipment	NA
Children's Activities	NA

Resort Features

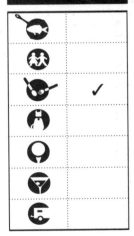

🐟	
👫	
🍳	✓
🔧	
☮	
🔻	
🚐	

PRICE CATEGORY: $$

SEASON: May through October.

TRANSPORTATION: Bangor (2 hour drive); Portland (2 hours).

FISHING: Where: Pierce Pond; 6 satellite ponds within walking distance; Pierce Pond Stream. **Type:** Fly fishing artificial lures only. **How:** Walk and wade; shore; boat. **Species:** Land locked salmon; brook trout. **Guides:** Guides are available with advance notice. **Equipment:** Boat rentals.

ACCOMMODATIONS : Log cabins with heated restroom/shower houses ($52 per day/person) includes all meals. Generator powered main lodge and dining room; canoe rentals.

AMENITIES AND ACTIVITIES: Hiking; boating; canoeing; swimming; birding.

PAYMENT: Personal checks; cash.

GUEST COMMENTS: "Great wilderness retreat." "Not a fancy lodge but it is tidy and very comfortable; the staff is excellent." "Owners couldn't be friendlier or more helpful." "Meals are not fancy; but they are very good," "superb and there is plenty of it." "Fishing is sometimes slow but you have the opportunity to catch a trophy native brook trout and/or landlocked salmon." "The fishing is good. You do not catch tons of fish but the ones you get are good fish." "Fishing is challenging with great rewards."

Guest Ratings

Room	🎣🎣🎣🎣
Staff	🎣🎣🎣🎣
Meals	NA
Outside areas	🎣🎣🎣
Fishing Guides	🎣🎣🎣🎣
Fishing Equipment	NA
Children's Activities	NA

Resort Features

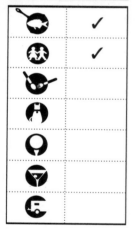

🐟	✓
👨‍👩‍👧	✓
🍳	
🍸	
♀	
🍷	
♿	

IDLEASE AND SHORELANDS GUEST RESORT

Route 9, Box 769 • Kennebunkport, ME 04046
Phone: 207-985-4460 • Reservations: 800-99BEACH
www.vrmedia.com/idlease/ • Email: idlease@mail.vrmedia.com

PRICE CATEGORY: $

SEASON: Year round.

TRANSPORTATION: Boston, Logan International Airport (1 1/2 hour drive.)

FISHING: Where: Mousam River; Atlantic Ocean. **Type:** Bait casting; spin casting; surf casting, fly casting. **How:** Shore; salt water charter boat; wade. **Species:** Mackerel, striper. **Guides:** Guided freshwater fishing; $250 per day 1 or 2 people includes boat; equipment; snack; drinks. Wading trip $175 for 2 people.

ACCOMMODATIONS: Cottages with kitchenettes; standard hotel style rooms (start at $39 double occupancy).

AMENITIES AND ACTIVITIES: Hot tub; pool; basketball court; shuffleboard; ping-pong; playground; board games; cafe; laundry; grills; lobster cookers. Baby-sitting available. Golf; tennis; canoeing; horseback riding; biking; hiking; whale-watching; antiquing; sailing; lobster boat cruises.

PAYMENT: MasterCard; Visa; cash.

GUEST COMMENTS: "Not primarily a fishing resort. Lots of families enjoy the beaches. However there is a wonderful river close by where guests fish pretty much year round." "Variety of fishing choices from saltwater charters to fresh water fly fishing close by." "Great service. Nice; cozy little place." "Clean; friendly and aesthetically pleasing." "Handicap equipped room very nice; attractive and functional." "Always improving resort facilities."

LIBBY CAMPS

PO Box V • Ashland, ME 04732
Phone: 207-435-8274 • Fax: 207-435-3230
libbycamps.com • email: Matt@libbycamps.com

Guest Ratings

Room	🎣🎣🎣🎣
Staff	🎣🎣🎣🎣
Meals	🎣🎣🎣🎣
Outside areas	🎣🎣🎣🎣
Fishing Guides	🎣🎣🎣
Fishing Equipment	🎣🎣🎣
Children's Activities	NA

Resort Features

🐟	
👥	✓
🍳	✓
🎧	
🔍	
▽	
🚐	

PRICE CATEGORY: $$

SEASON: May-December. Fishing season is May-September 30.

TRANSPORTATION: Bangor, ME (3 1/2 hour drive on gravel logging road). Shuttle to floatplane base for flight to lodge.

FISHING: Where: Aroostook River; Allagash River; Penobscot River. **Type:** Fly casting; bait casting; spin casting; fly out trips to other areas. **How:** Boat; shore; walk and wade. **Species:** Brook trout; landlocked salmon; lake trout; smallmouth bass. **Guides:** Orvis endorsed, Maine licensed guides. ($150 - $175 per day for 1-3 people.) **Equipment:** Orvis fly fishing rod, reel, vest and wader rentals.

ACCOMMODATIONS: Rustic log cabins ($115 per person/day) includes meals; full bath with shower; gas lights; wood stove; handmade quilts; all linens; use of boat; motor; canoe. Dining room; board games.

AMENITIES AND ACTIVITIES: Sailing; canoeing; hiking; artifact hunting; swimming; hunting packages. Baby-sitting available with advance notice.

PAYMENT: MasterCard; Visa; personal checks; cash.

GUEST COMMENTS: "An excellent place to enjoy backwoods Maine at it's very best...service as well as a network of outpost camps on a variety of ponds..." Staff: "friendly...concerned that all guests had a memorable visit." "Meals offer a lot of variety." Guides "knew where to find fish," "attentive." "Fly outs to remote ponds are great." "Although we did not hire a guide...staff shared advice on what to use and where to go." "Family run and family oriented. A high quality; but not fancy; and versatile camp."

Guest Ratings

Room	🎣🎣🎣
Staff	🎣🎣🎣🎣
Meals	🎣🎣🎣🎣
Outside areas	🎣🎣🎣🎣
Fishing Guides	NA
Fishing Equipment	NA
Children's Activities	NA

Resort Features

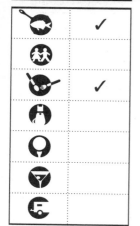

🐟	✓
👥	
🍳	✓
🍺	
♀	
🍸	
⛟	

MACANNAMAC CAMPS

Haymock Lake T8R11 • PO Box B FR • Patten, ME 04765
Phone: 207-528-2855

PRICE CATEGORY: $

SEASON: Year round.

TRANSPORTATION: Bangor, ME (3 hour drive).

FISHING: Where: Allagash Lakes Region including Haymock Lake; Cliff Lake; Spider Lake; Allagash River; Big Pleasant Lake; Big Eagle Lake; Churchill Lake. **Type:** Fly casting; bait casting; spin casting; trolling; ice fishing. **How:** Walk and wade; boat; shore. **Species:** Brook trout; whitefish; lake trout (togue); landlocked salmon. **Guides:** Guides available ($100 per person/ day). **Equipment:** Boat and motor rental; canoe rental.

ACCOMMODATIONS: Standard lodge rooms ($90 per person/day); includes 3 meals. Housekeeping cabins with kitchens (start at $25 per person/day).

AMENITIES AND ACTIVITIES: Canoeing; photography; white water rafting; hiking; hunting; wild flower trips; scenic plane rides; snowmobiling; cross country skiing. **Places to Visit:** Baxter State Park; historic sites.

PAYMENT: Personal checks; cash.

GUEST COMMENTS: "Cabins are great...built from massive local trees...on a large; remote lake with little development." "You rough it here; but all the wildlife you could ask for: bear; deer; moose; eagles." Staff was "knowledgeable...helpful and friendly." "We've had good luck summer and winter fishing." "Wonderful fishing; very few other fishermen on the lake." "Wide range of activities even if you don't want to fish."

MCNALLY'S ROSS STREAM CAMPS

HCR 71, Box 632 • Greenville, ME 04441
Phone: 207-944-5991

Guest Ratings

Room	🐟🐟🐟🐟
Staff	🐟🐟🐟🐟
Meals	🐟🐟🐟🐟
Outside areas	🐟🐟🐟
Fishing Guides	NA
Fishing Equipment	NA
Children's Activities	NA

Resort Features

🐟	✓
👥	
🍳	✓
🔧	
♀	
▽	
🔥	

PRICE CATEGORY: $

SEASON: May 15-November 22.

TRANSPORTATION: Bangor, ME (4 hour drive).

FISHING: Where: Allagash River; St. John River; Ross Stream; Cunliffe Lake; Long Lake; Umsaskis Lake. **Type:** Fly casting. **How:** Canoe; wade; trolling. **Species:** Lake trout; brook trout; whitefish. **Guides:** Maine licensed guides ($100 a day, 1-2 people) **Insider's Tip:** Excellent stream fly fishing during June. May flies and caddis work well.

ACCOMMODATIONS: Log cabins; all linens; flush toilets and showers; all meals ($70 per person/day).

AMENITIES AND ACTIVITIES: Canoe rentals; hunting; wildlife viewing; bird watching trips. **Places to Visit:** Baxter State Park; Allagash Wilderness Waterway.

PAYMENT: Personal check; cash.

GUEST COMMENTS: "Peaceful; quiet area with lots of wildlife." "Nicely kept log cabins with good river views." "Accommodating; friendly staff." "Good to excellent fly fishing for native brook trout." "Miles of rivers for canoeing with sections suited for everyone from beginner to expert."

Guest Ratings

Room	🎣🎣🎣🎣
Staff	🎣🎣🎣🎣
Meals	NA
Outside areas	🎣🎣🎣🎣
Fishing Guides	NA
Fishing Equipment	NA
Children's Activities	NA

Resort Features

🐟	✓
👫	
🍴	
♨	
⚲	
▽	
🔥	

MOOSE RIVER LANDING

PO Box 295 • Rockwood, ME 04478
Phone: 207-534-7577
Email: mrlmoose@aol.com

PRICE CATEGORY: $

SEASON: May 1st through mid-October.

TRANSPORTATION: Boston; MA (6 hour drive).

FISHING: Where: Moose River; Kennebac River. **Type:** Spin casting; fly casting; trolling. **How:** Shore; wade; boat. **Species:** Salmon; togue; brook trout. **Guides:** Local guides; start at $100 per person/day; includes rods; reels; boat; all equipment.

ACCOMMODATIONS: 1,2 and 3 bedroom waterfront cottages with fully equipped kitchens; linens; starts at $60 per day double occupancy.

AMENITIES AND ACTIVITIES: Private docks; rentals (fishing boat; pontoon; canoe; mountain bikes) wildlife cruise; photography; birding; hiking; biking; shopping; hunting. **Places to Visit:** Mt. Kineo; Moosehead Marine Museum; Pittston Farm; Big Squaw Mountain; Ripogenus Gorge and Gulf Hagas.

PAYMENT: MasterCard; Visa; personal check; cash.

GUEST COMMENTS: "Cabins are nice...," "Cozy; comfortable and tidy." "Outside areas are well maintained." Staff: "Used maps and gave us detailed instructions to best fishing spots." "Miles...of dirt roads for biking; nice hiking trail." "Don't...need to bring much...cards; board games...books...magazines in cabins." "Weather changes a lot up there so bring a variety of clothes." "There are several tackle shops in town so that you can buy what you forget." "Not a lot of tourists."

NAHMAKANTA LAKE CAMPS

PO Box 544 • Millinocket, ME 04462
Phone: 207-746-7356 (cell phone at camp)
www.maineguide.com/katahdin/nahmakanta

Guest Ratings

Room	♦♦♦
Staff	♦♦♦♦
Meals	♦♦♦♦
Outside areas	♦♦♦♦
Fishing Guides	♦♦♦♦
Fishing Equipment	♦♦♦♦
Children's Activities	NA

Resort Features

🐟	✓
👥	
🍳	
🔧	
◯	
▽	
🔔	

PRICE CATEGORY: $$

SEASON: Open all year. Family rates July and August.

TRANSPORTATION: Bangor, ME (2 1/2 hour drive); accessible by 4 wheel drive or float plane in summer. During winter last ten miles accessible via snowmobile only. Pick up available.

FISHING: Where: Nahmakanta Lake; surrounding streams and 10 remote ponds. **Type:** Spin casting; fly casting; ice fishing. **How:** Canoe; boat; shore; walk and wade. **Species:** Brook trout; salmon; lake trout. **Guides:** Insured, Maine registered guide starts at $100 per person/day. **Equipment:** Boat and motor rentals; canoe rentals; fishing licenses; lures; flies available in camp. **Insider's Tip:** Best fishing months May; June; early July and September.

ACCOMMODATIONS: Cabins with fully equipped kitchens; screened porches; wood stoves; outdoor privy; bed linens; common heated shower houses with flush toilets. Base rate is $35 per person/day; $75 per person with 3 meals per day or $55 per person for accommodations and dinner.

AMENITIES AND ACTIVITIES: Evening campfires; hiking; birding; wildlife viewing; swimming; canoeing; cross country skiing; snow shoeing; dog sled tours.

PAYMENT: Personal checks; cash.

GUEST COMMENTS: "Traditional Maine sporting camp cabins; basic but clean." "Water is supplied by spigots in front of your cabin...you have to heat water to do dishes." "No electricity...leave your blow dryer at home." "Meals... are healthy and delicious. Lots of fresh produce." "Exceptionally friendly staff that works hard..." "Very natural setting..." "Great variety of wildlife." "Several nice hiking trails that lead to other great fishing lakes." "Canoes available at several nearby lakes really expand fishing options."

Guest Ratings

Room	🐟🐟🐟🐟
Staff	🐟🐟🐟🐟
Meals	🐟🐟🐟🐟
Outside areas	🐟🐟🐟🐟
Fishing Guides	🐟🐟🐟🐟
Fishing Equipment	NA
Children's Activities	NA

Resort Features

🍳	✓
👫	
🥘	✓
🎣	
⚲	
⛵	
♿	

NUGENT'S CHAMBERLAIN LAKE CAMPS

HCR 76, Box 632 • Greenville, ME 04441
Phone: 207-944-5991
www.mainguides.com/members/nugents-camp/welcome.htm

PRICE CATEGORY: $ - $$

SEASON: Open all year.

TRANSPORTATION: Bangor, ME (3 hour drive).

FISHING: Where: Allagash River; West Branch Penobscot River; Chamberlain Lake; Eagle Lake. **Type:** Bait casting; spin casting; fly casting. **How:** Boat; shore; walk and wade; ice fishing. **Species:** Lake trout; brook trout; whitefish. **Guides:** Maine licensed ($100 per person/day). **Insider's Tip:** Trolling streamers and lures that imitate smelt are your best bet.

ACCOMMODATIONS: Cabins with kitchens; all linens and wood stoves ($25 per person/day). American plan—cabin; three meals ($60 per person/day). All cabins are served by privies and a community bath house.

AMENTIES AND ACTIVITIES: Canoeing; sailing; hunting; wildlife viewing. **Places to Visit:** Baxter State Park; Allagash Wilderness Waterway.

PAYMENT: Personal check; cash.

GUEST COMMENTS: "Great staff; knowledgeable about area wildlife and fishing techniques." "Good food; basic but plentiful." "Cabins are comfortable and kitchens well equipped for cooking." "No running water." "Don't forget the bug dope." "No licenses are available at the camp so buy them before you come." "Quiet; peaceful; a look at an earlier; simpler way of life. A treat in every way."

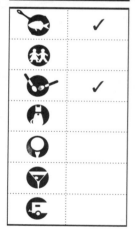

RIDEOUT'S LODGE AND COTTAGES

East Grand Lake • Danforth, ME 04424
Phone: 800-594-5391 • e-mail: Lorigan @ eastgrand.net

Guest Ratings

Room	🐟🐟🐟
Staff	🐟🐟🐟🐟
Meals	🐟🐟🐟
Outside areas	🐟🐟🐟
Fishing Guides	NA
Fishing Equipment	🐟🐟🐟
Children's Activities	NA

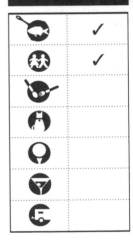

Resort Features

🐟	✓
👫	✓
🍳	
🦇	
♀	
▽	
Ⓕ	

PRICE CATEGORY: $ - $$

SEASON: Early May (ice out) through September 30.

TRANSPORTATION: Bangor International; ME (2 hour drive).

FISHING: Where: East Grand Lake. **Type:** Trolling (streamer flies); spin casting; down rigging; fly casting. **How:** Boat; shore. **Species:** Small mouth bass; landlocked salmon; lake trout. **Guides:** Maine registered guides scheduled upon request. **Equipment:** Rentals (16 foot aluminum boats with 15 hp motors; covered cabin cruisers; canoes; spin casting equipment; deep trolling equipment); Maine and Canadian fishing licenses available at the lodge; marine fuel; live bait; 2 docks (one over 200 ft. long); small tackle shop.

ACCOMMODATIONS: Cabins with full bath (shower); linens; heat; some with kitchens. American plan is $70.00 per person/per day and includes three meals; daily maid service; dock service (starting; cleaning; gassing rental boats; fish cleaning). Housekeeping plan starts at $400 per week.

AMENITIES AND ACTIVITIES: Hunting; hiking; climbing (Katahdin); boating; swimming; antiquing. **Places to Visit:** New Brunswick; Baxter State Park.

PAYMENT: Visa; MasterCard; personal checks; cash.

GUEST COMMENTS: "One of the best of the old fashioned fishing camps." "Situated on a quiet sheltered cove." Staff: "friendly and helpful." Accommodations are "clean but basic, a comfortable place to get a good night's rest...hot shower..." Meals are "very good; but not quite excellent. We...go up there to fish...not sample gourmet cuisine." "Boats and facility...well maintained." One guest: "enjoys scuba diving in the large clear lake." Overall: "...uncrowded; secluded; quality fishing at an affordable price."

175

Guest Ratings

Room	🐟🐟🐟🐟
Staff	🐟🐟🐟🐟
Meals	🐟🐟🐟
Outside areas	🐟🐟🐟🐟
Fishing Guides	🐟🐟🐟
Fishing Equipment	🐟🐟🐟◗
Children's Activities	NA

Resort Features

🐟	✓
👥	
🍳	✓
🎣	✓
⭕	
▼	
🔵	

THE LAKESIDE - COUNTRY INN AND SPORTING CAMPS

PO Box 36 • 2 Park Street • Princeton, ME 04668
Phone: 207-796-2324

PRICE CATEGORY: $

SEASON: Open all year.

TRANSPORTATION: Bangor, ME (1 hour 45 minute drive).

FISHING: Where: Big Lake; Long Lake; Lewey Lake; Grand Falls Flowage; St. Croix River; West Grand Lake; Grand Lake Stream; Pocomoonshine Lake; West Musquash Lake; Crawford Lake; area streams and rivers. **Type:** Fly, bait, spin casting; ice fishing. **How:** Boat; shore; walk and wade. **Species:** Smallmouth, largemouth bass; landlocked salmon; brook, lake trout; Atlantic salmon; bass. **Guides:** Maine certified ($130 per person/per day and up) w/boat; motor, tackle. **Equipment:** Boat; motor, canoe rental; non-resident fishing/hunting licenses.

ACCOMMODATIONS: Housekeeping cabins with electricity; gas stove and heat; flush toilet; hot and cold running water; start at $50 per day double occupancy, add $35 per day/per person for American plan (includes 3 meals; maid service).

AMENITIES AND ACTIVITIES: Pool table; parlor with fireplace; hiking; mountain biking; golfing; historical sights; boutiques; whale watching trips; float plane rides; boating; snowmobiling; cross country skiing.

PAYMENT: MasterCard; Visa; personal checks; cash.

GUEST COMMENTS: "Scenic views." "Basic, comfortable cabins." "Smallmouth bass fishing is definitely worth the tip." "Cabins are very close to the water." "Feeling of being out away from people, but still close to all the amenities of a small town." "Traditional country inn and sporting camp that preserves a bygone era of classic Maine."

THE PINES SPORTING CAMP

PO Box 158 • Grand Lake Stream, ME 04637
Phone: 207-796-5006
Email: pinespair@juno.com

Guest Ratings

Room	🎣🎣🎣🎣
Staff	🎣🎣🎣🎣
Meals	🎣🎣🎣🎣
Outside areas	🎣🎣🎣🎣
Fishing Guides	NA
Fishing Equipment	NA
Children's Activities	NA

Resort Features

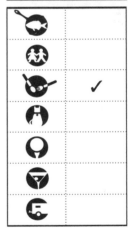

🐟	
👥	
🍴	✓
🔌	
⭕	
▼	
🅴	

PRICE CATEGORY: $$

SEASON: Early May through September.

TRANSPORTATION: Bangor, ME (2 hours).

FISHING: Where: Sysladobsis Lake; Pocumcuss Lake; West Grand Lake; Fourth Machias; Grand Lake Stream. **Type:** Fly casting; spin casting; bait casting. **How:** Walk and wade; boat; shore. **Species:** Smallmouth bass; landlocked salmon. **Guides:** Local guides available with advance request ($125 per day/up to 2 people) lunch; grand lake canoe. **Insider's Tip:** Book early for May and June smallmouth bass fishing peak.

ACCOMMODATIONS: Cabins or lodge rooms with 3 meals per day start at $60 per person/per night. 2 island housekeeping camps; $380 per week.

AMENITIES AND ACTIVITIES: Boat and motor rental; canoe rentals; dining room; camp store; library; hiking; swimming; climbing. **Places to Visit:** New Brunswick, Canada; Campabello Island.

PAYMENT: Personal checks; cash.

GUEST COMMENTS: "Beautiful location." "Built in the 1880's and has a charm and aura that is truly unique." "Food and service were excellent." "Meals perfect and delicious." "Excellent food and hospitality." "Cabins were very well equipped as well as comfortable." "Fishing was productive." "Really super bass fishing." "A wonderful place to get away from the crowds. The loudest sounds are the loons."

Guest Ratings

Room	♦♦♦♦
Staff	♦♦♦♦
Meals	♦♦♦♦
Outside areas	♦♦♦
Fishing Guides	♦♦♦
Fishing Equipment	♦♦♦
Children's Activities	NA

Resort Features

WHEATON'S LODGE

HC 81, Box 120 • Brookton, ME 04413
Summer Phone: 207-448-7723 • Winter Phone: 207-843-5732

PRICE CATEGORY: $$

SEASON: Early May through October 1st. 10% family discount July and August.

TRANSPORTATION: Bangor; ME (2 hour drive). Houlton Airport for small aircraft.

FISHING: Where: East Grand Lake; Spednik Lake; Baskahegan Lake; Upper St. Croix watershed and streams. **Type:** Bait fishing; spin casting; fly casting; fly trolling. **How:** Boat; shore; walk and wade. **Species:** Landlocked salmon; smallmouth bass. **Guides:** Maine registered guides ($125.00 per person/day) includes grand lake canoe; hot lunch. **Equipment:** Boat and motor rentals. **Insider's Tip:** Wheaton's will lend you whatever you need or forget to bring.

ACCOMMODATIONS: Private cottages with screened porches; $80 per person/day; includes breakfast; picnic lunch; dinner.

AMENITIES AND ACTIVITIES: Baby-sitting available upon request. Fly tying classes; fly casting clinics; swimming; boating; private beach; hiking; horseshoe court; windsurfer; canoes; basketball half court. **Places to Visit:** New Brunswick, Canada.

PAYMENT: MasterCard; Visa; personal checks; cash.

GUEST COMMENTS: "This is a fishing camp and an excellent one." "Wheaton's is for those who love the out-of-doors." "Well spaced cabins" are "rustic" and "so clean you could eat off the floor." "More than enough good; wholesome food to satisfy the biggest appetites." "Hot cooked shore lunch is incredible; worth the trip in itself;" "a real highlight." Guides "very knowledgeable and adaptable to changing conditions; patient; strong conservation ethic." "Fishing is fishing; sometimes great; sometimes you have to work at it." "Small mouth bass fishing unsurpassed in East." "Option of fishing lake or river outlet" with "plenty of different lakes to fish." "This is the consummate fishing experience; don't miss the guides or shore lunches." "No baloney Maine fishing trip."

MARYLAND · MASSACHUSETTS · MICHIGAN

Guest Ratings

Room	🐟🐟🐟🐟
Staff	🐟🐟🐟🐟
Meals	🐟🐟🐟🐟
Outside areas	🐟🐟🐟
Fishing Guides	NA
Fishing Equipment	🐟🐟
Children's Activities	NA

Resort Features

🐟	
👫	
🍳	✓
🍸	
🔦	
⊗	✓
🚐	

CARMEL COVE INN

PO Box 644 • Oakland, MD 21550
Phone: 301-387-0067
www.carmelcoveinn.com • Email: carmelcove@aol.com

PRICE CATEGORY: $$

SEASON: Open all year.

TRANSPORTATION: Washington, D.C. (2 hour drive). Pittsburgh, PA (1 1/2 hour drive).

FISHING: Where: Deep Creek Lake; Youghiogheny River; Youghiogheny Reservoir. **Type:** Fly, bait and spin casting; trolling. **How:** Boat; shore; walk and wade. **Species:** Trout; bass; walleye; crappie; pickerel; catfish. **Equipment:** Well equipped tackle box, worms/minnows for guests; canoes; fishing poles. **Insider's Tip:** The Inn is on a 'no-wake' cove.

ACCOMMODATIONS: Bed and breakfast in a restored and renovated Carmelite monastery ($80 and up; double occupancy), includes breakfast; private bath.

AMENITIES AND ACTIVITIES: Swimming dock; sauna; canoes; tandem bike; hot tub; common room; boating; hunting; golf; paddle boats; whitewater rafting; antiquing; downhill and cross country skiing. **Places to Visit:** Swallow Falls; Deep Creek Lake State Park; Fallingwater (Frank Lloyd Wright's home).

PAYMENT: Mastercard; Visa; Discover; personal check; cash.

GUEST COMMENTS: "Quiet; couples-only kind of resort." "Wooded area...six state parks in the immediate vicinity." "Lots of...deer; bear and wild turkeys." "...their dock juts out far enough into the cove to give access to some of the large stumps." "The quiet can be deafening...the view is breathtaking."

THE LODGE AT SAWMILL HOLLOW

400 Sawmill Hollow Road • Swanton, MD 21561
Phone: 301-387-8455 • Fax: 301-387-5039
www.gcnet.net • Email: tarvoc@erols.com

Guest Ratings

Room	♦♦♦♦
Staff	♦♦♦♦
Meals	NA
Outside areas	♦♦♦
Fishing Guides	
Fishing Equipment	♦♦♦
Children's Activities	NA

Resort Features

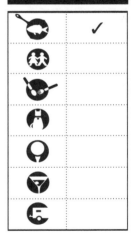

PRICE CATEGORY: $

SEASON: Open all year.

TRANSPORTATION: Cumberland, MD (1 hour drive).

FISHING: Where: Deep Creek Lake; Youghiogheny River; Casselman River; Savage River; Jennings-Randolf Lake. **Type:** Bait casting; spin casting; fly casting. **How:** Boat; shore; walk and wade. **Species:** Bass; bluegill; carp; catfish; crappie; perch; pickerel; pike; walleye; trout. **Guides:** Local guide with 17 years experience. **Equipment:** Bait; fishing rod; hook; sinkers; bobbers available at the lodge. **Insider's Tip:** Live bait is your best bait. Best fishing April through June.

ACCOMMODATIONS: Lodge rooms, all handicapped accessible; ($35 per person per day; towels and bedding extra $5 per day) Entire lodge is usually rented by groups of 4 or more. Kitchen; dining room; great room; conference room; recreation room; screened in porch; deck; satellite TV; VCR; Jacuzzi.

AMENITIES AND ACTIVITIES: Hayrides; pontoon; storytelling; folk music; nature study; craft activities; swimming; hiking; skiing. **Places to Visit:** Big Run State Park; Casselman State Park; Deep Creek Lake State Park; Herrington Manor State Park; New Germany State Park; Swallow Falls State Park.

PAYMENT: Personal checks; cash.

GUEST COMMENTS: "Great facility for meetings and groups." "Clean; well appointed accommodations; carefully designed to be accessible for everyone." "Average fishing but fun because there is so much variety; you can fly cast on a river in the morning and troll Deep Creek Lake in the afternoon." "Exceptional staff; well trained and caring."

Guest Ratings

Room	♦♦♦♦
Staff	♦♦♦♦
Meals	♦♦♦
Outside areas	♦♦♦♦
Fishing Guides	♦♦♦♦
Fishing Equipment	NA
Children's Activities	♦♦♦♦

Resort Features

🐟	
🧒	✓
🍳	
♨	
🍷	✓
▼	✓
⛽	

WISP RESORT

290 Marsh Hill Rd. • McHenry, MD 21541
Phone: 800-462-9477 • Fax: 301-387-4127
www.wisp-resort.com • Email: wisp@gcnet.net

PRICE CATEGORY: $$$

SEASON: Open all year.

TRANSPORTATION: Washington DC or Baltimore, MD (3 hour drive). Pittsburgh, PA (2 hour drive.)

FISHING: Where: Deep Creek Lake; North branch of Potomac; Youghiogheny River; Savage River. **Type:** Bait casting; fly casting; spin casting; ice fishing. **How:** Shore; walk and wade; boat. **Species:** Perch; smallmouth bass; large-mouth bass; bluegill; walleye; trout; chain pickerel; northern pike. **Guides:** Guides can be arranged through resort; $75 per person per day includes boat; bait and guide.

ACCOMMODATIONS: Suites; mini-suites (start at $129 double occupancy).

AMENITIES AND ACTIVITIES: 18 hole golf course; 23 ski runs; conference facilities; 2 restaurants; 2 lounges; tennis courts; pool; hot tub; fitness center. Maryland licensed daycare offers "Kid's Camp" program for ages 3-11. Hiking; biking; cross country skiing; in-line skating; horseback riding; water skiing; laser tag; rafting. **Places to Visit:** Deep Creek Lake State Park; Swallow Falls State Park; Herrington Manor State Park.

PAYMENT: MasterCard; Visa; Discover; American Express; personal checks; cash.

GUEST COMMENTS: "Not really a fishing resort but the wife and kids enjoyed resort activities and I set off for a different fishing hole each morning." "Take the kids fishing...a great introduction...not to mention some...quality one on one time." "The kid's program is nice. I get a break and the kids talk about their adventures for months after we return home." "Heated indoor pool is a great way to wind down..."

THE WILLIAMSVILLE INN

Route 41 • West Stockbridge, MA 01266
Phone: 413-274-6118 • Fax: 413-274-3539

Guest Ratings

Room	🎣🎣🎣🎣
Staff	🎣🎣🎣🎣
Meals	🎣🎣🎣🎣
Outside areas	NA
Fishing Guides	🎣🎣🎣
Fishing Equipment	NA
Children's Activities	NA

Resort Features

🍳	
👥	✓
🍽	✓
🍸	✓

PRICE CATEGORY: $$

SEASON: Open all year.

TRANSPORTATION: Hartford, CT (1hr. 15 min. drive).

FISHING: Where: Williams River; Housatonic River; Green River; Laurel Lake; Stockbridge Bowl. **Type:** Fly casting; bait casting; spin casting. **How:** Shore; walk and wade. **Species:** Brook trout; brown trout; rainbow trout; bass; pickerel; perch. **Guides:** Local guides ($195 per person/day) includes lunch and equipment. **Tip:** Peak fishing season April–June.

ACCOMMODATIONS: Inn rooms with private baths ($120-$150 double occupancy) included breakfast.

AMENITIES AND ACTIVITIES: Baby-sitting can be arranged. Swimming pool; parlor; restaurant; tavern; gardens; tennis court; meeting facilities; 10 acres of lawns; gardens; wood; hiking; biking. **Places to Visit:** Tanglewood (Boston Symphony Orchestra); Shakespeare and Company; Norman Rockwell Museum; Hancock Shaker Village.

PAYMENT: MasterCard; Visa; American Express; personal check; cash.

GUEST COMMENTS: Rooms are "snuggily and cozy;" "neat as a pin." "Terrific food;" "popovers to die for." "More activities available here than at most bed and breakfasts." "More like a gentleman's estate than a typical bed and breakfast. Lots of places to explore." "He can go fishing, and the outlet mall is only 10 minutes away."

Guest Ratings

Room	🐟🐟🐟
Staff	🐟🐟🐟🐟
Meals	NA
Outside areas	🐟🐟🐟🐟
Fishing Guides	🐟🐟🐟🐟
Fishing Equipment	NA
Children's Activities	NA

Resort Features

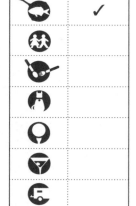

🐟	✓
👥	
🍳	
🏌	
☀	
⛳	
€	

RIVERSIDE MOTEL AND MARINA

520 Water St. • Manistee, MI 49660
Phone: 616-723-3554 • jackpine.com/~krweb/riverside
EMail: Riversid @ manistee-isd.k12.mi.us

PRICE CATEGORY: $

SEASON: All year.

TRANSPORTATION: Manistee Blacker Airport (1/2 hour drive).

FISHING: Where: Lake Michigan; Big Manistee River. **Type:** Spin casting; bait casting. **How:** Shore; boat; pier. **Species:** Brown trout; salmon; steelhead; lake trout. **Guides:** Insured; US Coast Guard Licensed guides ($475 / day 1-6 people). **Equipment:** Boat dock; fish cleaning station.

ACCOMMODATIONS: Motel rooms with walk out patios; color TV; phones; air conditioning ($40 and up).

AMENITIES AND ACTIVITIES: Pool; golf; antiquing. **Places to Visit:** Parks; museums; historic homes; festivals.

PAYMENT: MasterCard; Visa; American Express; personal check; cash.

GUEST COMMENTS: "The rooms are nothing special; but clean; comfortable..." Staff: "friendly and efficient." "We really liked having our boat docked right outside our room." "...walking distance of the Lake Michigan beach and restaurants..." Equipment was: "...latest technology and very well maintained." "A nice; well managed little motel. Reasonably priced; an exceptional location for fishermen."

MINNESOTA · MISSOURI · MONTANA

Guest Ratings

Room	🐟🐟🐟🐟
Staff	🐟🐟🐟🐟
Meals	🐟🐟🐟
Outside areas	🐟🐟🐟🐟
Fishing Guides	🐟🐟🐟🐟
Fishing Equipment	NA
Children's Activities	NA

Resort Features

🍳	✓
👫	
🍲	
🎣	
⛾	
🍸	
🚐	

ANGLE OUTPOST RESORT

RR 1, Box 36 • Angle Inlet, MN 56711
Phone: 218-233-8101 • Reservations: 800-441-5014
Website: FishandGame.com/angleoutpost

PRICE CATEGORY: $ - $$$

SEASON: Open all year. Transportation: Winnipeg; Manitoba (2 1/2 hour drive).

FISHING: Where: Lake of the Woods. **Type:** spin casting; trolling. **How:** Boat; shore; ice fishing. **Species:** Walleye; smallmouth bass; sauger; jumbo perch. **Guides:** US Coast Guard licensed guides ($155 per person / day); includes boat; motor; fillet service and bait. **Equipment:** Boat and motor rental; marina; boat dock; tackle and grocery store.

ACCOMMODATIONS: Private cottages overlooking Lake of the Woods; equipped with full kitchens; microwave; linens; full bath. Cabin only ($36 per person / per day); European Plan ($48 per person); American Plan ($66 per person); Deluxe American plan includes cabin; maid service; 3 meals; guide; boat; motor; gas; bait and fillet service($159 per person).

AMENIRIES AND ACTIVITIES: Golf; picnicking; recreation; swimming; wildlife viewing; cross country skiing and snow mobiling; hunting. Places to Visit: Winnipeg; Kenora; Ft. St. Charles.

PAYMENT: MasterCard; Visa; personal checks ; cash.

GUEST COMMENTS: "The food was exceptional; the service was great." "Clean; comfortable; modern accommodations." "Nights are refreshingly quiet. You might want to bring a book or some board games..." "We have never caught and released so many fish; in addition to taking home the legal limit." "Fishing here is primarily for muskie and walleye; although we did have good luck with bass - they are real fighters." "

BIG LAKE WILDERNESS LODGE

PO Box 359 • Ely; MN 55731 Phone: 800-446-9080
E-mail address: biglake@northernet.com

Guest Ratings

Room	🐟🐟🐟
Staff	🐟🐟🐟🐟
Meals	NA
Outside areas	🐟🐟🐟
Fishing Guides	🐟🐟🐟🐟
Fishing Equipment	NA
Children's Activities	NA

Resort Features

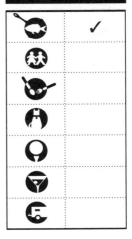

🐟	✓
👫	
🍳	
🍸	
⛄	
🍷	
🔥	

PRICE CATEGORY: $

SEASON: Early May through November. Transportation: Ely; MN (50 minute drive).

FISHING: Where: Big Lake; Lapond Lake; Big Rice Lake; other Boundary Waters Canoe Area lakes. **Type:** Bait casting; spin casting. **How:** Boat; shore; dock. Species: Walleye; smallmouth Bass; northern pike; yellow perch. **Guides:** Experienced; local guides are available for about $165.00 per day. Equipment: Small supply of fishing tackle and equipment in lodge; boat rentals. **Insider's Tip:** "Sunday morning orientation... included tour of the lake on a pontoon. Great time to meet other guests."

ACCOMMODATIONS: Housekeeping cabins with fully equipped kitchen; full bath ($595.00 per week double occupancy) includes 14 foot fishing boat. Tent camps on islands located in Superior National Forest; equipped with cabin style tents; cots; pads; sleeping bags; dock; picnic table; propane cook stove; cooking gear and fresh water. Daily ice; dry firewood and fresh water delivery ($495 per week up to 4 people).

AMENITIES AND ACTIVITIES: Lounge/game room; sauna; laundry room. Children's Nature Program/ playground. Pontoon rentals; canoes; kayaks; paddle boats;fire rings; swim raft; hiking; mountain biking; naturalist talks. Places to Visit: International Wolf Center; Vince Shute Bear Sanctuary

PAYMENT: MasterCard; Visa; Discover; American Express; checks; cash.

GUEST COMMENTS: Cabins: "extremely rustic" but "squeaky clean and well stocked." "Excellent naturalist program for kids." "Lots of wildlife." "Definitely a family resort." Fishing got mixed reviews: "Big ones; millions of them," to "fishing was just OK," "fish tend to be on the small side - but plentiful." "Unspoiled wilderness; relaxing; tremendous."

Guest Ratings

Room	🐟🐟🐟🐟
Staff	🐟🐟🐟🐟
Meals	NA
Outside areas	🐟🐟🐟◢
Fishing Guides	🐟🐟🐟
Fishing Equipment	NA
Children's Activities	NA

Resort Features

🐟 (pan)	✓
👪	✓
🍳	
🍸	
♀	
▼	
⑤	

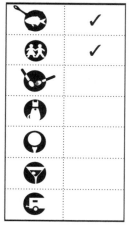

NORTHLAND LODGE

HCR 84, Box 376 • Walker, MN 45684
Phone: 218-836-2332 • Reservations: 800-247-1719

PRICE CATEGORY: $

SEASON: Open all year.

TRANSPORTATION: Minneapolis (3 hour drive).

FISHING: Where: Leech Lake. **Type:** Bait casting; spin casting ice fishing. **How:** Boat; shore. **Species:** Walleye; muskie; bass; northern pike. **Equipment:** Protected dock; boat ramp; boat and motor rentals; tackle shop; fish cleaning station. **Insider's Tip:** Best fishing May and September.

ACCOMMODATIONS: Log lake homes ($25 per person/day) with kitchens; screened deck; barbecue grill; TV; VCR.

AMENITIES AND ACTIVITIES: Daily children's activities and baby-sitting available. Game room; sand beach; sauna; fire pit; sand volleyball; playground; paddleboats; kayaks; basketball. Swimming; volleyball; hiking; biking; water skiing; golf; horseback riding; cross country skiing; snowmobiling. **Places to Visit:** Ithasca State Park; Chain Saw Carver; Casino; Mine tours; Forest History Center; Paul Bunyan Land.

PAYMENT: Visa; MasterCard; Discover; personal checks; cash.

GUEST COMMENTS: "Fresh; attractive homes;" "Kitchen was ..well equipped even a popcorn popper." "Terrific children's activities." Fishing ranged from "poor" to "very good" and "excellent." "...sheltered dock facility." "Plenty to do for those who don't fish. Ideal ..for family reunions." "Secluded...modern conveniences... best of both worlds."

THE QUARTERDECK ON GULL

1588 Quarterdeck Road • West Nisswa, MN 56468
Phone: 800-950-5596
Website: www.quarterdeckongulllake.com • Email: quarterdeck@brainerdonline.com

Guest Ratings

Room	🐟🐟🐟
Staff	🐟🐟🐟🐟
Meals	NA
Outside areas	🐟🐟🐟◣
Fishing Guides	🐟🐟🐟🐟
Fishing Equipment	NA
Children's Activities	NA

Resort Features

🐟	✓
👫	
🍳	
⚲	
🍸	
🚐	

PRICE CATEGORY: $

SEASON: Open all year. Discounts offered August 23rd to June 27th. Transportation: Minneapolis; MN (3 hour drive). Brainerd; MN (shuttle to resort).

FISHING: Where: Gull Lake; Gull Lake Chain. **Type:** Bait casting; spin casting; fly casting; trolling; ice fishing. **How:** Boat; shore. **Species:** Bass; walleye; northern pike; crappie; bluegill; rock bass; perch; bullheads. **Guides:** Local guide with 30 years experience ($150 per half day for 1-3 people,w/boat; bait; tackle; rods/reels. **Equipment:** Bait and tackle shop; ice fishing huts; fish cleaning house; boat docks; fishing boat rental; fish locator rentals; boat ramp. **Insider's Tip:** Gull Lake is rated one of the top ten fishing lakes in MN for walleye and bass (late May-June peak time).

ACCOMMODATIONS: Lakeside 2,3 and 4 bedroom vacation homes; luxury villas; fireplaces in most; housekeeping units with bed linens; towel rental available. Quad occupancy per 2-bedroom from $30 - $44 per person per night.

AMENITIES AND ACTIVITIES: Structured children's program,babysitter available. Conference facilities; hot tub; sauna; restaurant; recreation center; basketball court; volleyball court; horseshoes; beach; movies; bowling; children's park; raceway; golf; baseball; softball; snowmobile; cross country skiing; bird watching; hiking; antiquing; nature hikes. **Places to Visit:** Paul Bunyon hiking and biking trail; Pillsbury State Forest.

PAYMENT: MasterCard; Visa; personal check; cash;

GUEST COMMENTS: "Clean; attractive accommodations." "Tremendous staff; bent over backwards to make sure our vacation was great." "Well supervised children's activities." "Easy for kids to land a good string of panfish while the more advanced fisherman goes after a trophy walleye." "Variety of activities... and plentiful lake."

Guest Ratings

Room	🐟🐟🐟🐟
Staff	🐟🐟🐟🐟
Meals	NA
Outside areas	🐟🐟🐟🐟
Fishing Guides	🐟🐟🐟
Fishing Equipment	NA
Children's Activities	NA

Resort Features

🐟	✓
👨‍👩‍👧	
🍳	
🧍	
🍷	
▽	
🛥	

CEDAR RESORT

HCR 9, Box 1418 • Lake 265-12 • Branson, MO 65616
Phone: 417-338-2653 • Reservations: 800-788-4651
www.page: nations.com/motelscedar

PRICE CATEGORY: $

SEASON: Open all year; discounts offered November - February.

TRANSPORTATION: Branson-Springfield Airport (1 hour drive).

FISHING: Where: Table Rock Lake. **Type:** Bait casting; spin casting. **How:** Boat; shore. **Species:** Walleye; crappie; smallmouth, largemouth bass; catfish. **Guides:** List of recommended guides available. **Equipment:** Lighted; covered boat dock; concrete boat ramp; fishing boat and motor rentals; small tackle shop.

ACCOMMODATIONS: Kitchenette units with 1 - 8 bedrooms (start at $38 double occupancy).

AMENITIES AND ACTIVITIES: Picnic tables; barbecue grills; laundry; tetherball; game room; small convenience store; swimming pool; pontoon rentals; paddleboat rentals. Country music shows; golf; mini golf; go carts; hiking; biking. **Places to Visit:** Silver Dollar City; Shepherd of the Hills; Table Rock Dam Fish Hatchery; Branson Bell Showboat; White Water amusement park.

PAYMENT: MasterCard; Visa; Discover; cash.

GUEST COMMENTS: Accommodations were "clean; comfortable and spacious" with "well supplied kitchens." Staff was "...warm-hearted and gracious." "If you take a few balls and maybe a frisbee; the kids will find plenty to do... " "We caught enough fish to hold my grandson's attention." "Fish weren't huge but they were plentiful." Guests recommended side trips to country western music shows in Branson; the trout hatchery tour and Silver Dollar City. "A good family oriented get away that won't break the bank."

DEL MAR RESORT

1993 Lakeshore Drive • Branson, MO 65616
Phone: 417-334-6241 • Reservations: 800-892-9542

Guest Ratings

Room	🎣🎣🎣🎣
Staff	🎣🎣🎣🎣
Meals	NA
Outside areas	🎣🎣🎣
Fishing Guides	NA
Fishing Equipment	🎣🎣🎣🎣
Children's Activities	NA

Resort Features

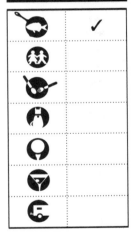

PRICE CATEGORY: $

SEASON: Open all year.

TRANSPORTATION: Springfield - Branson Airport (1 hour drive).

FISHING: Where: Lake Taneycomo. **Type:** Bait casting; spin casting; fly casting; trolling. **How:** Boat. **Species:** Rainbow trout; German brown trout. **Guides:** Local guides; ($85 - $125 per day) includes boat; rod/reel; bait. **Equipment:** Boat and motor rentals; small tackle shop; fuel; covered; 150 ft. lighted fishing dock with 3 fishing platforms and heated area.

ACCOMMODATIONS: Kitchenette units and cottages; fully equipped kitchens; all linens; color cable TV ($40 and up per day double occupancy. Discounts given for length of stay; $5 each additional person).

AMENITIES AND ACTIVITIES: Pool; video games; playground; horseshoes; volleyball; basketball; char coal grills; picnic tables; playground. Boating; live music and variety shows. **Places to Visit:** Silver Dollar City; White Water amusement park; Shepherd of the Hills Farm; Branson.

PAYMENT: Personal checks; cash.

GUEST COMMENTS: "Nothing real fancy but great for the money." The "owners do all they can to help us have a good time ..." "We really enjoy all the wildlife..." "The heated fishing dock is wonderful during the winter." "The lake is stocked every week so the trout fishing is normally good." "Boats; motors and pontoons are well kept." "The best place I know to catch your limit of trout...cook your supper relax or run to town..."

Guest Ratings

Room	🎣🎣🎣🎣
Staff	🎣🎣🎣🎣
Meals	NA
Outside areas	🎣🎣🎣🎣
Fishing Guides	🎣🎣🎣
Fishing Equipment	🎣🎣🎣🎣
Children's Activities	NA

Resort Features

🐟	✓
👫	
🥘	
🍴	
🍷	
🍸	
🔥	

EAGLE'S NEST AT LAKE POMME DE TERRE

HC 76, Box 2690 • Pittsburg, MO 65724
Phone: 800-259-6936

PRICE CATEGORY: $

SEASON: Open all year; lower rates offered November - March.

TRANSPORTATION: Springfield; MO (1 hour drive).

FISHING: Where: Lake Pomme de Terre. **Type:** Bait casting; spin casting. How: Shore; boat. **Species:** Bass; crappie; muskie. **Guides:** Local guides ($50 per person / half day). **Equipment:** Dock; Grumman bass boat with 35 hp motor; trolling motor; fish finder and tank of fuel ($75 per day). **Insider's Tip:** Best time for muskie is late August through early December. Crappie are best from late February through early May. Bass fishing best March through June.

ACCOMMODATIONS: Private cabins with full kitchens; propane grills; deck; linens ($65 and up double occupancy or $385 and up per week double occupancy.)

AMENITIES AND ACTIVITIES: Picnic area; fire ring; boat storage; hunting packages; canoeing; hiking; golf; movie theaters Branson music shows. Places to Visit: Trout Hatchery; Ha Ha Tonka; pioneer village.

PAYMENT: MasterCard; Discover; personal checks; cash.

GUEST COMMENTS: Cabins are "new; well kept and very comfortable." ".. kitchen was well equipped..." Staff was: "friendly and helpful; very accommodating." "Nice lake; good fishing." "The bass boat was extremely well maintained ..." "Fishing was excellent; both in terms of quantity and quality." "Very peaceful and relaxing in the evenings."

EDGEWATER BEACH RESORT AND MARINA

Box 159 • Lake Ozark, MO 56049
Phone: 800-822-6044

Guest Ratings

Room	🐟🐟🐟🐟
Staff	🐟🐟🐟🐟
Meals	NA
Outside areas	🐟🐟🐟🐟
Fishing Guides	NA
Fishing Equipment	🐟🐟🐟🐟
Children's Activities	NA

Resort Features

	✓

PRICE CATEGORY: $

SEASON: Open April through October.

TRANSPORTATION: St. Louis (2 1/2 hours); Springfield - Branson Airport (1 hour 45 minutes)

FISHING: Where: Lake of the Ozarks. **Type:** Spin casting; bait casting; trolling; bobber; fly casting. **How:** Boat; shore. **Species:** Drum; muskie; catfish; paddlefish; black crappie; white crappie; bass; bluegill; walleye. **Guides:** List of local guides available upon request. **Equipment:** Boat and motor rentals; fuel; covered boat slips; small tackle/boat equipment shop; fish cleaning station.

ACCOMODATIONS: Kitchenette units ($68 double occupancy); motel rooms ($47 double occupancy) all rooms have color TV and air conditioning.

AMENITIES AND ACTIVITIES: Swimming pool; playground; kiddie beach; rentals (jet ski; ski boat; pontoon). Golf; outlet shopping; spelunking; go carts; mini golf; movie theaters. **Places to Visit:** Factory Outlet Stores;

PAYMENT: Mastercard; Visa; cash.

GUEST COMMENTS: "Lots of entertainment within walking distance." "Located in the center of everything but very private." The staff "always has time to help." "Just about every spot has potential for a trophy fish; and I've caught plenty of them." "The dock areas and rental equipment is all well maintained. You don't have to worry about getting out on the water and breaking down." "The marina staff are also very friendly. "

Guest Ratings

Room	🐟🐟🐟
Staff	🐟🐟🐟🐟
Meals	NA
Outside areas	🐟🐟🐟🐟
Fishing Guides	NA
Fishing Equipment	🐟🐟🐟🐟
Children's Activities	NA

Resort Features

🐟	✓
👫	
🍴	
💡	

FISH HOOK RESORT

HCR 7; Box 1710 • Lake Road DD Hwy. • Reeds Spring; MO 65737
Phone: 417-338-2354

PRICE CATEGORY: $

SEASON: Open from March 1st through November 1st.

TRANSPORTATION: Springfield - Branson airport; (1 hour drive).

FISHING: Where: Table Rock Lake; Bull Shoals Lake; the Roaring Fork River; Beaver Lake; the James River and Tannycomo Lake. **Type:** Spin and bait casting; trolling. **How:** Boat; shore. **Species:** White, spotted, largemouth, smallmouth bass; spoonbill;walleye; crappie; catfish and panfish. **Guides:** Licensed; Coast Guard Approved guides can be recommended. **Equipment:** Covered and lighted dock; boat and motor rentals.

ACCOMMODATIONS: 1 and 2 bedroom duplex cottages ($42 and up) with kitchenette; air conditioning; television and covered porch. Off season rates start at $42.00 per night double occupancy. Discounts to guests staying seven days or longer and children under five stay free. During the off-season retired persons receive a complimentary rental boat or stall with lodging.

AMENITIES AND ACTIVITIES: Pool; playground; shuffleboard; game room; horseshoe court and small convenience store; white water rafting; horseback riding; golfing; spelunking or hiking. **Places to Visit:** Silver Dollar City; outlet shops; Branson MO; White Water amusement park; spring and fall festivals.

PAYMENT: MasterCard; Visa; in-state personal checks and cash. Discount for cash or travelers check.

GUEST COMMENTS: "The resort is always clean; the people are super and the fishing is good. "...the bathrooms are a little small ...very clean." "I always catch enough to head home happy." "... layout is very good; a gentle slope leads to the water." "We enjoy the secluded area; and it's just the right distance from Branson (about 20 minutes) and Silver Dollar City when we want more excitement." "...for the price; you can't beat it."

LAZY LEE'S RESORT

HC 7; Box 1840 • Reeds Springs; MO 65737
Phone: 417-338-2253 • Fax: 417-338-2546

Guest Ratings

Room	🐟🐟🐟
Staff	🐟🐟🐟🐟
Meals	NA
Outside areas	🐟🐟🐟🐟
Fishing Guides	NA
Fishing Equipment	🐟🐟🐟🐟
Children's Activities	NA

Resort Features

🍳🐟	✓
👫	
🍴	
🔧	
🔦	
♺	
🚐	

PRICE CATEGORY: $

SEASON: April through October.

TRANSPORTATION: Springfield/Branson Regional Airport (1 hour drive).

FISHING: Where: Table Rock Lake; Lake Taneycomo; Bull Shoals Lake; James River; White River. **Type:** Bait casting; spin casting; fly casting. **How:** Boat; shore; dock; walk and wade; limb lines. **Species:** Small mouth bass; crappie; catfish; walleye; sun-perch. **Guides:** List of licensed; insured guides available. **Equipment:** Small tackle shop on premises; boat and motor rentals. Insider's Tip: "The water is remarkably clear; so you need to adjust your fishing style to compensate."

ACCOMMODATIONS: 1-4 bedroom housekeeping units with deck; fully equipped kitchen; TV; air conditioning; linens (start at $46 per night).

AMENITIES AND ACTIVITIES: Game room; laundry; swimming pool; grill; picnic table; playground; covered boat dock; boat ramp. Boating; swimming; boat cruises; miniature golf; hiking trails; horseback riding; go carts; shopping. **Places to Visit:** Silver Dollar City; Shepherd of the Hills Theme Park; Branson; MO; Table Rock Dam.

PAYMENT: MasterCard; Visa; personal checks; cash.

GUEST COMMENTS: Rooms: nice views...short distance to the boat dock." Staff goes "out of their way for all of the guests." "It's close enough to Branson that you can sightsee; but far enough away to be quiet and peaceful." "Fishing is great." "It might be a good idea to get a guide your first time out... owners are really great about pointing out the good fishing spots." " The real difference ... is the personal and friendly service."

Guest Ratings

Room	♦♦♦
Staff	♦♦♦♦
Meals	NA
Outside areas	♦♦♦♦
Fishing Guides	NA
Fishing Equipment	♦♦♦♦
Children's Activities	NA

Resort Features

🐟	✓
👨‍👩‍👧	
🍳	

PLAZA BEACH RESORT

Rt. 76, Box 420 • Camdenton, MO 65020
Phone: 573-873-5308

PRICE CATEGORY: $

SEASON: Open all year; discounts offered May 23-June 6 and August 22-September 5.

TRANSPORTATION: St. Louis (2 1/2 hours); Springfield-Branson Airport (1 hour 45 minutes)

FISHING: Where: Lake of the Ozarks **Type:** Spin casting; bait casting; bobber. **How:** Boat; shore; enclosed dock. **Species:** Largemouth bass; white bass; crappie; catfish; bluegill; walleye. **Equipment:** Covered; padded dock; launching ramp; boat and motor rental; fish cleaning station.

ACCOMMODATIONS: Cottages with fully equipped kitchens; Weber grill; microwave; color cable TV; air conditioning; linens ($40 per day double occupancy).

AMENITIES AND ACTIVITIES: Swimming and sunbathing dock; gradual sand beach; playground; horseshoes; recreation room; picnic tables; lawn swings; pontoon rentals. Outlet shopping; country music shows; golfing; spelunking; mini golf; go carts; antiquing. **Places to Visit:** Water park.

PAYMENT: Cash; personal check.

GUEST COMMENTS: "Very nice waterfront area." "Rooms are a little bit dated;" "very clean and kitchen appliances are in good shape." "Boat docks are safe for people and boats." "We enjoy it here because it is a quieter area of the lake...seems the fish like the quiet too because we usually catch a stringer-full in the spring." "Kids really like the swim beach and rec. room." "Nice little playground for younger kids with benches where adults can sit and read."

ROBIN'S RESORT

4935 Robin's Circle • Osage Beach, MO 65065
Phone: 573-348-2275 • Fax: 573-348-1696
www . page: robins resort. com • E-mail: mark @ robinsresort.com

Guest Ratings

Room	♦♦♦♦
Staff	♦♦♦♦
Meals	NA
Outside areas	♦♦♦♦
Fishing Guides	NA
Fishing Equipment	♦♦♦♦
Children's Activities	NA

Resort Features

🐟	✓
👫	
🍳	
⚓	
🔦	
▼	
⌕	

PRICE CATEGORY: $`

SEASON: March through November. Discounts offered during "value weeks;" before Memorial Day and after Labor Day.

TRANSPORTATION: Branson; MO (2 hour drive).

FISHING: Where: Lake of the Ozarks. **Type:** Catfish line; spin casting; bait casting. **How:** Boat; shore; dock. **Species:** Catfish; walleye; spoonbill; bluegill; crappie; white bass; striper; hybrid bass; black bass. **Guides:** Local guides available ($120 per half day 1 or 2 people) includes boat; rods; bait; transportation. **Equipment:** Live bait sold on premises; boat dock; heated fishing dock; fish cleaning area; floating sun deck; boat and motor rental. **Insider's Tip:** Crappie best in late March to latte April. Whites good in June; September; October. Bass never a down time except winter. "Fishing from the point is excellent."

ACCOMMODATIONS: 1-4 bedroom units with complete kitchens; microwave; coffeepot; linens ($490 per week for 2-4 people).

AMENITIES & ACTIVITIES: Laundry facility; recreation room; basketball court; horseshoe court; shuffleboard court; pontoon rental; swimming pool; hiking; golf; spelunking; shopping swimming; boating. **Places to Visit:** Big Surf water park; Miner Mike's Adventures; Ha Ha Tonka State Park.

GUEST COMMENTS: "Not fancy; but always clean as a pin," "good location; convenient to area activities." Staff: "work very hard to make an excellent vacation." "Definitely a family oriented resort." "Very well maintained grounds; cabins and dock" "extra large boat slips;" "enclosed fishing deck;" "fish cover around the dock;" "ample; paved parking for boat trailer," "We usually limit and occasionally catch a wall hanger."

Guest Ratings

Room	🎣🎣🎣🎣
Staff	🎣🎣🎣🎣
Meals	NA
Outside areas	🎣🎣🎣🎣
Fishing Guides	NA
Fishing Equipment	🎣🎣🎣🎣
Children's Activities	NA

Resort Features

🐟	✓
👫	
🍳	
♨	
♀	
▼	
E	

SHORE ACRES RESORT

Rt. 4, Box 2010 • Reeds Spring, MO 65737
Phone: 417-338-2351
Website: Shoreacres.tablerocklake.net • Email: rosanne@tri-lakes.net

PRICE CATEGORY: $

SEASON: March 1st through December.

TRANSPORTATION: Springfield - Branson Airport (1 hour drive).

FISHING: Where: Table Rock Lake. **Type:** Bait casting; trolling. **How:** Boat; shore. **Species:** Bass; catfish; bluegill; crappie. **Guides:** Licensed; bonded guides. **Equipment:** Lighted boat dock; boat and motor rentals; bass boat rentals; small tackle shop; fuel; concrete launching ramp.

ACCOMMODATIONS: Cottages with fully equipped kitchens; covered front porches; linens; ($54 per night double occupancy).

AMENITIES AND ACTIVITIES: Swimming pool; laundry; game room; picnic tables; grills; playground; private kid's fishing pond; boating; horseback riding; antiquing; outlet shopping. **Places to Visit:** Silver Dollar City; Shepherd of the Hills; Branson Music Shows; Table Rock Dam; College of the Ozarks; Ralph Foster Museum; White Water theme park.

PAYMENT: MasterCard; Visa; personal check; cash.

GUEST COMMENTS: "Close to major attractions and ..right on the lake in a good fishing area." "Facilities are constantly being improved...," "rustic; comfortable;" "Owners are personable and helpful." "Great ...for fishermen and their traveling partners. Near ...activities in Branson and on an extremely clear area of the lake." "Safe; covered dock area." "Good fish cleaning station." "..we both caught some big ones."

STILL WATERS VACATION RESORT

HCR 1, Box 928 • Branson, MO 65616
Phone: 417-338-2323 • Reservations: 800-777-2320
E-Mail: StillWaters@Branson.net

Guest Ratings

Room	▮▮▮▮
Staff	▮▮▮▮
Meals	NA
Outside areas	▮▮▮▮
Fishing Guides	▮▮▮▮
Fishing Equipment	▮▮▮▮
Children's Activities	▮▮▮▮

Resort Features

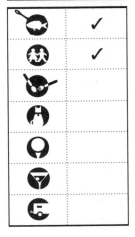

🐟	✓
👫	✓
🍴	
🔧	

PRICE CATEGORY: $$

SEASON: Open all year; discounts offered September - May/

TRANSPORTATION: Springfield - Branson; MO (1 1/2 hour drive).

FISHING: Where: Table Rock Lake. **Type:** Bait casting; Spin casting; fly casting. **How:** Boat; shore. **Species:** Largemouth, smallmouth bass; walleye; crappie; catfish. **Guides:** Local guides ($185 and up per person/ day) includes guide; boat; instruction. Gas and tackle extra. **Equipment:** Boat launch; 3 covered and lighted boat docks with electricity.

ACCOMMODATIONS: Hotel style rooms ($69 double occupancy); suites ($109 double occupancy); cottages ($59 double occupancy). Suites and cottages have fully equipped kitchens.

AMENITIES & ACTIVITIES: Structured daily "Kids Camp" during the summer. Rentals (ski boats; pontoons; fishing boats; jet skis); 2 swimming pools; 3 kiddie pools; 3 outdoor hot tubs; playgrounds; tennis court; horseshoes; basketball; volleyball; boat launch; game room; family reunion pavilion; swimming; boating; hiking; golf; horseback riding. **Places to Visit:** Silver Dollar City; Branson; MO.

PAYMENT: Visa; MasterCard; American Express; Discover; cash.

GUEST COMMENTS: "Very family oriented resort." "Exceptionally clean; well maintained pool ... playground area. " "Lots of different things to do on or near the resort." "My husband fished all day while the kids and I relaxed by the pool or went into town." Guides "knew how to find the bass." "A safe; well maintained docking facility." "I wouldn't hesitate to take children fishing in this area.". "Everything was top notch."

Guest Ratings

Room	🎣🎣🎣🎣
Staff	🎣🎣🎣🎣
Meals	
Outside areas	
Fishing Guides	
Fishing Equipment	
Children's Activities	

ALTA MEADOW RANCH

9975 West Fork Road • Darby, MT 59829
Phone: 406-349-2464 • Fax: 406-349-2018
Website: www.altameadow.com • Email: amr@montana.com

Resort Features

🐟	
👥	✓
🍴	
🚐	✓

PRICE CATEGORY: $$–$$$

SEASON: Alta Meadow is open all year.

TRANSPORTATION: Missoula, MT (2 hour drive).

FISHING: Where: Bitterroot River; Painted Rock Lake; beaver ponds along Deer Creek; private ponds. **Type:** Fly casting; bait or spin casting. **How:** Shore. **Species:** Cutthroat trout; rainbow trout; brown trout.

ACCOMMODATIONS: Log homes with fully equipped kitchens; laundry; TV; VCR; CD and tape deck; dishwasher. $150 per night for up to 4 guests.
Amenities and Activities: Babysitting available with advance notice. Catering service; horse boarding facilities for guests who bring their own horses. Hiking trails; wildlife viewing; Big Hole Battlefield; whitewater raft trips; native American Petroglyphs.

GUEST COMMENTS: "Very new cabins, owners who are extremely eager to please." "Kitchens are well stocked with staples and quality cooking equipment." "Spotless cabins and untouched, wild outside areas." "Owners treated us like we were the most important people." "Good, extremely private fishing." "Beaver ponds are fly fisherman's dream, tons of good hiding places for wily trout." "True test of skill." "Very family oriented atmosphere."

AVERILL'S FLATHEAD LAKE LODGE

150 Flathead Lake Lodge Road • Bigfork, MT 59911
Phone: 406-837-4391 • Fax: 406-837-6977
Email: fll@digisys.net

Guest Ratings

Room	🐟🐟🐟
Staff	🐟🐟🐟🐟
Meals	🐟🐟🐟
Outside areas	🐟🐟🐟🐟
Fishing Guides	🐟🐟🐟🐟
Fishing Equipment	🐟🐟🐟🐟
Children's Activities	NA

PRICE CATEGORY: $$$

SEASON: May through September. Discounts offered May 1 - June 15 and September 1 - October 10.

TRANSPORTATION: Glacier International Airport; MT (20 minute drive).

FISHING: Where: Flathead Lake; Van Lake; Swan Lake; Swan River. **Type:** Fly casting; bait casting. **How:** Walk and wade; boat; **Species:** Rainbow, lake, bull; cutthroat, brook trout. **Guides:** Local guides available; flyfishing is $85 per person per day for wade trips; includes waders; fly rods; flies; all equipment. Lake trips are $85 per person per day and include lures; all other equipment. **Equipment:** Fishing boats free to guests. **Insider's Tip:** Avid fishermen should bring own their own tackle. Best fishing is after June 15 when the water goes down.

ACCOMMODATIONS: Private cabins ($1792 per week for adults; teens $1344; ages 6-12 $1162; ages 3-5 $896; under 3 $96). Rates include all meals; horse-back riding and recreation facilities.

AMENITIES & ACTIVITIES: Baby-sitting available upon request. Pool; meeting rooms; sailboat; canoe; tennis courts; recreation room; hiking; wildlife viewing; golf; river kayaking; raft fishing trips. **Places to Visit:** Glacier National Park; National Bison Range; Jewel Basin primitive area; Bob Marshall Wilderness.

PAYMENT: MasterCard; Visa; American Express; personal checks; cash.

GUEST COMMENTS: "Not the Hilton... but certainly very comfortable. You have to remember you're in Montana; not New York." "Staff is energetic; friendly; attentive." "...guides know where to find fish and are concerned that you have a good time. Real good fishing." "All kinds of things to do a really wonderful family vacation." "Excellent location; very close to fairly large city; easy to get to and at the same time private."

Resort Features

🐟	
👥	✓
🍳	✓

Guest Ratings

Room	♦♦♦
Staff	♦♦♦♦
Meals	♦♦♦
Outside areas	NA
Fishing Guides	♦♦♦♦
Fishing Equipment	NA
Children's Activities	NA

Resort Features

🐟🍳	✓
👫	
🍴	✓
🐕	
🔍	
▼	
🎣	

BEARTOOTH PLATEAU OUTFITTERS

PO Box 1127 • Cooke City, MT 59020
Phone: 800-253-8545

PRICE CATEGORY: $$

SEASON: June 1 through September 15.

TRANSPORTATION: Billings, MT (2 ´ hour drive).

FISHING: Where: Slough Creek; Lamar River; Cache Creek; Miller Creek; Pebble Creek; several Alpine lakes in the Absaroka - Beartooth Wilderness. **Type:** Fly casting; spin casting. **How:** Walk and wade; float tube. **Species:** Cutthroat, brook, rainbow golden trout; arctic grayling. **Guides:** Local wrangler/guides included with pack trip packages. **Equipment:** Fly shop on premises.

ACCOMMODATIONS: Private log lodge with kitchen; $75 per night double occupancy. Tents in backcountry. Pack trips w/meals; guide; horses; airport shuttle; hotel lodging Sunday and Friday; week long pack trips start at $1250 per person; price per person decreases w/more people.

AMENITIES & ACTIVITIES: Hiking; back country pack trips; photography. Places to Visit: Yellowstone National Park; Buffalo Bill Museum.

PAYMENT: MasterCard; Visa; personal checks; cash.

GUEST COMMENTS: "Lodge is...nice place to crash ... before or after a pack trip." "Pack trips are great." "Fishing the isolated high country areas is unrivaled." "Trout fight hard and don't give up till they're landed." " Unbelievably peaceful and beautiful. Untouched." "Wranglers are clean cut...hard working," "...safety conscious but madeW sure we found the fish and had fun." "Perfect way to catch some great fish."

HAWLEY MOUNTAIN GUEST RANCH

Guest Ratings

Room	🐟🐟🐟🐟
Staff	🐟🐟🐟🐟
Meals	🐟🐟🐟
Outside areas	🐟🐟🐟🐟
Fishing Guides	🐟🐟🐟🐟
Fishing Equipment	NA
Children's Activities	NA

PO Box 4 • McLeod, MT 59052
Phone: 406-932-5791 • Fax: 406-932-5715
Website: www.duderanch.org/hawley/index.htm • Email: bblewett@aol.com

Resort Features

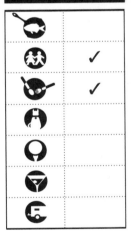

PRICE CATEGORY: $$$

SEASON: June through September. Discounts offered in June.

TRANSPORTATION: Bozeman; MT (2 1/2 hour drive). Airport pickup available.

FISHING: Where: Upper Boulder River; private stocked trout pond; Blue Lake; Silver Lake; Meatrack Creek; Yellowstone River (float trips). **Type:** Fly casting - mostly catch and release. **How:** Walk and wade; shore. **Species:** Cutthroat, rainbow, cutbow, brook trout. **Guides:** Included in package. **Equipment:** Fly rod and reel provided to guests. **Instruction:** Beginning fly casting lessons included in package. **Insider's Tip**: Most guests prefer waders. Peak season is August through September.

ACCOMMODATIONS: Lodge rooms ($1420 per person/week); cabins ($1660 per person/per week). Both lodge and cabin accommodations include all activities and meals.

AMENITIES & ACTIVITIES: Baby-sitting available with advance notice. Volleyball; horseshoes; calf roping; wildlife viewing; horseback riding; sightseeing picnics; hunting packages **Places to Visit:** Yellowstone Park.

PAYMENT: Personal checks; cash; travelers checks.

GUEST COMMENTS: "..quiet; isolated and rustic. We loved this but many would find it too remote." "Spectacular vistas... genuine old west living." Meals: "buffet style, delicious; large quantities." "Ratio of staff to guests was good," "...perfect for a couple where one...wants to fish 3 or 4 hours and the other... all day," ".. beginners get a lot of help; kids fish in a stocked pond." "If you can't catch fish here; you can't catch fish."

Guest Ratings

Room	♦♦♦♦
Staff	♦♦♦♦
Meals	NA
Outside areas	♦♦♦♦
Fishing Guides	NA
Fishing Equipment	NA
Children's Activities	NA

Resort Features

🐟	✓
👫	
🍳	
🐾	✓
♀	
▽	
🎣	

RED LODGING

PO Box 1477 • 115 West 9th • Red Lodge, MT 59068
Phone: 406-446-1272 • Reservations: 800-6-REDLODGE
Email: 5165,143@compuserve.com

PRICE CATEGORY: $

SEASON: Open all year.

TRANSPORTATION: Billings; MT (1 hour drive).

FISHING: Where: Yellowstone River; Stillwater River drainage; Rock Creek; Stillwater River; Wild Bill Lake; several high altitude lakes. **Type:** Fly casting; trolling; spin casting. **How:** Walk and wade; boat; shore. **Species:** Cutthroat, rainbow,; brook, golden trout. **Guides:** Local guides; starts around $275 for 1 or 2 people. Includes lunch; equipment and instruction. **Insider's Tip:** Many homes are streamside, all others within 15 minutes of great fishing. Light lines and leaders w/small lures are best.

ACCOMMODATIONS: Wide variety of private home rentals scattered throughout the community (rates start at $140 for 1-5 people). All homes have kitchens, most have TV/VCRs, all equipped and furnished. May include Jacuzzi; washer/dryer; direct creek access; on golf course; fireplace; swimming pool; pets allowed; stereo; deck.

AMENITIES AND ACTIVITIES: Mountain biking; hiking; golfing; auto tours; river rafting; live theatre. **Places to Visit:** Yellowstone National Park; Mystic Lake; Buffalo Bill Museum.

PAYMENT: MasterCard; Visa; Discover; American Express; personal checks; cash.

GUEST COMMENTS: "Delightful place to stay. We enjoyed the roominess; the proximity to both skiing and town; and the creek running under the bedroom window." "Service was great." "Extraordinary service on a Sunday evening; courteous and helpful." "Lots of house for the money." "Price was very fair. We had every amenity we could have wanted and plenty of room."

RUBY SPRINGS LODGE

PO Box 119 • Alder, MT 59710
Phone: 800-278-7829 • Fax: 406-842-5806
www.page: www.rubyspringlodge.com • E-mail: Info@rubyspringlodge.com

Guest Ratings

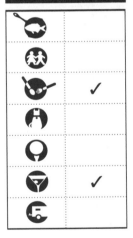

Room	🐟🐟🐟🐟
Staff	🐟🐟🐟🐟
Meals	🐟🐟🐟🐟
Outside areas	🐟🐟🐟🐟
Fishing Guides	🐟🐟🐟🐟
Fishing Equipment	🐟🐟🐟🐟
Children's Activities	NA

Resort Features

🐟		
👫		
🍳		✓
🔧		
🍷		
🔻		✓
🔥		

PRICE CATEGORY: $$$$

SEASON: May 1 through October 15.

TRANSPORTATION: Butte; Mt or Bozeman; MT.

FISHING: Where: Bighole River; Beaverhead River; Ruby River; Madison River; Jefferson River. **Type:** Fly casting. **How:** Walk and wade; shore; float trips. **Species:** Brown trout; rainbow trout; grayling. **Guides:** Professional licensed guides included in fishing package. **Equipment:** Lodge provides rod; reel; waders; boots.

ACCOMMODATIONS: Private cabins ($1150 per person for 3 nights 2 days); includes meals; accommodations; guided fishing; equipment; open bar. Facilities: Lounge; dining room; great room; large front porch.

AMENITIES AND ACTIVITIES: Golf; horseback riding; hiking; wildlife viewing. **Places to Visit:** Yellowstone National Park; Historic Virginia City.

PAYMENT: MasterCard; Visa; personal checks; cash.

GUEST COMMENTS: Staff was: "bright; eager and dedicated." "The dining is elegant without being pretentious" "...you are reasonably close to many prime fisheries." Guides are: "Skilled; funny; patient; and yes; they can catch fish anywhere." ".. did an excellent job of judging my skills and providing me a challenge at exactly the right level." "..variety of fishing venues is amazing." "...the lodge makes for a nice day alone; with the cabin and a sit down lunch very close. "

Guest Ratings

Room	🐟🐟🐟🐟
Staff	🐟🐟🐟🐟
Meals	🐟🐟🐟🐟
Outside areas	🐟🐟🐟🐟
Fishing Guides	🐟🐟🐟🐟
Fishing Equipment	NA
Children's Activities	NA

Resort Features

🍳🐟	
👥	
🍳🥄	✓
🎯	
💡	
▼	
🔵	

UNDER WILD SKIES LODGE AND OUTFITTERS

PO Box 849 • Philipsburg, MT 59858
Phone: 406-859-3000 • Fax: 406-859-3161
Email: underwildskies@juno.com

PRICE CATEGORY: $$

SEASON: May through December.

TRANSPORTATION: Butte, MT (1´ hour drive).

FISHING: Where: Rock Creek; Middle Fork River; Big Hole River; numerous high mountain lakes. **Type:** Fly casting; spin casting. **How:** Walk and wade; float tube; boat. **Species:** Mountain whitefish; dolly varden; rainbow, brook, cutthroat trout. **Guides:** Licensed; insured guides ($75 per day) includes lunch. **Equipment:** Some available for loan. **Insider's Tip:** High mountain lakes are accessable after July 1st. Hand tied flies are available at the ranch. Waders are recommended.

ACCOMMODATIONS: Lodge rooms; meals included; $80 per person/day; reduced rates for children. Tent camping on pack trips.

AMENIIES AND ACTIVITIES: Golf; hiking; hunting packages (bighorn sheep; elk; deer; mountain goat; bear; moose; antelope); horseback riding; pack trips; boating; panning for gold; digging for sapphires. **Places to Visit:** Anaconda Pintler Wilderness Area; Deer Lodge National Forest.

PAYMENT: Personal checks; cash.

GUEST COMMENTS: "Unstructured ranch...follows guest's schedule instead of the one ... most convenient for the staff." "Terrific fishing; great fishing spots from rivers to beaver ponds in the near vicinity." "Home cooking; plentiful portions." "Staff is outstanding... willing to accommodate special requests." "Not for someone who wants a ....super fast paced...trip. "..."a chance to become intimately familiar with a little slice of heaven."

NEW HAMPSHIRE · NEW MEXICO · NEW

Guest Ratings

Room	🐟🐟🐟🐟
Staff	🐟🐟🐟🐟
Meals	🐟🐟🐟🐟
Outside areas	🐟🐟🐟🐟
Fishing Guides	NA
Fishing Equipment	🐟🐟🐟🐟
Children's Activities	NA

Resort Features

🐟	
👨‍👩‍👧	✓
🍳	✓
🎣	
🍷	✓
🍸	✓
🚐	

THE BALSAMS GRAND RESORT HOTEL

Lake Gloriette • Route 26 • Dixville Notch, NH 03576
Phone: 603-225-3400
www.thebalsams.com • E-mail address: theBALSAMS@aol.com

PRICE CATEGORY: $$$

SEASON: Open all year.

TRANSPORTATION: Portland International; ME (2 1/2 hour drive).

FISHING: Where: Lake Gloriette (no license required; fly fishing only); Lake Umbagog; Connecticut Lakes; Mohawk River; Connecticut River; Androscoggin River; Magalloway River; Rapid Rivers. **Type:** Fly fishing; spin casting. **How:** Boat; shore. **Species:** Rainbow, brook, brown trout, salmon, pickerel; northern pike. **Guide Service:** Licensed New Hampshire guides. **Instruction:** A series of fly fishing schools is offered each spring, includes casting, knot tying, fly tying, entomology; equipment and cooking.

ACCOMMODATIONS: Historic Inn built in 1866 ($150 and up per person) includes three meals and unlimited use of facilities.

AMENITIES AND ACTIVITIES: Full day, structured childcare; 2 golf courses, putting greens, tennis courts, swimming pool, canoes, hiking and biking trails; basketball court. Games, contests, family activities, tours; wine tastings; guided nature walks, hikes, picnic tours; professional nightclub shows, lectures, concerts; movie theater; downhill and cross country skiing, snowshoeing and ice skating.

PAYMENT: Mastercard, Visa, American Express, personal checks and cash.

GUEST COMMENTS: "Balsams is not a fishing lodge per se; the meals; ambiance and other activities make it a truly grand resort." "Meals are outstanding; a highpoint." Staff: "is friendly; quick to help...unobtrusive." "The fly fishing school was very interesting; learned new techniques and a few tricks." "...enough variety to keep most anglers happy." "Fishing here isn't as good as Alaska; but the varied activities and luxurious setting make it a superb destination for groups with diverse interests."

WOODBOUND INN

Guest Ratings

Room	🎣🎣🎣
Staff	🎣🎣🎣🎣
Meals	🎣🎣🎣
Outside areas	🎣🎣🎣🎣
Fishing Guides	NA
Fishing Equipment	NA
Children's Activities	NA

62 Woodbound Rd. • Rindge, NH 03461
Phone: 603-532-8341 • Reservations: 800-688-7770
Email: Woodbound@aol.com

PRICE CATEGORY: $$ – $$$

SEASON: Open all year.

TRANSPORTATION: Boston, MA (1 hour 15 minute drive).

FISHING: Where: Lake Contoocook. **Type:** Spin casting; Fly casting. **How:** Boat; shore. **Species:** Bass; trout; various panfish. **Insider's Tip:** Fishing is best in spring or fall.

ACCOMMODATIONS: Lakefront cabins; Inn rooms ($79 per person) breakfast included.

AMENITIES AND ACTIVITIES: 9 hole golf course; putting green; tennis court; skating pond; playbarn; shuffleboard; picnic area; private beach; hiking trails; dining room; lounge; banquet room; meeting rooms. Swimming; golf; hiking; cross country skiing; summer concerts; greyhound races; theater. **Places to Visit:** Mt. Monadnock; Cathedral of the Pines; Friendly Farm (petting zoo).

PAYMENT: MasterCard; Visa; American Express; personal checks; cash.

GUEST COMMENTS: "Many big resort amenities...bed and breakfast atmosphere." "Rooms are very modern and attractive." "Bed and breakfast rooms are quaint." "Cabins...close to the water with good access." "Average to good fishing." "Fishing is done on your own...very nice, private and quiet." "Relaxing fishing with opportunity to catch and cook some nice, hard fighting panfish."

Resort Features

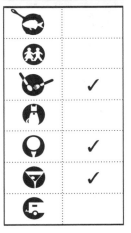

🐟	
👥	
🍳	✓
🍸	
⛳	✓
🍷	✓
⛷	

Guest Ratings

Room	🐟🐟🐟🐟
Staff	🐟🐟🐟🐟
Meals	🐟🐟🐟🐟
Outside areas	🐟🐟🐟
Fishing Guides	NA
Fishing Equipment	NA
Children's Activities	NA

Resort Features

🐟	✓
👥	
🍴	✓
🍷	
💡	
⛴	
♿	

BLACKFIRE FLYFISHING GUEST RANCH

Box 981 • Angel Fire; NM 87710
Phone: 505-377-6870 • Fax: 505-377-3807
www.newmex.com/blackfire • Email: blackfire@newmex.com

PRICE CATEGORY: $$$

SEASON: Mid-May through mid-October.

TRANSPORTATION: Albuquerque (3 hour drive).

FISHING: Where: Private lake on property. Cimarron River; Red River; Coyote Creek within easy driving distance. **Type:** Fly casting (catch and release only on property). **How:** Boat; float tubes; wade; shore. **Species:** Rainbow trout; brown trout; cutthroat trout. **Guides:** Local guides arranged through ranch ($220-$300 per person/day) include lunch and flies. **Equipment:** Small tackle shop; some rod/reel sets for guest use. **Insider's Tip:** July and August are the best months for dry fly action.

ACCOMMODATIONS: 3 bedroom, 2 bath guest house with sitting area; kitchen; (start at $125 per person/day) includes rod fee; lodging; meals. Meals are prepared; delivered and served in guest house.

AMENITIES AND ACTIVITIES: Nature walks; bird watching; self-guided auto tours. **Places to Visit:** Angel Fire Resort (golf; tennis; horseback riding; hot air ballooning); historic sites.

PAYMENT: Personal checks; cash.

GUEST COMMENTS: "The lodge is immaculate and very comfortable." Staff: "Very accommodating; helpful; friendly and personable." "Many large trout were caught; admired and released." "Blackfire's fish are strong and healthy; great fighters." "A fantastic; well maintained fishery." "Fish after giant fish." "Fishing was challenging; but not...frustrating or boring." "We especially enjoyed being the only group at the ranch. It gave the whole vacation a very personal; relaxed feel."

LOS PINOS RANCH

Rt. Box 8 • Terrero, NM 87573
Phone: 505-757-6213

Guest Ratings

Room	🐟🐟🐟
Staff	🐟🐟🐟🐟
Meals	🐟🐟🐟🐟
Outside areas	🐟🐟🐟
Fishing Guides	NA
Fishing Equipment	🐟🐟🐟
Children's Activities	NA

Resort Features

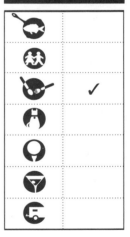

PRICE CATEGORY: $$$

SEASON: June 1st through Labor Day.

TRANSPORTATION: Santa Fe, NM (1 hour drive).

FISHING: Where: Pecos River and tributaries; Mora River; high mountain lakes. **Type:** Wet and dry fly fishing. **How:** Walk and wade; horseback to high mountain lakes. **Species:** Rainbow trout; pecos brown trout; cutthroat trout. **Guides:** Local guides ($100 per person for 1/2 day).

ACCOMMODATIONS: Private cabins ($95 per person/day) includes 3 meals.

AMENITIES AND ACTIVITIES: Hiking trails; great room; library; front porch. Horseback riding; hiking. **Places to Visit:** Indian Pueblos; Santa Fe; Pecos National Monument; Spanish Villages; Bandolier National Park.

PAYMENT: Cash; personal check.

GUEST COMMENTS: "Staying at Los Pinos takes you back in time. No TVs or telephones, the ambiance is from the 1920's." "I wouldn't classify this ranch as a fishing lodge; although the stream is right there and you can simply walk down the hill and drop a line." "...we were surprised at the superb dinner and manner in which it was served...both 5 stars." Staff: "very accommodating;" "Excellent fishing on the Pecos and Pecos headwaters." "You are free to ride; hike; fish or simply be lazy."

Guest Ratings

Room	🐟🐟🐟
Staff	🐟🐟🐟🐟
Meals	🐟🐟🐟
Outside areas	🐟🐟🐟
Fishing Guides	🐟🐟🐟
Fishing Equipment	NA
Children's Activities	NA

Resort Features

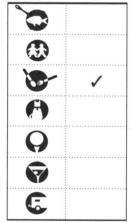

🐟	
👪	
🍳	✓
🎣	
♀	
🍸	
🚐	

INDIAN SPRINGS FLYFISHING CAMP

RR1, Box 200AA • Hancock, NY 13783
Phone: 215-679-5022 • Fax: 717-224-2708
Email: Leehrtmn@erols.com

PRICE CATEGORY: $$$

SEASON: May 1st-September 30th.

TRANSPORTATION: Binghamton; NY (1 hour drive).

FISHING: Where: Upper Delaware River. **Type:** Fly casting. **How:** Float; shore; walk and wade. **Species:** Rainbow trout; brown trout; shad. **Guides:** Experienced guide services included with lodging. **Equipment:** Some equipment available for loan. **Instruction:** 2 and 3 day fly fishing schools: equipment; knot tying; leader design; casting; entomology; releasing; nymphing tactics; dry fly tactics, lodging and meals.

ACCOMMODATIONS: Cabins with full baths (meals included). 2 day fly fishing school $390 2 day float package $580/1 or 2 anglers.

AMENITIES AND ACTIVITIES: Lodge; dining room. Trout casting and fishing pond; 1-3 day float trips; scenic river trips. **Places to Visit:** Catskill Fly Fishing Museum.

PAYMENT: Cash; personal checks.

GUEST COMMENTS: "A fishing camp for fishing people—no tourist frills." "Cabins are very nice; staying in the main house is not preferred." Guides: "...want you to catch fish." "...expert fishermen with extensive knowledge of the river." "Fishing on the Upper Delaware River is not easy." "...Dry fly anglers will be shut out if they will not fish nymphs; streamers and wets." "The fish are extremely selective; but when you do land one, it is a tremendous thrill," "...river was fabulous...the comforts and setting perfect."

K & G CHARTERS AND LODGE

94 Creamery Rd. • Oswego, NY 13126
Phone: 315-343-8171 • Reservations: 800-346-6533
www.mgfx.com/fishing/charters/K&G • Email: kgsportfishinglodge@reddragon.com

Guest Ratings

Room	🐟🐟🐟
Staff	🐟🐟🐟🐟
Meals	🐟🐟🐟🐟
Outside areas	🐟🐟🐟
Fishing Guides	🐟🐟🐟
Fishing Equipment	🐟🐟🐟🐟
Children's Activities	NA

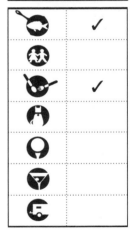

Resort Features

🐟	✓
👥	
🍳	✓
🔧	
♀	
▼	
₤	

PRICE CATEGORY: $$$

SEASON: Open all year.

TRANSPORTATION: Syracuse, NY (40 minute drive.)

FISHING: Where: Lake Ontario; Oswego River; Salmon River. **Type:** Bait casting; spin casting; fly casting. **How:** Boat; shore; walk and wade. **Species:** Smallmouth bass; salmon; steelhead; brown trout. **Guides:** US Coast Guard certified charters or New York State licensed guides included in lodging packages. **Equipment :** All spin and trolling tackle. **Insider's Tip:** "...many different fish at various times...browns in March...ending with steelhead in December...in between are lakers; coho; king salmon. "

ACCOMMODATIONS: 2 bedroom suites with complete kitchens; living room; towels; linens; color cable TV; AC; heat. ($200 per person/day) includes guide and lodging. Meal packages also available.

AMENITIES & ACTIVITIES: Golf; sporting clays; maritime museum; Harborfest (4 day water front event last weekend in July).

PAYMENT: Personal checks; cash.

GUEST COMMENTS: "The area is not remote...offers a multitude of fine restaurants and other activities." "Comfortable; no frill rooms." "Spacious lodging with full kitchen." "Excellent equipment and boats." "The host and guide was courteous; friendly and knowledgeable; willing to do anything to make the trip a success." "Prices are very competitive." "You'll have a great time and catch great fish."

213

Guest Ratings

Room	🐟🐟🐟🐟
Staff	🐟🐟🐟🐟
Meals	🐟🐟🐟🐟
Outside areas	🐟🐟🐟🐟
Fishing Guides	NA
Fishing Equipment	NA
Children's Activities	NA

Resort Features

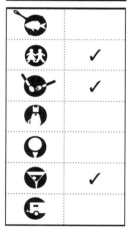

🐟	
👥	✓
🍳	✓
🎣	
⛱	
🚤	✓
⛽	

LAKE PLACID LODGE

PO Box 550 • Lake Placid, NY 12946
Phone: 518-523-2700 • Fax: 518-523-1124
www.lakeplacidlodge.com • Email: info@lakeplacidlodge.com

PRICE CATEGORY: $$$$

SEASON: Open all year.

TRANSPORTATION: New York City (5 1/2 hour drive), Adirondack Regional Airport (small aircraft/commuter flights).

FISHING: Where: West Branch AuSable River; Lake Placid. **Type:** Fly casting; spin casting; bait casting. **How:** Walk and wade; boat; shore. **Species:** Trout rainbow; lake (togue); brook; cutthroat; pike; largemouth bass; smallmouth bass. **Guides:** Guide packages are custom priced depending on individual requirements.

ACCOMMODATIONS: Lodge rooms; 1 and 2 bedroom cabins; starts at $225 double occupancy. Full breakfast included with all accommodations.

AMENITIES AND ACTIVITIES: Baby sitting upon request. Restaurant; sandy swimming area; sundeck; mountain bike rentals; Lake Placid sightseeing cruise; golf; tennis; canoeing; biking; hiking; hunting; ice skating; skiing; bobsledding. **Places to Visit:** Olympic Museum; Lake Placid Village; Whiteface Club (fishing boat rentals; canoe rentals; golf; tennis); Adirondack State Park.

PAYMENT: MasterCard; Visa; American Express; cash; personal checks.

GUEST COMMENTS: "Excellent accommodations with unexpected extras like fresh flowers; iced sparkling bubbly; fresh fruit and pastries." "Staff was attentive; quick and always willing to please. I never heard the word 'no'." "Grounds are immaculate right down to the docks at the lake." "Attention paid to every detail." "The lodge is beautiful and warm; the scenic setting is perfect."

THOUSAND ISLANDS INN

335 Riverside Drive • PO Box 69 • Clayton, NY 13624-0069
Phone: 315-686-3030 • Reservations: 800-544-4241
www.1000-islands.com • email: tiinn@1000-islands.com

Guest Ratings

Room	🎣🎣🎣
Staff	🎣🎣🎣🎣
Meals	🎣🎣🎣🎣
Outside areas	🎣🎣🎣
Fishing Guides	🎣🎣🎣🎣
Fishing Equipment	🎣🎣🎣🎣
Children's Activities	NA

Resort Features

🐟	
👨‍👩‍👧	✓
🍴	✓
🎿	
🏌	
🍷	✓
🚐	

PRICE CATEGORY: $ – $$$$

SEASON: Third Friday in May through last Sunday in September.

TRANSPORTATION: Syracuse, NY (1 hour 15 minute drive).

FISHING: Where: New York and Ontario regions of the St. Lawrence River. **Type:** Trolling; sight fishing; drift boat. **How:** Boat. **Species:** Smallmouth bass; northern pike; walleye; muskie. **Guide:** US Coast Guard licensed guides ($150 per person per day) can accommodate large groups. Includes; bait; tackle; boat and guide. **Equipment:** All equipment is provided on fishing package trips. Typically 6 1/2 ft. Shimano Sensilite rod with 8# test line.

ACCOMMODATIONS: Historic Inn built in 1897 ($43.50 per person; bed and breakfast) or Fishing packages (start at $360 per person for group of 4-6; rates vary based on party size) includes 2 nights lodging; all meals; 2 days guided fishing; tackle and bait.

AMENITIES AND ACTIVITIES: Restaurant; lounge; babysitting services. Golfing; white-water rafting; tennis; boat tours. **Places to Visit:** Antique Boat Museum.

PAYMENT: MasterCard; Visa; Discover; American Express.

GUEST COMMENTS: "Rooms are old but nicely furnished," "Wide choice of meals; well prepared and plenty..." "—try the prime rib; it's legendary." "We always catch enough fish to satisfy." "I caught and released over thirty fish in a day and a half. Mostly smallmouth bass...plus one big catfish." "Knowledgeable guide who works hard for the guests" "Very comfortable boat for fishing." "All tackle top of the line; looked brand new." "The packages including boat; guide; bait; tackle and meals...excellent value."

OREGON

Guest Ratings

Room	🐟🐟🐟🐟
Staff	🐟🐟🐟🐟
Meals	🐟🐟🐟◗
Outside areas	🐟🐟🐟
Fishing Guides	🐟🐟🐟🐟
Fishing Equipment	NA
Children's Activities	NA

Resort Features

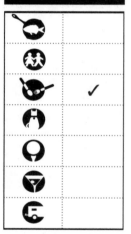

🐟	
👥	
🍳	✓
🎣	
⚲	
▼	
₵	

THE CJ LODGE

PO Box 130 • Maupin, OR 97037
Phone: 541-395-2404 • Fax: 541-395-2494
Email: cnjlodge@aol.com

PRICE CATEGORY: $$

SEASON: Open all year.

TRANSPORTATION: Portland, OR (2 hour drive).

FISHING: Where: Deschutes River. **Type:** Fly casting; catch and release; artificial lures. **How:** Boat; shore. **Species:** Redside trout; steelhead; salmon. **Guides:** List of local guides available at lodge. **Instruction:** Hour long casting classes and all day entomology seminars are available through fishing guides. **Tip:** Native redside trout fishing good all year. Steelhead best summer and fall.

ACCOMMODATIONS: Guest rooms with private entries and private baths ($65 double occupancy) includes breakfast.

AMENITIES AND ACTIVITIES: Picnic tables; fly tying bench; dining room; common area. Whitewater raft trips; self-guided driving tours; biking; canyon hiking; hunting; clay shoots; walking; rock hunting. **Places to Visit:** Waterfalls; Indian Museum; Discovery Center.

PAYMENT: MasterCard; Visa; American Express; personal check or cash.

GUEST COMMENTS: "Bed and breakfast not a fishing lodge; but probably the best place...in Maupin...great river access," "...nice and homey; not fancy." "Very clean; always." "Fishing excellent." "Great people; like family." "Wonderful large lawn; right down to the river." "Wife caught 3 steelhead on a fly in one day all over 31 inches." "White water rafting is fantastic; food is great; scenery is beautiful; everything is done for you- you can't help but relax and enjoy."

HORSESHOE RANCH

PO Box 495 • Fort Klamath, OR 97626
Phone: 541-381-2297 • Fax: 541-381-2258

Guest Ratings

Room	🎣🎣🎣
Staff	🎣🎣🎣🎣
Meals	🎣🎣🎣🎣
Outside areas	🎣🎣🎣🎣
Fishing Guides	🎣🎣🎣🎣
Fishing Equipment	NA
Children's Activities	NA

Resort Features

🍳🐟	
👪	
🍴	✓
🎣	✓
🔦	
⛳	
🚵	

PRICE CATEGORY: $$$

SEASON: Open all year. Fishing season is May through October.

TRANSPORTATION: Medford, OR (1 1/2 hour drive). Klamath Falls, OR (45 minute drive).

FISHING: Where: Wood River (private access), Williamson River; Sprague River; Klamath Lake; Agency Lake; various spring creeks. **Type:** Fly casting (catch and release; artificial lures). **How:** Shore; boat; float tube. **Species:** Rainbow, German brown, brook trout. **Guides:** Licensed; insured; local guides; $250 1 or 2 people per day; includes boat; tackle. **Equipment:** A few loaner rods, reels and flies are available; fly tying bench. **Insider's Tip:** 9' ; 6# rods average, dry and wet line. Peak season: September and October. There should be good hopper action in August.

ACCOMMODATIONS: Historic ranch house ($200 per day/person) includes fishing, breakfast, dinner and access to Wood River; ($125 per day/person) without access to Wood River.

AMENITIES & ACTIVITIES: Sun room; living room; horse facilities; rodeo; golf; skiing; canoeing; boating; biking; hiking; horseback riding; cutting; birding. **Places to Visit:** Crater Lake.

PAYMENT: MasterCard; Visa; personal checks; cash.

GUEST COMMENTS: "Exceptionally clean always." "Staff is friendly and professional. Always on the ball." "Meals were good to excellent." "Fishing was excellent to off-the-charts." "Magnum sized trout swim here." "These fish fight and fight hard." "Beautiful unspoiled setting."

Guest Ratings

Room	♦♦♦
Staff	♦♦♦♦
Meals	♦♦♦
Outside areas	♦♦♦♦
Fishing Guides	NA
Fishing Equipment	NA
Children's Activities	NA

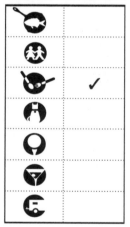

Resort Features

🐟	
👥	
🍳	✓
🎣	
♀	
▽	
🛞	

PARADISE LODGE

PO Box 456 • Gold Beach, OR 97444
Phone: 541-247-6022 • Reservations: 800-525-2161 • Fax: 541-247-7714
www.paradise-rogue.com • Email: rrr97@harborside.com

PRICE CATEGORY: $$

SEASON: Year round.

TRANSPORTATION: Commercial flight to Coos Bay/North Bend or Crescent City, CA. Lodge is accessible only via boat or foot—reservations made through Rogue River Trip Center—503-247-6022.

FISHING: Where: Rogue River; Paradise Creek; Jackson Creek. **Type:** Bait casting; spin casting; fly casting. **How:** Wade; shore. **Species:** Coho salmon; steelhead; trout.

ACCOMMODATIONS: Standard hotel rooms and cabins; $138 per adult—includes one night's lodging, round trip transportation; 4 meals.

AMENITIES AND ACTIVITIES: Hiking; river rafting; photography; volleyball; horseshoes; board games. **Insider's Tip:** "Bring extra film. Only limited supply at the lodge and it's not possible to just run to the store."

PAYMENT: Visa; MasterCard; personal checks; cash.

GUEST COMMENTS: "Extremely secluded yet easy to get to." "Jet boat ride is fairly comfortable and extremely scenic." "Rooms are excellent considering the remoteness of the location." "Good solid meals, excellent staff." "Fishing areas are not crowded, very private." "Remote and unique, if you're looking for something off the beaten path but don't want to rough it too much this may be the right place for you."

SUMMER LAKE BED AND BREAKFAST INN

Room	🐟🐟🐟🐟
Staff	🐟🐟🐟🐟
Meals	🐟🐟🐟🐟
Outside areas	🐟🐟🐟🐟
Fishing Guides	NA
Fishing Equipment	NA
Children's Activities	NA

31501 Hwy. 31 • Summer Lake, OR 97640
Phone: 541-943-3983 • Reservations: 800-261-2778
www.presys.com/comm/summerlakeinn • Email: dseven@presys.com

Resort Features

🐟	✓
👥	
🍳	✓
🎣	✓
◐	
▼	
€	

PRICE CATEGORIES: $-$$

SEASON: Open all year.

TRANSPORTATION: Redmond, OR (2 hour drive). Paisley Airport (private aircraft).

FISHING: Where: Ana River; Ana Reservoir; Chewacan River; Sycan River; Sprague River; Thompson Reservoir. **Type:** Bait casting; spin casting; fly casting (catch and release only on Jack's Lake). **How:** Boat; float tube; shore. **Species:** Rainbow trout; brook trout; brown trout. **Equipment:** Canoe; small boat; or float tube free to guests.

ACCOMMODATIONS: Inn rooms; $60 double occupancy; Cedar cabins, four with fully equipped kitchen facilities ($85 and up double occupancy without meals; $185 with meals).

AMENITIES AND ACTIVITIES: Laundry; horse boarding facilities; library; hot tub; picnic table; horseshoe pits; canoes; small boats. Rock hunting; bird watching; hiking; photography. **Places to Visit:** Chewaucan Marsh; Summer Lake Hot Springs; Five Mile Caves; Gearheart Wilderness Area; Warner Valley.

PAYMENT: Visa; MasterCard; American Express; personal checks; cash.

GUEST COMMENTS: "Clean, comfortable, luxurious lodging." "Beautifully decorated." "Generous portions at mealtime." "Because Jack's Lake is private, fishing pressure is low and you don't have to fight other anglers for space." "The pond is a good place for beginners to practice fly casting." "Wide variety of water to challenge most fishermen of varying abilities." "Plenty for nonfishers to do" "Nice quiet area, professional staff, delicious meals and fabulous fishing."

Guest Ratings

Room	🐟🐟🐟
Staff	🐟🐟🐟🐟
Meals	NA
Outside areas	🐟🐟🐟🐟
Fishing Guides	NA
Fishing Equipment	NA
Children's Activities	NA

Resort Features

🐟	
👥	
🍴	✓
🎿	
♀	
▽	
♿	✓

THE LODGE AT SUMMER LAKE

36980 Hwy. 31 • Summer Lake, OR 97640
Phone: 541-943-3993

PRICE CATEGORY: $-$$

SEASON: Open all year.

TRANSPORTATION: Redmond, OR (2 hour drive).

FISHING: Where: Ana Reservoir; Ana River; Chewaucan River; private catch and release bass pond. **Type:** Fly casting; bait casting; spin casting. **How:** Shore; boat; walk and wade. **Species:** Bass; rainbow trout; brook trout; brown trout.

ACCOMMODATIONS: Motel Units $39 per person/night. Lodge units $55 per person/night with breakfast or $25 per person without breakfast. RV hookups ($10 double occupancy).

AMENITIES AND ACTIVITIES: Restaurant; horse boarding facilities; birding; wildlife viewing; horseback riding; hiking. **Places to Visit:** Summer Lake Hot Springs; self-guided petroglyph tours.

PAYMENT: MasterCard; Visa; personal checks.

GUEST COMMENTS: "The accommodations are very basic; a place to sleep but not much more." "Extremely clean...better than you'd expect for the...price." "Lots of different places to fish." "You really have a shot at catching trophy bass in this area." "Outstanding fishing." "Staff...can help you find the most productive places and ways to fish." "We enjoy hiking out to the lesser known hot springs. "

YAMSI RANCH

Box 371 • Chiloquin, OR 97624
Phone: 541-783-2403

Guest Ratings

Room	🐟🐟🐟
Staff	🐟🐟🐟🐟
Meals	🐟🐟🐟🐟
Outside areas	🐟🐟🐟🐟
Fishing Guides	🐟🐟🐟
Fishing Equipment	🐟🐟🐟
Children's Activities	NA

Resort Features

🐟	
👫	
🍴	✓
🔧	
🏌	
🚁	
🚐	

PRICE CATEGORY: $$$

SEASON: May 1st through November 1st.

TRANSPORTATION: Klamath Falls, OR (1 hour drive). Medford, OR (1 1/2 hour drive).

FISHING: Where: Williamson River headwaters (8 miles of private access); Spring Creek. **Type:** Catch and release fly fishing only. **How:** Bank and some wading. **Species:** Rainbow trout; brook trout. **Guides:** Professional, local guides ($100 per day.) **Equipment:** Some equipment available for rent. Flies; leaders and tippets for sale. **Instruction:** Fly casting instruction available.

ACCOMMODATIONS: Main ranch house; 5 bedrooms; shared bath. Cabin (5-7 people) ($200 per person/day; 3 night minimum).

AMENITIES AND ACTIVITIES: Library; living room; meeting room. Hiking; biking; wildlife viewing; canoeing; ranch activities. **Places to Visit:** Crater Lake National Park

PAYMENT: Cash; personal checks.

GUEST COMMENTS: "It's a working cattle ranch...you have breakfast and dinner with your hosts...fish all day," "uncrowded lodge in a beautiful setting." "Outstanding meals." "The staff works around the guest's schedule..." "not the easiest fishing; but...some of the best." "Most...is site fishing to observable fish...most...from the banks." Guides: "...knew where the trout liked to lie...related well to fishermen and women...novice to the best." "...hostess delightful; the house unique...no...'b.s.' (except in the pasture)."

Guest Ratings

Room	⚓⚓⚓
Staff	⚓⚓⚓⚓
Meals	⚓⚓
Outside areas	⚓⚓
Fishing Guides	NA
Fishing Equipment	NA
Children's Activities	NA

Resort Features

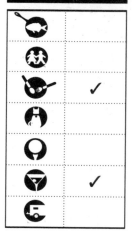

🐟	
👥	
🍳	✓
🎧	
♀	
🍸	✓
🚐	

KANE MANOR COUNTRY INN

230 Clay St. • Kane, PA 16735
Phone: 814-837-6522 • Fax: 814-837-6664

PRICE CATEGORY: $$

SEASON: Open all year.

TRANSPORTATION: Pittsburg; PA (3 hour drive.)

FISHING: Where: Kinzua Resevoir; Tionesta Creek—East Branch; Tionesta Creek—South Branch; Chappel Fork; Mead Run; several other small streams and tributaries. **Type:** Spin casting; fly casting; bait casting. **How:** Boat; shore; walk and wade. **Species:** Trout; salmon; bass; muskielunge; walleye. **Insider's Tip:** Call Commonwealth of Pennsylvania Fish and Boat Commission for current year license fees; seasons and regulations (717) 657-4518.

ACCOMMODATIONS: Historic bed and breakfast inn; period furnishing; private baths; ($99 double occupancy) includes breakfast.

AMENITIES & ACTIVITIES: Hiking; golfing; cross country skiing; mystery clue weekend; canoeing; boating; swimming; mountain biking; horseback riding; waterslides; Knox Kane Kinzua excursion train. **Places to Visit:** Holgate Toy Company; Kinzua Bridge; Zippo Family Store: Tionesta Scenic Area.

PAYMENT: MasterCard; Visa; American Express; personal checks.

GUEST COMMENTS: "Very peaceful and refreshing." "Staff extra helpful; always available to lend a hand." "Lots of great civil war period furnishing. Like stepping back in time without giving up any modern day conveniences." "Grounds are lovely with lots of hidey holes to explore." "Lots of good fishing in the area." "Nice place for a romantic getaway/fishing weekend."

YELLOW BREECHES HOUSE

PO Box 221 • 213 Front St. • Boiling Springs, PA 17007
Phone: 800-258-1639 • Fax: 717-258-9882
www.pa.net/flyfish • Email: flyfish@pa.net

Guest Ratings

Room	🎣🎣🎣🎣
Staff	🎣🎣🎣🎣
Meals	🎣🎣🎣🎣
Outside areas	🎣🎣🎣
Fishing Guides	🎣🎣🎣
Fishing Equipment	🎣🎣🎣
Children's Activities	NA

Resort Features

🐟	
👥	
🍳	✓
🔧	
⚲	
▽	
€	

PRICE CATEGORY: $$

SEASON: April 1st through November 30th.

TRANSPORTATION: Harrisburg International (1/2 hour drive). Dulles, D.C. (2 hour drive).

FISHING: Where: Yellow Breeches; Letort; Big Spring; Green Spring; Clarks Creek. **Type:** Fly casting; spin casting. **How:** Walk and wade. **Species:** Brown trout; brook trout; rainbow trout; palomino trout. **Guides:** Included in packages or hired separately ($285 per day for 1 or two people includes lunch and equipment.) **Equipment:** Free full outfitting on guided and learn to fly-fish package. **Instruction:** 2 day fly fishing school covers equipment; casting; entomology; fly tying.

ACCOMMODATIONS: Bed and breakfast style rooms decorated with fly fishing theme; breakfast included. Fly fishing school starts at $375 per person (2 nights lodging; instruction; 4 meals; wine and cheese reception). Lodging & breakfast starts at $90 for 1 or 2 people.

AMENITIES & ACTIVITIES: Dining room; library; sitting room with cable TV; sun porch; tackle room; fly shop; antiquing; hiking; dinner theater; biking; swimming; golfing. **Places to Visit:** Hershey Theme Park; Gettysburg Battlefield; Lancaster Dutch Country.

PAYMENT: MasterCard; Visa; American Express; personal checks; cash.

GUEST COMMENTS: "Quaint bed and breakfast with relaxed atmosphere." "Clean rooms, good food, but the real highlight is fishing and gracious hosts." "Learned so much about fly fishing; really a great experience." "Great guide; patient teacher; very knowledgeable." "Great; personalized instruction." "Low student teacher ratio."

Guest Ratings

Room	♦♦♦
Staff	♦♦♦
Meals	NA
Outside areas	♦♦♦♦
Fishing Guides	NA
Fishing Equipment	NA
Children's Activities	NA

Resort Features

🐟	✓
👪	
🍳	
🎣	
⛵	
🔻	
🔥	✓

SANTEE STATE PARK

251 State Park Rd. • Santee, SC 29142
Phone: 803-854-2408 • Fax: 803-854-4834

PRICE CATEGORY: $

SEASON: Open all year.

TRANSPORTATION: Charleston, SC (1 hour drive).

FISHING: Where: Lake Marion; Lake Moultrie; Santee River. **Type:** Spin casting; bait casting; fly casting; bobber. **How:** Shore; boat; pier. **Species:** Largemouth bass; striped bass; black crappie; bream; catfish. **Equipment:** Boat rentals (guests provide motors); tackle shop; boat ramp. **Insider's Tip:** Fishing best spring and fall.

ACCOMMODATIONS: Campsites with water and electric ($14); vacation cabins with kitchens; linens ($360 per week for 1-4 people).

AMENITIES AND ACTIVITIES: Conference facilities; interpretive center; restaurant; pedal boats; sheltered picnic area; nature trails; lake and swamp tours; golf; naturalist program; hiking; biking; birding. **Places to Visit:** Santee National Wildlife Refuge.

PAYMENT: MasterCard; Visa; Discover; personal checks; cash

GUEST COMMENTS: "Cabins are functional and clean," "...entire park is extremely well maintained and managed." "Lots of activities...but you never feel crowded or rushed." "Naturalist programs are really interesting." "Bass are great fighters." "We like to bring our own boat and rent one of the pier cabins that have a dock. It's convenient and inexpensive." "Haven't been able to find a better deal for do it yourself fishing."

Guest Ratings

Room	🎣🎣🎣
Staff	🎣🎣🎣🎣
Meals	🎣🎣🎣
Outside areas	🎣🎣🎣🎣
Fishing Guides	🎣🎣🎣🎣
Fishing Equipment	🎣🎣🎣
Children's Activities	NA

CEDAR HILL RESORT

2371 Cedar Hill Rd. • Celina, TN 38551
Phone: 615-243-2301 • Reservations: 1-800-872-8393

Resort Features

🐟	✓
👪	
🍳	
⚓	✓
🔦	
⛴	
🚐	

PRICE CATEGORY: $

SEASON: Open mid March through December 1st.

TRANSPORTATION: Nashville, TN (2 hour drive).

FISHING: Where: Dale Hollow Lake. **Type:** Spin casting; bait casting; trolling; bobber. **How:** Boat; shore. **Species:** Smallmouth bass; walleye; bluegill; crappie; catfish; trout. **Guides:** Experienced; local guides ($150 per day). **Equipment:** Dock; fishing boat rentals. **Insider's Tip:** The world record smallmouth bass; weighing in at 11 lbs. 15 oz.; was caught by a Cedar Hill guest on Dale Hollow Lake.

ACCOMMODATIONS: 1-3 bedroom cottages with fully equipped kitchens and decks facing the lake ($95 per day double occupancy). Standard motel rooms ($62 per day double occupancy); houseboat rentals ($650 and up for 4 days) Houseboats include 15 foot fishing boat; linens; fully equipped kitchen and deck furniture.

AMENITIES AND ACTIVITIES: Swimming pool; restaurant; rentals (jet skis; ski boats; pontoons). Hiking; picnic; boating. **Places to Visit:** Stone State Park.

PAYMENT: MasterCard; Visa; personal checks and cash.

GUEST COMMENTS: "Staff members make us feel like family." "Lots of fried foods...in the restaurant; but what the heck, you're on vacation." "Walleye are great to catch and better to eat," "...many guides to chose from...different prices..." "The water in Dale Hollow Lake is exceptionally clean..." "The houseboat is always clean; well equipped and ready to go when we get there." "Fish early; late...catch plenty of fish. Then during the day; have a great time on the lake with the family."

LEATHERWOOD RESORT AND MARINA

751 Leatherwood Bay Rd. • Dover, TN 37058
Phone: 931-232-5137 • Fax: 931-232-2339

Guest Ratings

Room	🐟🐟🐟
Staff	🐟🐟🐟🐟
Meals	🐟🐟🐟
Outside areas	🐟🐟🐟
Fishing Guides	🐟🐟🐟
Fishing Equipment	🐟🐟🐟🐟
Children's Activities	NA

Resort Features

🐟	✓
🏃	
🍳	
🏨	
⬤	
▽	
€	✓

PRICE CATEGORY: $

SEASON: Open all year. Discounts offered December-February.

TRANSPORTATION: Nashville (2 hour drive).

FISHING: Where: Kentucky Lake; Lake Barkley. **Type:** Bait casting; spin casting; fly casting. **How:** Boat; shore. **Species:** Largemouth bass; smallmouth bass; catfish; crappie; bluegill; white bass. **Guides:** Local guides (start at $175 per day for 1 or 2 people) Includes guide and boat. **Equipment:** Small tackle shop on premises; boat slip; boat ramp; fishing licenses; bait; fish cleaning station; boat and motor rentals.

ACCOMMODATIONS: 2 bedroom cottages ($67 per night/2 people); 3 bedroom log cabins ($125 per night/up to 6 people) equipped with color TV; fully equipped kitchen; air conditioning; picnic table; grill; linens. Full RV sites $15; primitive camping $7.

AMENITIES AND ACTIVITIES: Swimming pool; restaurant; playground; gameroom; basketball; volleyball; horseshoes; hiking trails; rentals (pontoons; paddle boats). Golf; boating; antiquing; horseback riding; hiking. **Places to Visit**: Land Between the Lakes National Park; Fort Donelson National Park; Home Place.

PAYMENT: Visa; MasterCard; American Express; personal checks; cash.

GUEST COMMENTS: "It's clean; close the water...," "well suited to the needs of fishermen." Staff is "friendly...very helpful." "Food is very good...served with a smile." "There's plenty to do..." "...family fun as well as for die-hard fishermen." "Night fishing...exceptional." "Some crappie over 2 lbs. We average about 150 per week..." "You'll love the way the Marina is laid out..."."Reasonable...well maintained boats." "...covered and open boat slips...good food; large protected bay and good fishing." "It's secluded enough for a quiet weekend, but it can be lively if friends are along."

Guest Ratings

Room	♦♦♦
Staff	♦♦♦♦
Meals	NA
Outside areas	♦♦♦♦
Fishing Guides	♦♦♦♦
Fishing Equipment	♦♦♦♦
Children's Activities	NA

Resort Features

🐟	✓
👪	
🍳	
🏋	✓
♀	
⛵	
🎣	✓

MOUNTAIN LAKE MARINA AND CAMPGROUND

136 Campground Rd. • Lake City, TN 37769
Phone: 423-426-6510 • Fax: 423-426-7360
www.norrislake.com • Email: mtnlakketn@aol.com

PRICE CATEGORY: $

SEASON: Open all year, discounts offered November 1 through Easter.

TRANSPORTATION: McGhee Tyson Airport (1 hour drive).

FISHING: Where: Clinch River; Norris Lake. **Type:** Spin casting; bait casting; fly casting. **How:** Boat; shore; walk and wade. **Species:** Walleye; crappie; small mouth bass; largemouth bass; striper. **Guides:** Local guides available (Start at $150 per person per day) includes boat; bait and instruction. **Equipment:** Tackle shop at marina; covered dock; rentals (bass boat; fishing boat; motor; depth finder); fish cleaning station.

ACCOMMODATIONS: Cabins with fully equipped kitchens; TV; linens; ($82.50 double occupancy); Full RV hook up ($15.00); primitive camp site ($11.50).

AMENITIES AND ACTIVITIES: Swimming pool; meeting room; playground; game room; horseshoe pit; shuffleboard; volleyball; laundry. Boating; biking; swimming. **Places to Visit:** Oakridge American Museum of Science and Energy; Museum of Appalachia; Grist Mill; Norris Dam State Park; Gatlinburg; Pigeon Forge; Lenoir Museum.

PAYMENT: MasterCard; Visa; cash.

GUEST COMMENTS: "Well managed family oriented resort with attractive; wooded RV sites." "Helpful staff...willing to share fishing tips." "Everything you need...in one place. Park your car and start your boat." "Clean; well arranged grounds." "Fishing was...at times excellent." "Guide always found fish." "Marina is well laid out and easy to get to." "Unhurried and plenty to do." "Beautiful in all seasons."

SUGAR HOLLOW DOCK

Rt. 2, Box 344 H • Lafollete, TN 37766
Phone: 423-562-3466
www.norrislake.com • Email: Docklady@aol.com

Guest Ratings

Room	🐟🐟🐟
Staff	🐟🐟🐟🐟
Meals	NA
Outside areas	🐟🐟🐟
Fishing Guides	NA
Fishing Equipment	NA
Children's Activities	NA

Resort Features

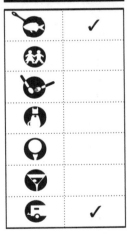

🍳	✓
👥	
🍳	
🛏	
🎣	
🚐	
🐾	✓

PRICE CATEGORY: $

SEASON: Open all year.

TRANSPORTATION: Knoxville, TN (1 hour 15 minute drive).

FISHING: Where: Norris Lake. **Type:** Bait casting; spin casting. **How:** Boat; shore. **Species:** Smallmouth bass; largemouth bass; rock bass; crappie. **Equipment:** Covered boat slips; small tackle shop; boat and motor rentals; fishing licenses.

ACCOMMODATIONS: Standard motel rooms ($55 double occupancy); house ($600 per weekend or $1200 per week); houseboats ($55 and up per night); camp sites ($15 per night).

AMENITIES AND ACTIVITIES: Laundry; rentals (pontoon; jet skis; houseboat); swimming; boating; biking; hiking. **Places to Visit:** Gatlinburg; Knoxville; Appalachian Museum.

PAYMENT: MasterCard; Visa; Discover; personal checks; cash.

GUEST COMMENTS: "Nice; clean rooms with basic furnishing." "We really enjoyed the stationary houseboat. The kitchen was equipped with everything we needed to prepare meals." "The staff is just wonderful. Friendly and quick to help." "The campground offers a nice view of the lake." "Fishing is very good for rock bass in March and early April." "Crappie fishing is fantastic in the spring." "Nice fishing resort on a quiet lake."

Guest Ratings

Room	♦♦♦◊
Staff	♦♦♦♦
Meals	♦♦♦
Outside areas	♦♦♦♦
Fishing Guides	♦♦♦♦
Fishing Equipment	♦♦♦♦
Children's Activities	NA

Resort Features

🐟	✓
👫	
🍳	

SUNSET MARINA AND RESORT

2040 Sunset Dock Rd. • Byrdstown, TN 38549
Phone: 931-864-3146 • Fax: 931-864-7441
www.sunsetmarina.com • Email: reservations@sunsetmarina.com

PRICE CATEGORY: $

SEASON: March 1st through November 15th.

TRANSPORTATION: Nashville, TN (2 hour drive). Private planes can fly into Livingston, TN.

FISHING: Where: Dale Hollow Lake; Pendergrass Creek; Hurricane Creek; Big Eagle Creek; Franklin Creek. **Type:** Spin casting; bait casting; trolling. **How:** Boat; shore. **Species:** Smallmouth bass; largemouth bass; Kentucky bass; muskie; walleye; bluegill; crappie; catfish and trout. **Guides:** Seasoned guides ($75 per half day) includes tackle and bait. **Equipment:** Fishing boat and motor rentals; launch ramps; open and covered boat slips.

ACCOMMODATIONS: One and two bedroom cottages include fully equipped kitchens; outdoor charcoal grills; picnic table and cable TV ($55 and up).

AMENITIES AND ACTIVITIES: Forty-four to seventy foot long houseboats; rentals (pontoons; ski boats; personal water craft; ski equipment; knee boards; tubes; canoes and paddle boats); large store; floating restaurant; water skiing; boating; swimming.

PAYMENT: MasterCard; Visa; American Express; personal checks; cash.

GUEST COMMENTS: "Our cabin was neat as a pin...very well equipped for cooking." "Staff went well beyond the call of duty," "...an outstanding location for activities like water skiing and tubing." "A quiet place with few mosquitoes." "All of the resources at the facility are very conveniently located." "Fishing is best in early spring and fall." "The dock area is clean; safe and well maintained." "They have an excellent mechanic should your...boat break down." "Reasonably priced; quiet and well run."

777 RANCH INC.

777-P.R. 5327 • Hondo, TX 78861-5445
Phone: 830-426-3476 • Fax: 830-426-4821
www.777ranch.com • e-mail address: 777ranch@777ranch.com

Guest Ratings

Room	🐟🐟🐟🐟
Staff	🐟🐟🐟🐟
Meals	🐟🐟🐟
Outside areas	🐟🐟🐟
Fishing Guides	🐟🐟🐟
Fishing Equipment	🐟🐟🐟🐟
Children's Activities	NA

Resort Features

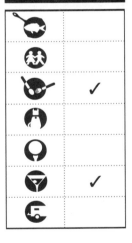

🍳🐟	
👪	
🍳	✓
🛎	
🔦	
⛵	✓
🎣	

PRICE CATEGORY: $$$

SEASON: Open all year.

TRANSPORTATION: San Antonio; (1 hour drive).

FISHING: Where: 30 private lakes and ponds. **Type:** Bait casting; fly casting; catch and release. **How:** Boat; shore. **Species:** Largemouth bass. **Guide Service:** Included in daily rate. **Instruction:** Fishing instruction provided. **Insider's Tip:** Ranch record for largemouth is 13 lbs. 6 ozs.

ACCOMMODATIONS: Hotel style rooms ($200 double occupancy; $250 single occupancy) includes three meals; guided jeep tour; boat; motor; rods; reels; fishing guide.

AMENITIES AND ACTIVITIES: The ranch is home to over 50 species of game from Africa; India; Europe; the middle east and the orient including springbok; dama gazelle; scimitar-horned oryx and bongo antelope. Tennis court; swimming pool; ranch store; bird watching; skeet shooting; photo safaris; hunting packages; jeep tour. **Places to Visit:** San Antonio; The Alamo; Sea World; Six Flags.

PAYMENT: Cash; cashiers check; personal check (if received 10 days in advance).

GUEST COMMENTS: Rooms: "well maintained and spacious; rustic setting with all the amenities." "Great cooking; served with unmatched hospitality." "The staff went above and beyond to make us feel comfortable." "A great family experience. The staff is excellent and the facility is first class." "The landscaping was gorgeous and well kept." "The game viewing on route to the fishing holes was amazing...tremendous variety of game species." "Behometh bass in a truly unique setting."

Guest Ratings

Room	♦♦♦
Staff	♦♦♦♦
Meals	♦♦♦♦
Outside areas	♦♦♦♦
Fishing Guides	♦♦♦♦
Fishing Equipment	NA
Children's Activities	NA

Resort Features

🐟	
👫	
🍳	✓
🦮	
♀	
▽	
ℇ	

LAKE FORK LODGE BASS AND BREAKFAST

PO Box 160 • Alba, TX 75410
Phone: 903-473-7236
www.lakeforklodge.com • E-Mail Address: lakefork@koyote.com

PRICE CATEGORY: $$

SEASON: Open all year.

TRANSPORTATION: Dallas-Fort Worth Airport (1 hour drive).

FISHING: Where: Lake Fork. **Type:** Spin casting. **How:** Boat; shore. **Species:** Bass, crappie, bluegill; catfish. **Guide Service:** Can be arranged through the lodge, start at $250 per day for up to two people. **Equipment:** Fully equipped Skeeter bass boat; $145 per day. **Insider's Tip:** Lake Fork has produced 19 of Texas' top 25 bass! Crappie fishing hits its peak from mid September to January.

ACCOMMODATIONS: Bed and breakfast style rooms with private baths. Includes early morning continental breakfast, full breakfast at 10:30 a.m. or both (start at $75 per night double occupancy). Large groups can rent the entire lodge starting at $695 per night.

AMENITIES AND ACTIVITIES: Two hot tubs; an outdoor patio; fishing pier; fish cleaning facilities; pontoon rentals; dog kennels and a game room. **Places to Visit:** Antique malls; Wild Willy's Mountain; outlet malls and Canton's First Monday Trades Day—the world's largest flea market.

PAYMENT: MasterCard; Visa; American Express; personal checks; cash.

GUEST COMMENTS: "Special place to get away from everyday stress and strain." "Wonderful; hospitable staff." "Lots of great antique stores in the area." "Incredible bass fishing." "The bass I catch here are; on average; bigger; harder fighters than anywhere else I've fished."

THE BACK FORTY RANCH OF FREDERICKSBURG

457 Bob Moritz Dr. • Fredericksburg, TX 78624
Phone: 830-997-6373 • Fax: 830-997-9986
www.fredericksburg-texas.com/backfort.html • Email: backforty@ktc.com

Guest Ratings

Room	♦♦♦♦
Staff	♦♦♦♦
Meals	♦♦♦
Outside areas	♦♦♦♦
Fishing Guides	♦♦♦♦
Fishing Equipment	NA
Children's Activities	NA

Resort Features

🐟	✔
👥	
🍳	✔
🔧	
🔍	
🍷	
🅵	

PRICE CATEGORY: $$

SEASON: Open all year.

TRANSPORTATION: San Antonio (1 hour 20 minute drive); Austin (5 1/2 hour drive).

FISHING: Where: Private lakes; Baron's Creek. **How:** Fly casting; bait casting; spin casting. **How:** Shore; boat; walk and wade. **Species:** Hybrid bass; bluegill; catfish. **Guide Service:** Certified guides ($160-200 per day).

ACCOMMODATIONS: 2 unique rock buildings originally built in 1860 and completely modernized and restored in 1993. Features include kitchen; fireplace; private patio; full bath. Both include continental breakfast and use of boat on private lake ($125 per person per night).

AMENITIES AND ACTIVITIES: Week long art classes in oil painting; watercolor and acrylics; campfire ring; nature walks; birding; rock hunting; 18 hole golf course nearby; antique shops and boutiques. **Places to Visit:** Historic Fredericksburg; Enchanted Rock State Park; Gillespie County Horse Races; Lindon B. Johnson Park and Pool

PAYMENT: Personal checks; cash.

GUEST COMMENTS: "Good place to sneak away for a romantic weekend with a little early morning fly fishing." "Cabins are cozy and well appointed." Staff: "...friendly and quietly efficient." "Saw to all the details and offered advice on ...places to visit...good fishing spots—...never intrusive." "Fly fishing is...not exceptional, but relaxing." "...creek running through the ranch is uncrowded and peaceful." "...probably won't catch a trophy here, but you will leave relaxed..."

Guest Ratings

Room	🎣🎣🎣🎣
Staff	🎣🎣🎣🎣
Meals	🎣🎣🎣
Outside areas	🎣🎣🎣🎣
Fishing Guides	🎣🎣🎣🎣
Fishing Equipment	NA
Children's Activities	NA

Resort Features

🐟	
🧑‍🤝‍🧑	
🍳	✓
🎿	
⛏	
⛵	
🎯	

BOULDER MOUNTAIN LODGE

PO Box 1397 • Boulder, UT 84716
Phone: 801-335-7460 • Fax: 801-335-7461
www.boulder-utah.com • e-mail: bmlut@color-country.com

PRICE CATEGORY: $$

SEASON: Open all year.

TRANSPORTATION: Salt Lake City (4 1/2 hour drive); Las Vegas (6 1/2 hour drive).

FISHING: Where: High elevation alpine lakes and streams; low elevation canyon streams. **How:** Shore; float tube; walk and wade. **Type:** Bait casting; fly casting. **Species:** Rainbow trout; brook trout; brown trout; cutthroat trout. **Guide Service:** Licensed; insured guides (start at $95 per person/day) includes lunch; instruction; tackle. Helicopter and remote camp-out guide packages available.

ACCOMMODATIONS: Private rooms in several separate buildings around 15 acre private waterfowl sanctuary ($74 and up; double occupancy).

AMENITIES AND ACTIVITIES: Dining room; great room; library. Horseback riding; mountain biking; hiking; canoeing. **Places to Visit:** Capitol Reef National Park; Bryce Canyon National Park; Zion National Park; Calf Creek Falls; Burr Trail; Muley Twist and Kodachrome Basin. **Insider's Tip:** Guests can save money and enjoy the many parks in the area by buying a National Parks yearly pass.

PAYMENT: MasterCard; Visa; personal checks; cash.

GUEST COMMENTS: Lodge is "exceptionally clean" with "comfortable western decor." The pond is a "beautiful place to just sit and admire nature." Meals were "adequate"; the dining facility "excellent." "The lodge's proximity to public lands made it a good base for day hikes and photography." Guides: "personable," "knowledgeable" and one beginning angler noted "very patient."

DEER TRAIL LODGE

PO Box 647 • Clear Creek Canyon Rd. • Panguitch Lake, UT 84759
Phone: 435-676-2211 • Reservations: 888-DTL-2211
www.deertrail.com • e-mail: bigfish@color-country.net

Guest Ratings

Room	🐟🐟🐟
Staff	🐟🐟🐟🐟
Meals	NA
Outside areas	🐟🐟🐟🐟
Fishing Guides	NA
Fishing Equipment	NA
Children's Activities	NA

PRICE CATEGORY: $

SEASON: Open all year.

TRANSPORTATION: Salt Lake City (4 1/2 hour drive); Las Vegas (4 hour drive).

FISHING: Where: Panguitch Creek; Sevier River; Clear Creek; Panguitch Lake; Mammoth Creek. **Type:** Fly casting; spin casting; bait casting; ice fishing. **How:** Walk and wade; boat; shore. **Species:** Rainbow trout; German trout; cutthroat trout; brown trout. **Equipment:** Fishing licenses available; fish cleaning station.

ACCOMMODATIONS: Cabins ($50); some with kitchenettes; RV sites ($15); tent sites ($9.50).

AMENITIES AND ACTIVITIES: Barbecue area; lodge. Nature walks; hiking; boating; hunting; mountain biking; horseback riding; snowmobiling; cross country skiing; snow shoeing. **Places to Visit:** Bryce Canyon National Park; Zion National Park.

PAYMENT: Visa; MasterCard; cash.

GUEST COMMENTS: Cabins are "rustic"; "functional" and "clean, but spartan," "the decor was fine—they are cabins; not the Hilton." Hosts were "friendly," could tell them "where and how the fish were biting." Fishing areas were "not crowded." Area fishing varied: "excellent"; "slow, until we rented a boat"; "fish are small but plentiful" and "outstanding, everyone in our group of four had a limit catch our first day." Most guests rated Deer Trail Lodge as "somewhat" or "much better" that other lodges and said they would consider a return trip.

Resort Features

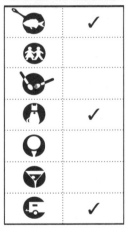

🐟	✓
👥	
🍳	
🎣	✓
⛵	
▼	
🚐	✓

Guest Ratings

Room	🎣🎣🎣⅃
Staff	🎣🎣🎣🎣
Meals	🎣🎣🎣
Outside areas	🎣🎣🎣
Fishing Guides	🎣🎣🎣🎣
Fishing Equipment	NA
Children's Activities	NA

Resort Features

🐟	✓
👫	
🍳	
🔌	
🍸	
▽	
🚐	

FLAMING GORGE LODGE

155 Greendale, US 191 • Dutch John, UT 84023
Phone: 435-889-3773 • Fax: 435-889-3788
www.flaminggorgelodge.com • Email : greenriverherald@union-tel.com

PRICE CATEGORY: $$

SEASON: Open all year.

TRANSPORTATION: Salt Lake City (3 hour drive).

FISHING: Where: Green River; Flaming Gorge Reservoir; private ponds located at the Bar S Ranch. **Type:** Fly casting; spin casting. **How:** Float; shore; walk and wade. **Species:** Kokanee salmon; rainbow; brown; lake; brook; cutthroat trout; smallmouth bass. **Guide Service:** Local guides (start at $225 per person/day) w/transportation; lunch; instruction. **Equipment:** Rentals (rods; reels; waders); fishing licenses; tackle shop. **Insider's Tip:** The current state record holding Kokanee salmon; rainbow trout; brown trout and lake trout were all pulled from Flaming Gorge Reservoir.

ACCOMMODATIONS: 1 bedroom condominiums with fully equipped kitchens; phone; VCR; air conditioning ($98); motel rooms ($58).

AMENITIES AND ACTIVITIES: General store; fuel; liquor store; restaurant; raft rentals. Hiking; mountain biking; Green River float trips; water skiing; swimming; snowmobiling; cross-country skiing.

PAYMENT: MasterCard; Visa; American Express; personal checks; cash.

GUEST COMMENTS: Rooms were: "clean; adequate," "clean but plain," "...not the 4 Seasons, but that's OK." Meals were: "adequate," "this lodge was not chosen for gourmet food, but...access to a great river." Guides: "very knowledgeable"; "the best guide I've ever used"; "...my grandsons were not experienced fly fishermen. The first day the youngest was awarded a special cap for a 22 inch trout caught and released. I relaxed and had a great time."

L.C. RANCH

Room	🐟🐟🐟🐟
Staff	🐟🐟🐟🐟
Meals	🐟🐟🐟🐟
Outside areas	🐟🐟🐟
Fishing Guides	🐟🐟🐟🐟
Fishing Equipment	NA
Children's Activities	NA

PO Box 63 • Altamont, UT 84001
Phone: 435-454-3750
www: aros.net/~achap/Nick_html • Email: LCRanch@uwin.com

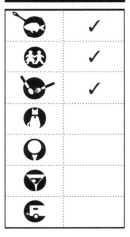

Resort Features

🍳	✓
👨‍👩‍👧	✓
🍴	✓
🎣	
⚲	
▽	
⅁	

PRICE CATEGORY: $$$

SEASON: Open all year; fishing available April through October.

TRANSPORTATION: Salt Lake International Airport (2 hour drive).

FISHING: Where: 28 private lakes and ponds. **Type:** Fly fishing. **How:** Float; shore. **Species:** Brook, rainbow, brown trout. **Guide Service:** Arranged through Western Rivers Flyfisher ($175 per person/ per day) w/lunch, float tube, individual instruction. Full service trips ($255 per person/day) include one night's lodging; three meals plus above. **Insider's Tip:** A carefully monitored catch and release policy is in place and has paid off: average L.C. Ranch trout is 18".

ACCOMMODATIONS: Cabins with fully equipped kitchen; TV; VCR; satellite; stereo; barbecue grill and picnic table ($40 per person/day; group discounts available).

AMENITIES AND ACTIVITIES: Baby-sitting available. Owner offers catering service for family reunions; business meetings etc.(up to 50 people). Hiking; birding; mountain biking. **Places to Visit:** Sand Wash Reservoir; Dinosaurland; Nine Mile Canyon petroglyphs; Ute Indian reservation: Flaming Gorge recreation area.

PAYMENT: MasterCard; Visa; personal checks; cash.

GUEST COMMENTS: Cabins were "spacious and light"; "top notch" and "unique". Staff: "hard working" by more than one guest. "A lot of different water and fishing conditions, dries and droppers to buggers down deep...some real bruisers on occasion." "Strong, healthy fish. This was not a "gimme" experience. Casting; hook setting and reel playing tested our ability." "Still water fishing at its best." Guides: "experienced.," "patient with first timer," let them "fish til you drop!" "world class fishing; food and hospitality."

VERMONT · VIRGINIA

Guest Ratings

Room	🐟🐟🐟🐟
Staff	🐟🐟🐟🐟
Meals	🐟🐟🐟🐟
Outside areas	🐟🐟🐟🐟
Fishing Guides	🐟🐟🐟🐟
Fishing Equipment	🐟🐟🐟
Children's Activities	NA

Resort Features

🍳	
👫	
🍳	✓
🎣	
♀	
▽	
🄴	

GOLDEN MAPLE INN

Rt. 15, Main St. • Wolcott Village; VT 05680-0035
Phone: 800-639-5234
www. members.aol.com/GoldnMaple/index.html • E mail: goldnmaple @aol.com

PRICE CATEGORY: $

SEASON: May through October.

TRANSPORTATION: Burlington International Airport, VT (one hour drive). Morrisville Stowe Regional airport (15 minute drive).

FISHING: Where: Lamoille River; Winooski River; Dog River; Black River; Clyde River; area ponds and lakes. **Type:** Fly casting. **How:** Walk and wade; canoe. **Species:** Rainbow, brook, brown trout. **Guides:** Insured; Vermont licensed guides ($100 per person per half day). **Equipment:** Tackle shop, the Dry Fly, on premises. Factory demo rods can be borrowed. **Instruction:** 3 day fly fishing schools, on and off water instruction. Includes lodging and meals ($450 per student). **Insider'sTip:** Four to 6 weight; 8 to 9 foot rods are ideal. Reserve ahead for fall foliage season: September 15 through October 15.

ACCOMMODATIONS: Historic landmark inn on the Lamoille River; built in 1865. Bed and breakfast guest rooms with private baths ($64 and up double occupancy) includes full breakfast.

AMENITIES AND ACTIVITIES: Antiquing; golfing; glider rides. **Places to Visit:** Ben and Jerry's Ice Cream Factory; Cabot Cheese Creamery; Green Mountain Chocolates; Cold Hollow Cider Mill; Stowe Village Shopping.

PAYMENT: Visa; MasterCard; American Express; Discover; personal checks; cash.

GUEST COMMENTS: Accommodations were "clean and comfortable;" with "lovely and interesting period furnishings." Staff: "friendly;" "helpful." Meals were "well prepared; delicious." Fishing was "excellent;" "traditional fly casting setting;" "easy enough for a novice; challenging enough to entertain a more experienced angler." "There was an adequate supply of equipment..." "A great place to fish, relax and get away from it all."

VERMONT SPORTSMAN LODGE

HCR 70, Box 42 • Morgan, VT
Phone and Fax: 802-895-4209

Guest Ratings

Room	🎣🎣🎣🎣
Staff	🎣🎣🎣🎣
Meals	🎣🎣🎣🎣
Outside areas	🎣🎣🎣🎣
Fishing Guides	🎣🎣🎣🎣
Fishing Equipment	NA
Children's Activities	NA

Resort Features

🐟	
👫	✓
🍴	✓

PRICE CATEGORY: $ - $$

SEASON: Open all year.

TRANSPORTATION: Burlington, VT (2 hour drive.)

FISHING: Where: Lake Seymour; Lake Memphremagog; Echo Lake; the Connecticut River. **Type:** Fly casting; spin casting; ice fishing. **How:** Boat; shore. **Guides:** Local guides ($150 1 or 2 people per day) includes picnic lunch. **Equipment:** Fly rods and spinning tackle available for loan; ice fishing shanty; boat dock. **Instruction:** Fly tying and fly casting instruction.

ACCOMMODATIONS: Lodge rooms. Full service ($105 double occupancy) includes breakfast and dinner; bed and breakfast ($70 double occupancy); room only ($60 double occupancy).

AMENITIES AND ACTIVITIES: Babysitting available. Private beach; nature walks; canoe; library and game room; bicycle tours; boating; hunting; canoeing; hiking; campfires; fly tying classes; moose watches; antiquing; downhill or cross country skiing; snowmobiling; ice skating; hiking; swimming.

PAYMENT: Personal checks; cash.

GUEST COMMENTS: "If you are looking to get away from the everyday hustle; this is the place" "beautiful lakes and quiet nights." Staff: "always there to answer questions and help." "Absolutely can't beat the home cooking; eat as much as you want." Guides are "always willing to go the extra mile." "If you aren't catching fish; ask one of the staff for advice. If you follow the advice and still don't catch any you probably won't catch fish anywhere." "Beautiful scenery;" "a good time."

Guest Ratings

Room	♦♦♦♦
Staff	♦♦♦♦
Meals	♦♦♦◢
Outside areas	♦♦♦♦
Fishing Guides	♦♦♦♦
Fishing Equipment	NA
Children's Activities	NA

Resort Features

🍳	
👪	
🍴	✓
🎽	
🔦	
▽	
€	

THE INN AT NARROW PASSAGE

PO Box 608 • Woodstock, VA 22664
Phone: 540-459-8000 • Reservations: 800-459-8000 • Fax: 540-459-8001
www. InnAtNarrowPassage.com • Email: Innkeeper @InnAtNarrowPassage.com

PRICE CATEGORY: $$

SEASON: Open all year.

TRANSPORTATION: Washington, DC/ Dulles (90 minute drive).

FISHING: Where: Shenandoah River. **Type:** Fly Casting; spin casting. **How:** Walk and wade; shore; canoe. **Species:** Smallmouth bass; perch; bluegill. **Guides:** Local guide; ($150 per person per day) includes guide; instruction and transportation.

ACCOMMODATIONS: Historic Colonial Inn ($95-$110 double occupancy); breakfast included.

AMENITIES AND ACTIVITIES: Conference facilities; dining room; hiking; golf; horseback riding; antiquing; canoeing. **Places to Visit:** Shenandoah Valley Music Festival concerts during summer; civil war sites; vineyards.

PAYMENT: MasterCard; Visa; Discover; personal checks; cash.

GUEST COMMENTS: "Clean; comfortable; attractive rooms...for a reasonable price." "Friendly staff...don't mind seeing to the extra details..." "Superb smallmouth bass fishing." "Great access to the Shenandoah river and brook trout..." "Canoe drift fishing for smallmouth bass and pan fish is excellent" "Although I would not characterize the Inn at Narrow Passage as a fishing lodge per se; I recommend it highly....While my friends and I fish...our wives find enough to do that we can return year after year."

SEA GULL COTTAGES AND MARINA

PO Box 182 • Wachapreague, VA 23480
Phone: 757-787-4848

Guest Ratings

Room	♦♦♦♦
Staff	♦♦♦♦
Meals	NA
Outside areas	♦♦♦♦
Fishing Guides	♦♦♦
Fishing Equipment	NA
Children's Activities	NA

Resort Features

🐟	✓
👥	
🍳	
🍺	
🔍	
▼	✓
€	

PRICE CATEGORY: $

SEASON: Open all year.

TRANSPORTATION: Norfolk, VA (90 minute drive); Salisbury, MD (90 minute drive).

FISHING: Where: Atlantic Ocean; Brad Ford Bay; Burton Bay. **Type:** Fly casting; spin casting; bait casting. **How:** Boat; pier. **Species:** Flounder; trout; spot; croaker; shark; tuna; dolphin; marlin. **Guides:** Coast Guard licensed guides available. Flounder charters ($350 per day for 1-6 people). Off shore charters ($400-$800 for 6 people). **Equipment:** Marina/tackle shop nearby. **Insider's Tip:** Flounder fishing April through November. Offshore fishing: end of June through October. Trout; spot and croaker: June; July and August. Bring your own equipment.

ACCOMMODATIONS: Private cottages with cable TV; microwave; linens; air conditioning; $50 per night for 1-4 guests. 1 large cottage: full kitchen; screened porch; etc. $400 per week for 1-4 people. Bed and Breakfast rooms: $65 and up double occupancy.

AMENITIES AND ACTIVITIES: Boating; bird watching; swimming; biking; Tangeir Island cruise. **Places to Visit:** Chincoteague Island; Assateague Island.

PAYMENT: MasterCard; Visa; personal checks; cash.

GUEST COMMENTS: Accommodations were: "large; clean and nicely furnished." Outside areas "well maintained" with "beautiful flowers...remarkable gardens." Cottages were "conveniently located to visit the quaint fishing village of Wachapreague and to fishing." Guest after guest remarked that the hosts were "accommodating;" "friendly;" and "helpful." Guides were: "knowledgeable; friendly and helpful." "A good; reasonably priced home base;" "one of a kind spot perfect."

WASHINGTON · WISCONSIN · WYOMING

Guest Ratings

Room	♦♦♦♦
Staff	♦♦♦♦
Meals	NA
Outside areas	♦♦♦♦
Fishing Guides	♦♦♦
Fishing Equipment	NA
Children's Activities	NA

Resort Features

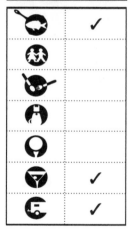

🍳	✓
👪	
🍳	
🎣	
⊙	
▽	✓
☰	✓

RAIN FOREST RESORT VILLAGE

516 South Shore Rd. • PO Box 40 • Quinault, WA 98575
Phone: 360-288-2535 • Reservations: 800-255-6936

PRICE CATEGORY: $ - $$

SEASON: Open all year; fishing season is mid April through October.

TRANSPORTATION: Seattle, WA (3 1/2 hour drive).

FISHING: Where: Lake Quinault; Queets River; Hoh River; Bogachiel River. **Type:** Fly casting; bait casting; spin casting. **How:** Boat; shore. **Species:** Rainbow trout; cutthroat trout; dolly varden; salmon; steelhead. **Insider's Tip:** Because Lake Quinault is part of the Quinault Indian Reservation; an Indian fishing permit is required.

ACCOMMODATIONS: Cabins ($115 double occupancy); motel rooms ($60 and up double occupancy). RV Sites (start at $15).

AMENITIES AND ACTIVITIES: Restaurant; general store; gift shop; driving range; hiking trails (some are barrier free handicapped accessible); boating; sailing; horseback riding; biking; guided nature walks; hunting. **Places to Visit:** Olympic National Park.

PAYMENT: Mastercard; Visa; Discover; American Express; personal checks; cash.

GUEST COMMENTS: "Tidy; comfortable cabins." "Tastefully decorated." Staff: "Proficient"; "never pushy or hurried." "Outside areas and RV sites immaculately maintained." "Lots of rain in this area; so don't forget rain gear." "Salmon and trout fishing is good to excellent." "Strong hatches that must be matched for successful fly fishing." "Caught and released a few good-sized steelhead." "Relaxed atmosphere; long mornings on area streams; leisurely afternoon hikes and good meals at the resort's restaurant."

ROCHE HARBOR RESORT AND MARINA

Guest Ratings

Room	🐟🐟🐟🐟
Staff	🐟🐟🐟🐟
Meals	🐟🐟🐟🐟
Outside areas	🐟🐟🐟🐟
Fishing Guides	🐟🐟🐟🐟
Fishing Equipment	🐟🐟🐟🐟
Children's Activities	NA

PO Box 4397 • Roche Harbor, WA 98250
Phone: 360-378-2155 • Fax: 360-378-6809
www.rocheharbor.com

Resort Features

🍳	✓
👥	
🥘	
🍸	
☕	
🍷	✓
🎿	

PRICE CATEGORY: $ - $$

SEASON: Year around. Discounted rates October-April.

TRANSPORTATION: Seattle; WA (2 hour drive to ferry; 2 hour ferry ride).

FISHING: Where: Pacific Ocean near San Juan Island. **Type:** Bait casting; spin casting; bottom fishing. **How:** Boat. **Species:** Rock cod; ling cod; various bottom fish; humpies; silver salmon; king salmon; coho salmon. **Guides:** Private charters ($79.00 for four hours) includes bait; tackle; boat; guide.

ACCOMMODATIONS: Hotel room with private bath ($85 for 1 or 2 people). Condominium with fully equipped kitchen ($145, up to 4 people). Cottage with fully equipped kitchens ($130 for up to 4 people).

AMENITIES AND ACTIVITIES: Gift shop; grocery and marine supply; swimming pool; tennis court; restaurant; meeting rooms; moorage; fuel facilities; laundromat; rentals (canoe; kayak; motorboat). Golf; photography, kayak treks; whale and wildlife discovery cruise; whale watch cruise; swimming; tennis; historic walking tour.

PAYMENT: Visa: MasterCard; American Express; personal checks; cash.

GUEST COMMENTS: "The entire resort is picture perfect." "Beautifully decorated cabins; always clean." "Fishing is spectacular." "Protected harbor is immaculate and well maintained." "Charter captain was terrific...everything a good guide should be." "Grounds are...breathtaking." "Although there is a tremendous array of different activities; the pace is relaxed and casual." "Our family of four had a grand resort level vacation for Holiday Inn prices."

Guest Ratings

Room	♣♣♣♣
Staff	♣♣♣♣
Meals	NA
Outside areas	♣♣♣◗
Fishing Guides	NA
Fishing Equipment	♣♣♣◗
Children's Activities	NA

Resort Features

🐟	✓
👪	✓
🍳	
🎣	
♀	
▽	✓
🄴	

GHOST LAKE LODGE

Rt. 7, Box 7450 • Hayward, WI 54843
Phone: 715-462-3939 • Fax: 715-462-3939
www.ghostlakelodge.com • Email: ghost@win.bright.net

PRICE CATEGORY: $ - $$

SEASON: May 1 through October 30; discounts May, September, October.

TRANSPORTATION: St. Paul/Minneapolis; (3 hours by car) Duluth, MN (2 hours by car) Small aircraft; Hayward, WI (20 minutes by car).

FISHING: Where: Ghost Lake; Chippewa River; Chippewa Flowage; Teal Lake; Lost Land Lake. **Type:** Bait casting; fly casting; spin casting. **How:** Wade; fishing boat; canoe; shore. **Species:** Muskie; bass; crappie; walleye; bluegill; perch. **Guides:** Licensed; professional guides ($150 to $250 per day for up to 2 people) **Equipment:** Muskie bait casting rental equipment; fishing boat rentals; fish cleaning house.

ACCOMMODATIONS: Private cabins with 1 to 3 bedrooms; equipped with full kitchens; fireplaces; 14' boat; private pier; barbecue grill; firewood; color TV; microwave; coffee pot; all linens; some whirlpool units. Rates start at $85 double occupancy per night; $485 per week.

AMENITIES AND ACTIVITIES: Baby-sitting available. Heated pool; tennis court; rental bikes; basketball court; nature trails; shuffleboard; recreation room; 3 playgrounds; restaurant; cocktail bar; swim raft. Tennis; biking; hiking; bird watching; horseback riding; golf; hunting. **Places to Visit:** Hayward's Fishing Hall of Fame; Chequamegon National Forest; Wood Carvers Museum; Waterslide.

PAYMENT: MasterCard; Visa; Diner's Club; personal checks; cash.

GUEST COMMENTS: "Quiet and comfortable...a variety of things to do." "Very secluded and quiet." "Cabins somewhat dated;" "Rustic and roomy;" "Hosts: "very friendly and accommodating." "...rustic experience with the luxury of an in-ground, heated pool." "Special cook out night to meet other guests." "Get up early; you'll have the lake to yourself (unless I'm there too)."

LOZIER'S BOX R RANCH

Guest Ratings

Room	♦♦♦
Staff	♦♦♦♦
Meals	♦♦♦♦
Outside areas	♦♦♦
Fishing Guides	♦♦♦
Fishing Equipment	NA
Children's Activities	NA

Box 100 • Cora, WY 82925
Phone: 307-367-4868 • Fax: 307-367-6260
www. Guestranches.com/boxr • E-mail: boxr @wyoming.com

Resort Features

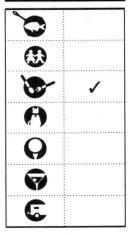

PRICE CATEGORY: $$

SEASON: Memorial day through mid-September.

TRANSPORTATION: Jackson Hole (free transfer to ranch Sundays and Wednesdays).

FISHING: Where: Willow Creek; Willow Lake; Green River Lakes; Green River; New Fork Lakes; New Fork River; several alpine lakes (pack trips). **Type:** Fly casting; spin casting. **How:** Wading; shore. **Species:** Brook, German, cutthroat, golden, lake, rainbow trout; grayling. **Equipment:** Not available. **Insider's Tip:** Bring your own tackle or buy an inexpensive set in town when you arrive. Purchase license in Jackson Hole or Pinedale before you arrive at the ranch.

ACCOMMODATIONS: 1,2,or 3 bedroom cabins; ($895 per person/week) includes all meals, linens; maid services.

AMENITIES AND ACTIVITIES: Game room; dining room; horseback riding; hiking; photography; 2-10 night pack trips from ranch; wild life viewing; cattle drives; moonlight picnic; breakfast cookout; golf; hiking; rafting; rodeo; sightseeing. **Places to Visit:** Yellowstone National Park; Teton National Park.

PAYMENT: MasterCard; Visa; Discover; cash; checks.

GUEST COMMENTS: Accommodations: "rustic but clean...everything we needed." Staff: "friendly" "helpful." "Meals were better than I expected..." "It should be noted (this)...is a guest ranch first; a fishing destination second." "Fishing on pack trips is excellent...usually have the entire lake...to yourself." Guide: knowledgeable...but not about fly patterns." "An outstanding all around family vacation. Great horseback riding garnished with unique fishing opportunities."

WHERE TO FIND GUEST-RATED RESORTS:
- ALPHABETICALLY
- BY PRICE CATEGORY
- BY STATE
- BY FISH SPECIES
- BY BODY OF WATER/ GEOGRAPHIC AREA
- BY RESORT FEATURES

ALPHABETIC LISTING OF GUEST-RATED RESORTS

RESORT BY PRICE CATEGORY

RESORTS BY STATE

RESORTS BY FISH SPECIES

RESORTS BY BODY OF WATER/GEOGRAPHIC AREA

RESORT FEATURES

A

Art Classes, 237

B

Baby-Sitting, 89, 112, 118, 141, 142, 144, 146, 158, 159, 168, 170, 178, 183, 188, 201, 203, 243, 254

Bed And Breakfast, 99, 129, 144, 180, 183, 209, 215, 218, 221, 226, 227, 236, 246, 247, 249

Birding, 89, 96, 112, 142, 143, 167, 173, 174, 219, 222, 228, 237, 243

C

Catch And Release, 100, 124, 127, 133, 152, 203, 210, 218, 219, 221, 222, 223, 235, 243

Catering, 116, 200, 243

Clamming, 93, 95, 106

Condominiums, 132, 144, 150, 158, 159, 162, 242

Covered Boat Slips, 112, 158, 160, 193, 233, 234

Crabbing, 93, 95

Cross Country Skiing, 154, 156, 166, 169, 171, 174, 180, 182, 186, 188, 189, 208, 209, 226, 241, 244, 247

D

Deep Sea Fishing, 106, 137, 140

Digging For Sapphires, 206

E

Elderhostel, 93

Entomology Seminars, 218

F

Family Reunion, 188, 199, 243

Fishing Tournaments, 115, 141

Fitness Center, 125, 136, 142, 148, 182

Float Trips, 93, 94, 114, 151, 203, 205, 212, 242

Fly Fishing Schools, 146, 147, 208, 212, 244, 246

Fly Out Fishing, 89, 103, 105

Fly Tying, 89, 90, 93, 94, 105, 147, 178, 208, 218, 219, 227, 247

G

Guest Ranch, 117, 127, 203, 210, 255

H

Heated Fishing Dock, 191, 197

Horse Boarding Facilities, 221, 222

Hot Springs, 93, 111, 221, 222

Houseboat Rentals, 159, 230

Hunting, 89, 118, 133, 151, 152, 154, 164, 165, 166, 169, 170, 171, 172, 173, 175, 176, 180, 186, 192, 203, 206, 214, 218, 221, 235, 237, 241, 244, 247, 252, 254

I

Ice Fishing, 166, 171, 174, 175, 182, 186, 188, 189, 241, 247

M

Meals Included, 89, 90, 91, 93, 94, 96, 97, 100, 101, 102, 103, 104, 105, 106, 107, 152, 153, 206, 212, 213

ATTENTION FISHING ENTHUSIASTS !!

Have you stayed at a fishing camp, bed and breakfast, inn, lodge or resort within the last year? If so, and you would like to review or recommend a facility for the next edition of **Fishing Vacations For All Budgets**, please contact:

Pilot Books
PO Box 2102
Greenport, NY 11944
1-800-797-4568

We 'd love to hear from fishing resort guests like you, who are willing to share your experiences with other readers. We'll send you a survey so you can give us your unbiased ratings and comments—good or bad—about your latest fishing vacation.

If you love a fishing getaway but expect good value for your money...regardless of your budget, join the hundreds of fishing resort guests who "tell all" about their favorite (or least favorite) fishing vacation.

Or

If you own a camp, inn, resort or lodge that caters to fishing clientele and would like your facility to be included in the next edition of **Fishing Vacations For All Budgets**, please contact Pilot Books for an application. There is absolutely no charge for listing in the Directory or Guide and all overnight fishing facilities are welcome to contact us.